In a unique study of rural administration in the Ottoman empire, Amy Singer explores the relationship between Palestinian peasants and Ottoman provincial officials around Jerusalem in the mid-sixteenth century. Using local court records, as well as imperial surveys and decrees, the author provides detailed information on local conditions of production, the mechanisms for assessing and collecting taxes, and the strategies peasants evolved for evading them. Rural administration functioned as a process of negotiation and compromise between peasants and military-administrative officials, often mediated through the *kadi* who was the formal judicial authority in virtually all matters. The book emphasizes the complex, colourful, and interactive nature of Ottoman provincial administration, which, while obliged to extract revenues from the peasants and impress them with the power of imperial authority, was nevertheless profoundly influenced by local conditions and traditional practices in its dealings with the populace.

Cambridge Studies in Islamic Civilization

Palestinian peasants and Ottoman officials

Cambridge Studies in Islamic Civilization

Titles in the series

B. F. MUSSALLAM. *Sex and society in Islam: birth control before the nineteenth century*
SURAIYA FAROQHI. *Towns and townsmen of Ottoman Anatolia: trade, crafts and food production in an urban setting, 1520–1650*
SURAIYA FAROQHI. *Men of modest substance: house owners and house property in seventeenth-century Ankara and Kayseri*
PATRICIA CRONE. *Roman, provincial and Islamic law: the origins of the Islamic patronate*
STEFAN SPERL. *Mannerism in Arabic poetry: a structural analysis of selected texts, 3rd century AH/9th century AD–5th century AH/11th century AD*
BEATRICE FORBES MANZ. *The rise and rule of Tamerlane*
AMNON COHEN. *Economic life in Ottoman Jerusalem*
PAUL E. WALKER. *Early philosophical Shiism: the Ismaili Neoplatonism of Abū Ya'qūb al-Sijistānī*
BOAZ SHOSHAN. *Popular culture in medieval Cairo*
STEPHEN FREDERIC DALE. *Indian merchants and Eurasian trade, 1600–1750*

Palestinian peasants and Ottoman officials

Rural administration around sixteenth-century Jerusalem

AMY SINGER
Tel Aviv University

CAMBRIDGE
UNIVERSITY PRESS

Published by the Press Syndicate of the University of Cambridge
The Pitt Building, Trumpington Street, Cambridge CB2 1RP
40 West 20th Street, New York, NY 10011-4211, USA
10 Stamford Road, Oakleigh, Melbourne 3166, Australia

First published 1994

Printed in Great Britain at the University Press, Cambridge

A catalogue record for this book is available from the British Library

Library of Congress cataloguing in publication data

Singer, Amy
Palestinian peasants and Ottoman officials: rural administration around sixteenth-century Jerusalem / Amy Singer.
p. cm. – (Cambridge studies in Islamic civilization)
Includes bibliographical references.
ISBN 0 521 45238 4
1. Peasants – Jerusalem Region – History – 16th century.
2. Peasantry – Taxation – Jerusalem Region – History – 16th century.
3. Military government – Jerusalem Region – History – 16th century.
4. Court records – Jerusalem Region – History – 16th cent.
I. Title. II. Series.
HD1537. J4S56 1994
305.5′633′09569442–dc20 93-38441 CIP

ISBN 0 521 45238 4 hardback
ISBN 0 521 47679 8 paperback

CE

To my parents, who have always treated my endeavors seriously, while attempting to instill in me a sense of humor with which to face life and work, thanks are never enough.

Contents

Maps

Tables

Preface

While this manuscript was in the advanced stages of preparation, my continuing researches in the Ottoman archives yielded several types of documents related to village administration which I had not previously seen concerning the villages in this study. All of these documents relate to the administration of the endowment of Hurrem Sultan in Jerusalem. In all likelihood, they will add a further dimension to our understanding of how rural administration was effected. However, my present assessment is that they will not modify significantly the basic propositions and conclusions of this study. Therefore, it seems proper to leave their presentation and analysis to future publications.

Likewise, during this same period, new works on peasants in the Ottoman empire, on peasants in other societies and ages, and on Ottoman history have appeared which I have not been able to consider in the present work. Doubtless, they would have further enriched the discussion in my study; my future work will benefit from their insights. Such is the nature of scholarship.

Bernard Lewis was my principal advisor for the dissertation which engendered this book, and to him I owe my deepest gratitude for the enormous commitment and wisdom with which he fulfilled that role. He and Amnon Cohen of the Hebrew University of Jerusalem infected me with their enthusiasm for the challenge of Ottoman history and archival research. Peasants first drew my attention in a Russian history seminar in college, where it became clear to me that the village-based agrarian population of a huge empire was not necessarily a willing partner to that empire's ambitions. Brigitte and Gerard Nicolino, and the people of Alleins convinced me of the enduring disparity between state regulations of rural administration and rural compliance.

My years of graduate study were generously supported by Princeton University, and made easier by the help of all the staff of the Department of Near Eastern Studies. For the financial support of the research for this book, I would like to thank the American Research Institute in Turkey, the Lady Davis Fellowship Trust, and the Institute of Turkish Studies.

In Turkey, I wish to thank the staffs of the Başbakanlık Arşivi in Istanbul and the Tapu ve Kadastro Umum Müdürlüğü in Ankara for their professional assistance. At the archives in Istanbul, I took advantage of the generous assistance, freely offered, by many scholars working there. Halil Inalcik, Halil Sahillioğlu, Suraiya Faroqhi, Mehmet Genç, Donald Quataert, Dan Goffman, and the late Jean-Pierre Thieck all suffered patiently the endless queries of the novice researcher.

In Jerusalem, I owe special thanks to the clerks of the Jerusalem *maḥkama al-sharʿiyya*, especially Chief Clerk Zayn al-Dīn al-ʿAlamī. They accepted my presence and graciously shared their desks in a limited space during a difficult time. Shaykh Asʿad al-Imām al-Ḥusaynī was often my guide through the seemingly illegible pages of the Jerusalem *sijill*s. I am indebted for their help as well to my other colleagues there – ʿAdel Mannaʿ, Itzhak Reiter, and Dror Ze'evi.

My colleagues at Tel Aviv University have provided much support and encouragement since I joined them. In particular I thank Zvi Razi, Ehud Toledano, David Wasserstein, and Gadi Algazi for helping me find my way through some thorny spots in revising this manuscript. I would like to express my appreciation to the Yigal Alon Fund, which has supported the work of revising the original thesis.

I offer my sincere thanks to Marigold Acland and the production staff of Cambridge University Press for her patient assistance and professional guidance in the preparation of the final text for publication.

Many friends have made the writing and re-writing of this book far easier and more enjoyable than I anticipated or deserved. I am fortunate to have had your companionship, advice, and support. As I persist in having the final say on my work, any remaining errors are my own.

Note on Transliteration

Documents in both Ottoman Turkish and Arabic served as source materials for this book. As a result there is a mixture of citations in both languages. However, I have attempted to follow consistently certain principles when referring to institutions, persons, and places. All references to institutions, persons, and offices which were part of the Ottoman empire have been rendered in Turkish transliteration. For example: *tımar*, *vakıf*, *sancak*. References from documents in Ottoman Turkish have also been rendered in Turkish transliteration. References from documents in Arabic appear in Arabic transliteration, including the names of all villages and peasants from the *sancak* of Jerusalem. Place names such as Jerusalem, Hebron, etc. have been given their more familiar English form, although all villages appear in Arabic transliteration. For example: *ra'īs al-fallāḥīn*, Bayt Laḥm (Bethlehem), Rīḥā (Jericho).

The transliteration system of the *International Journal of Middle East Studies* was followed as a standard. Inconsistencies in transliterations from titles and citations from other works are due to the variety of systems used at different times and in different places around the world.

Note on Money, Weights, and Measures

One of the most confusing and complicated aspects of any research involving counting and measuring in early Ottoman history is the standardization and conversion of terminology. A plethora of coins was in circulation and containers varied in size, if not in name, over very small distances. As research in the *sijill* series from the Arab towns of the Ottoman empire proceeds, we will gradually collect the data necessary for a more definitive tabulation of the various coins, weights, and measures used there. No attempts were made here to quantify and convert measures to present-day equivalents.

A general notion of the size of these measures will accordingly suffice. Since the relative worth of monies or measures is germane to certain discussions, the following table is provided as a simplified guide. Brief reminders will be inserted in the footnotes where it is more convenient to have the relative values immediately available.

(A) Money

1 gold coin =	40 pieces of silver =	80 small silver coins
**sulṭānī*	**qiṭʿa*	**akçe*
qibrisī	*para*	*akçe-i ʿuthmānī*
dīnār	*fiḍḍa*	*ʿuthmānī akçe*
sikke		*asper*
sikke-i hasane		

The term starred (*) at the top of each column is the one found most commonly in the Jerusalem *sijill* during the period covered here. The three terms – *sulṭānī*, *qiṭʿa*, and *akçe* – will be used consistently throughout this work. Equivalents were established using other works of Ottoman history and from internal references found in the *sijill*.[1] The terms *sulṭānī*, *sikke*, *qibrisī*, and gold *dīnār* are all used interchangeably in *sijill* documents relating to the countryside. What may be true for this area in these years does not necessarily apply to the empire in any larger sense. In other instances, these terms may describe coins of different values, but the substitution of one term for the other within the same document, or their equivalence to 40 silver *para* noted on different occasions, leaves little doubt of their synonymous use here.

These rates give a rough approximation of the relative worth of gold to silver used in figuring accounts. The rate of 1 gold piece:80 silver *akçe* is used quite consistently in the *sijill* for the years under study. At the beginning of Ottoman rule in Syria, a rate of 1 gold piece:60 *akçe* obtained, while by the end of the sixteenth century the rate was 1:90, as evidenced by the *cizye* rates in the Jerusalem survey registers. In this way, the silver *akçe* was used as a "money of account." Imperial records were calculated in Istanbul using this currency and these rates. When taxes were collected at the local level, therefore, imperial currency had to be converted into local equivalents.[2]

(B) Weights

1 *qinṭār* = 50 *mann* = 100 *raṭl*
A *qinṭār* varied in weight from place to place, depending on the weight of the local *raṭl*. One estimate says a Syrian *qinṭār* was approximately 182 kilos.[3]
Used to weigh: olive oil, grape syrup, vegetables, fruits

(C) Measures of capacity

1 *ghirāra* = 72 *mudd*[4]
One Jerusalem *ghirāra* was equal to three of Damascus; these latter are estimated at 200 kilos of wheat, or 250 liters.[5]
Used to measure: grains, here primarily wheat and barley.
kile: This term has two meanings. It can mean simply "a measure" which was then defined to be a *ghirāra*, or whatever. Or, it can be the name of a particular measure, whose size varied. The *İstanbul kilesi* was a standard imperial measure.[6]

CHAPTER 1

Peasants, Palestine, and the Ottoman Empire

On August 9, 1555, Ilyas *sipahi* (cavalry officer), acknowledged before the kadi of Jerusalem that he had received 19 gold *dinar*s and 35 silver pieces from the villagers of ʿAyn Silwān. The peasants had owed him a total of 27 gold *dinar*s as taxes on the revenues from their annual crops and therefore a debt of 7 gold *dinar*s and 5 silver pieces remained outstanding.[1] All of this was carefully noted in the kadi's ledger.

In December 1554, Nasif *sipahi* sued Aḥmad of the village of Bayt Dhakariyya, which was part of Nasif's *tımar* (income grant), claiming that Aḥmad had been living in another village for two years although he was registered among the peasants of Bayt Dhakariyya. When the district survey register was produced before the kadi in Aḥmad's presence, it confirmed Nasif's claim and he thus requested that Aḥmad be required to return to Bayt Dhakariyya. Aḥmad, for his part, claimed that he could prove his residence in the other village but then conceded that he was still legally a resident of Bayt Dhakariyya, having left the village only three years earlier. Whereupon the kadi ordered him to return to his village and pay his back taxes to Nasif.[2]

Seven peasants who cultivated lands around Jerusalem came before the kadi on July 11, 1553 and sued Mehmet, the official responsible for the immediate surroundings of the city. They claimed that he was abusive and illegally levied arbitrary amounts of grain and straw from their threshing floors. Mehmet maintained that they had voluntarily donated the grain and straw to him, but the peasants insisted that he had forced them to hand it over and they produced two more witnesses to attest to this fact. The kadi ordered that Mehmet be prevented from such acts in future.[3]

Each of these three cases from the Muslim court of Jerusalem involved an Ottoman official, the kadi of Jerusalem, and one or more local peasants. As was often the case, peasants were brought by officials to settle accounts or else they came seeking redress against the abuses of these same officials. The kadi heard the facts of the case, issued a judgment and determined the fine or punishment required. In the Ottoman provincial regime, one important function of the kadi was to serve as an arbiter between the military and fiscal administrators, and the local population. His jurisdiction ranged from the mundane mediation and cataloguing of debts and payments to much more dramatic incidents of abuse and wrongdoing. Local peasants were not a rare curiosity in the kadi's chambers. The ledger entries of the Jerusalem kadi recorded hundreds of cases which exposed the details of peasant–official relations during the period of Ottoman rule.

Peasants, millions of people living in Anatolia, the Balkans, Eastern Europe, the Fertile Crescent, Egypt, and North Africa, were the majority population of the Ottoman empire. In official chronicles they figure most often – if at all – as the backdrop to the great persons and events of imperial history. In official documents, peasants appear as lists of taxpayers, transmuted into quantities of grain, oil, meat, fruit, or silver coins. The villages and villagers filled in as grey between the colors of the great cities and provincial towns, below and around the ruling elite, the military, religious and commercial notables, the urban populace and the nomads. Yet the peasant populations were one foundation of the Ottoman empire, an integral component of its strength. Mostly Muslims and Christians, they formed the bulk of the *re'aya*, the taxpaying class. Their agricultural labors were the basis of the state's wealth, producing subsistence for themselves and revenues for the ruling *askeri* class, the military, administrative and religious functionaries.

From the perspective of a lifetime of research, Halil Inalcik has said:

> the peasant family labor farm, which was the cell of the socio-economic structure in most of the so-called Asiatic empires, determined the formation and was responsible for the survival of these empires ... In fact, if we reverse our usual point of view, it would be no exaggeration to call them peasant empires ... It is our contention that without open or tacit support of the peasant masses, the Ottoman empire could not have come into existence and could not have survived. In other words, it was a compromise that gave rise to this particular polity.[4]

What sort of a compromise was it which obtained "the open or tacit support of the peasant masses"? Inalcik implies that the compromise was made possible by the very nature of Ottoman administration, specifically the agrarian regime. There was, however, no great historic negotiation which mediated this arrangement, a meeting at long tables with the peasants on one side, and the sultan and his men on the other. The settlement was essentially imposed from above, by force when necessary. However, the compromise was continually and implicitly renegotiated to produce a temporary equilibrium between the forces and needs of the administration and the forces and needs of the local agrarian, taxpaying populations, in any particular place, for any given month or year or decade.

Compromise and equilibrium, however, sound both tranquil and vague. Abuse and unrest were to be found at opposite ends of the spectrum of official–peasant relations, and could escalate to cruel oppression and outright revolt. Indeed, peasants have most often figured prominently in historic annals as the victims of oppression or the heroes/villains of insurrection. Yet it was not always in such instances that the peasants were most successful at affecting their situations. Rather, the more routine actions of these millions, individual acts on a minute scale, added up to influence the nature of government. Through them the peasants negotiated their side of the nebulous compromise.

The Palestinian peasants were incorporated into the imperial network of Ottoman provincial administration with the conquests of the early sixteenth century. Names of villages familiar to local residents even today were first recorded in the Ottoman tax registers around 1520. This process was not abrupt or disjunctive, but was part of the gradual integration of the Arab provinces into the Ottoman empire, thereby informing another aspect of the underlying compromise. Ottoman provincial administrative mechanisms did not replace existing structures of local government and taxation in conquered areas. Initially, they imposed only a general framework; gradually Ottoman practices were introduced, simultaneously incorporating useful and appropriate aspects of local custom. The resulting administration was clearly Ottoman, adapted to suit local conditions.

This book explores the relationship between provincial officials and local peasants in order to analyze the day-to-day workings of Ottoman rural administration. It concentrates, as far as possible, on the village and the villagers, how the peasants responded to officials and how they were treated by these representatives of the imperial administration. The aim is to attain a perspective of rural administration closer to that of the peasants themselves, both its immediate personification and its imperial persona, and to build a new empirical basis for understanding the actual administration of the countryside. Having done this, one must further ask, to what extent the administration of Palestine typified Ottoman provincial administration of the period. Finally, any reconsideration of peasant–official relations implies a re-evaluation of our conception of Ottoman imperial authority and its relations with the societies which maintained it.

Palestine and the Ottoman Empire

When the Ottomans conquered the lands of the Fertile Crescent and Egypt from the Mamluks in the early sixteenth century, the Mamluk provinces (*niyābāt*) of Gaza and Safad were often provincial outposts and places of exile for unruly commanders in the Cairo-based empire. Under the Mamluks, Jerusalem had been part of the province centered on the town of Gaza. The Mamluk sultan preferred to banish his commanders to Jerusalem because the region was isolated, yet nearby, and lacked a strong garrison or fort from which to base a revolt. The commanders themselves favored Jerusalem as a place of exile for its climate and the concentration of religious sites and scholars there.[5]

These southern provinces of Syria were vividly described in fifteenth-century writings.[6] Bedouin raiding was a chronic problem, plaguing local residents and travelers alike. For ten years at the beginning of the sixteenth century, the Muslim pilgrimage to Mecca (*ḥajj*) was impossible from Jerusalem due to Bedouin brigandage on the road leading south from the city.[7] Nor did the Mamluk sultan have complete control over his own officers here. The frequent change of governors wore on the local population as each one successively sought to reimburse his private treasury for the price of his governorship. By the fifteenth century, the local Jerusalem economy was depressed due to a general lack of income. The city was populated by "the poor and the pious," Muslims, Christians, and Jews alike. Even the many *vakıf*s (pious foundations) which had been created to support Muslim schools were impoverished.[8] Jerusalem itself was not an important economic center, and lay off the official post and regular coastal trade route from Damascus to Egypt through Gaza. People there subsisted on meager earnings from agriculture, or employ in basic services and manufactures.[9]

In 1516–17, the Ottoman sultan Selim I (1512–20) led his army in a rapid campaign south from Anatolia through Syria to Egypt and the Hejaz, incorporating the provinces of the Mamluk empire into the Ottoman empire. Selim's conquest was a continuation of the policies of his grandfather Mehmet the Conqueror (1451–81) and his great-grandfather Murat II (1421–51), who spent the better part of the fifteenth century consolidating the gains of their predecessors while pushing out the boundaries of the empire in Europe and Asia. Selim's son Süleyman (1520–66) continued to extend these borders, adding Bosnia, Hungary, Podolia, the Crimea, Azerbaijan, Iraq, Yemen, and North Africa up to Morocco.[10]

In general, after an area was conquered, the Ottomans at first ruled it indirectly through the agency of some local lord. Meanwhile, the local revenues were thoroughly investigated and assessed, recorded town by town and village by village in the Ottoman survey registers of population and revenue (*tapu tahrir defterleri*).[11] On the basis of these registers, the Ottoman government then set up a more direct administration, assigning the revenues from local sources as income to Ottoman officials appointed locally, as well as to *sipahi*s, cavalry officers of the sultan's army. Some of the revenues were reserved to the state treasury, while others belonged to pious foundations such as mosques, schools, hospitals, or hospices.

The towns of Palestine were taken late in 1516 with relatively little destruction or force. A rumor of Ottoman defeat prompted revolt in the towns of Safad, Ramle, and Gaza, but the rumor proved false and a massacre quashed the resistance. Jerusalem seems not to have been involved in these episodes.[12] Nor were the city and its hinterland touched greatly by the short-lived revolt of the governor-general of Damascus, Jānbirdī al-Ghazālī, which followed the death of Selim I in 1520. Indirect rule in Syria lasted through this revolt, and the former Mamluk al-Ghazālī was replaced in Damascus by an Ottoman career officer.

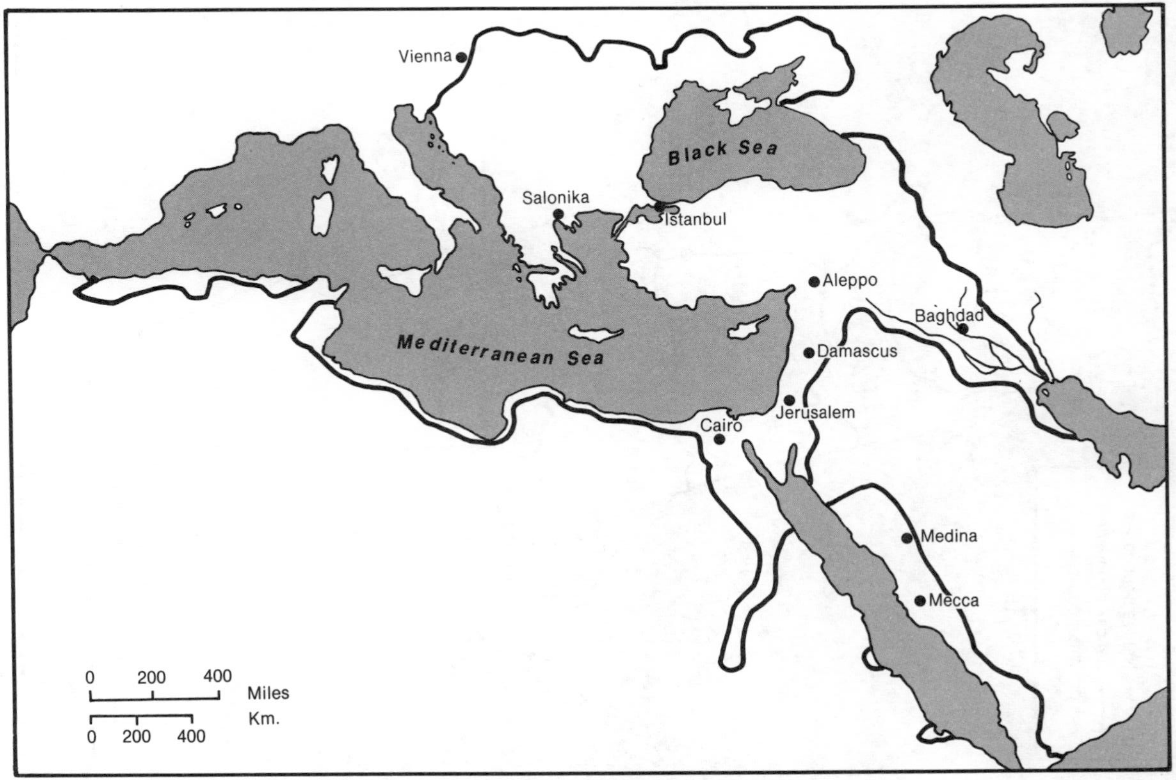

Map 1 The Ottoman empire in 1566

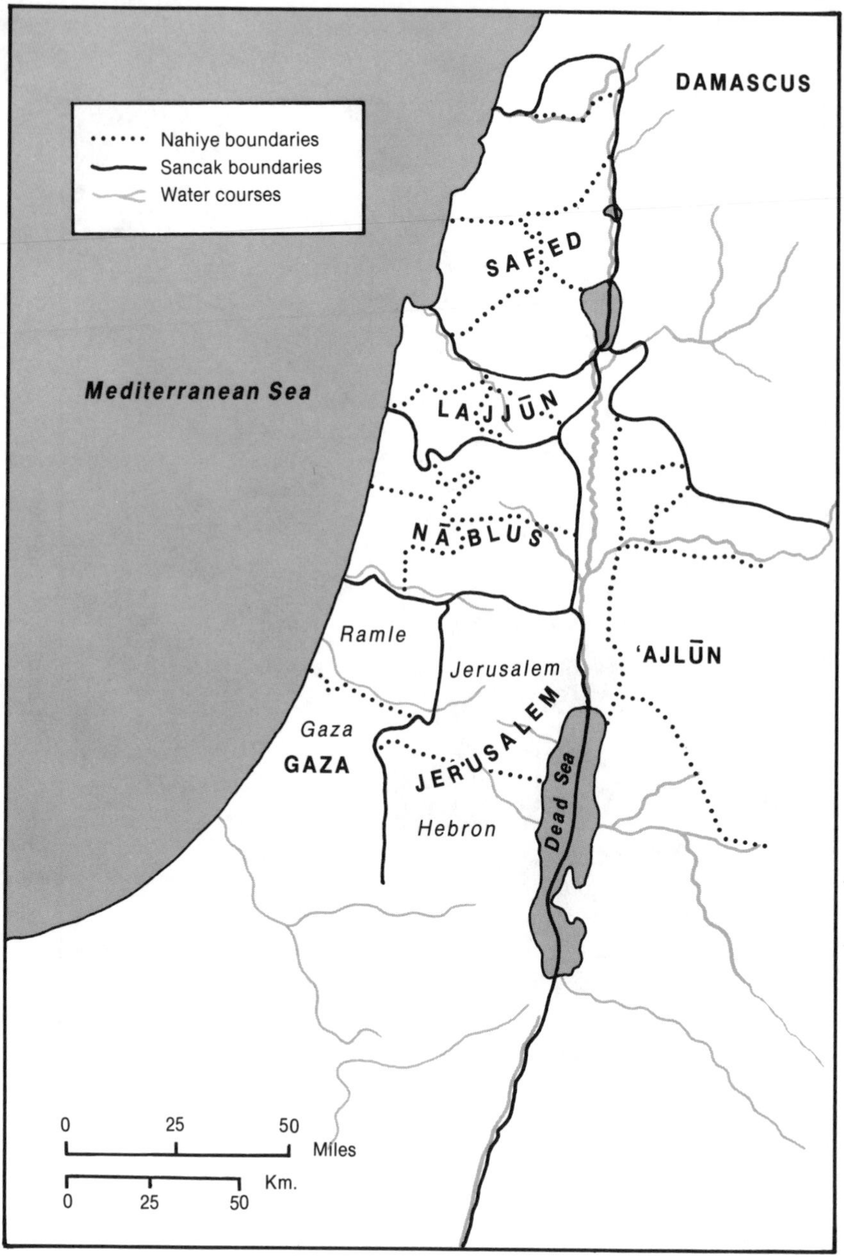

Map 2 Administrative divisions of southern Syria (sixteenth century)

Under Kânûnî Süleyman (the Lawgiver) – known in the West as "the Magnificent" – the Ottomans assimilated their new territory into the administrative framework of the empire. The Syrian lands were divided and incorporated as regular provinces, while Egypt was administered separately. A list of the provinces and their governors from 933/1527 shows that the province (*beylerbeylik*) of Damascus was composed of fifteen districts (*sancaks*).[13] Jerusalem and Gaza were the southernmost *sancaks* of the province. Gaza lay to the west, along the Mediterranean shore, while Jerusalem was bounded by the desert to the east and south, and by the *sancak* of Nablus in the north. The *sancak* of Jerusalem was sub-divided into the two sub-districts (*nahiyes*) of Jerusalem and Hebron, each centered on its eponymous town.

Far from the imperial capital in Istanbul, beyond the borders of the modern Republic of Turkey in Anatolia, the lands which include today's Syria, Lebanon, Jordan, Iraq, Israel, Egypt, and parts of Saudi Arabia played a supporting role to the central provinces of the empire. These lands offered variously: wheat, rice, textiles, dried fruits, cotton, olive oil, and soap. Their vast area expanded the territory which provided revenues to support the running of the empire. Arabia and Egypt also constituted key points of entry to the empire for imported goods from Africa, the Indian Ocean, and the Far East. Spices, slaves, gold, ceramics, and every other precious thing arrived by ship and camel and were forwarded to the sultan's court and the thriving bazaars of Istanbul.

Lying wholly inside the Ottoman realm, the important land routes through Syria and Egypt to the Muslim holy cities of Mecca and Medina were now the responsibility and privilege of the Ottomans. Organizing supplies for the annual *ḥajj* caravans from Damascus and Cairo to the Hejaz and back, as well as ensuring the security of tens of thousands of pilgrims, became a major preoccupation of Ottoman officials in these provinces. Protection of the caravan was not only a religious duty; the *ḥajj* was an important economic event where goods from all over the Muslim world were exchanged.[14] Jerusalem, holy to Muslims, Christians, and Jews, attracted patrician and plebeian pilgrims from every direction. Numerous holy sites and religious centers outside of Jerusalem – in Hebron, Bethlehem, Nabī Mūsā, Nazareth, Safad, and by the shores of the Sea of Galilee – were a further draw to Palestine for pilgrims.

Initially, the Syrian countryside benefitted from the increased order and security established by the new authority. The Ottomans managed better than their predecessors to contain and control the marauding activities of the various Bedouin and Turcoman tribes who lived throughout the area.[15] They were eager to ensure safe passage of the *ḥajj* caravan and the overland trade routes from Arabia and beyond. The restoration and maintenance of the annual pilgrimage were fundamental to the Ottoman image as the supreme Muslim state. Substantial economic advantages accrued to the whole of Syria as this enormous caravan requisitioned supplies to outfit and stock itself for the trek from Damascus to the holy cities and back again.[16]

Jerusalem was sometimes included on the *ḥajj* route, although the main caravan did not pass through the city, but rather through the desert to the east. The traditional route from Damascus to Cairo passed the Sea of Galilee westwards to the Mediterranean coastal plain and then turned south following the sea. The Ottomans took care to repair and reinforce the network of defenses along this route, and the regular presence of imperial troops improved security there. Syria, however, took second place to Egypt in military importance for the Ottomans, as Egypt was a more sensitive frontier of the empire.[17]

Nonetheless, because of its holiness and attraction for Muslim pilgrims, and because of the steady if thin stream of foreign Christians and Jews to Jerusalem, Süleyman spent much time, effort, and money on the reconstruction and refurbishment of the city. The walls, which stand today, were completed in the mid-1530s.[18] Numerous *sabīl*s, fountains for drinking and holy ablutions, were built within the city. The long aqueducts, repaired in the fifteenth century by the Mamluks, were completely restored to ensure the city's water supply.[19]

Partly in response to more settled conditions, the rural population gradually expanded, reoccupying abandoned sites and cultivating new areas. The *sancak*s of Palestine clearly exemplified these trends. Settlement outside the major towns grew through the first half of the sixteenth century, and expanded down into the coastal plains from the sheltering heights of the mountain ridge which stretched from Hebron north through Jerusalem to Nablus. The area was not extraordinarily fertile, but agricultural output here rose, as did the revenues from commercial transit taxes and levies on Christian and Jewish pilgrims.

The increased security, order, and production which followed the Ottoman conquest probably improved general conditions for the rural population of the provinces of southern Syria as well. Many aspects of the new regime, however, did not constitute a radical departure from Mamluk times. An Ottoman sultan ruled in place of the Mamluk sultan, but both the former and the latter were ethnically Turkish. Although Turkish was the official language of government under the Ottomans, the local vernacular remained Arabic. And, the Ottomans, like the Mamluks, were Sunni Muslims. For the peasants who were now under Ottoman rule, life proceeded on much the same basis as it had before. Administration and tax collection seem initially to have been more regular, and so perhaps less abusive. The growth and expansion of settlement and production were experienced within an established framework. The change of government was perhaps felt more by the local urban elites, who had to accommodate the Ottoman officials sent from the capital to perform the military, judicial, and financial tasks of administration.

It is difficult to assess the extent to which peasants knew, understood, and appreciated the change from the unrelated succession of Mamluk sultans to the long-established dynasty of the Ottomans. They certainly recognized some differences between the Mamluks and the Ottomans. The physical presence and clash of armies announced the conquest to all; the imperial seat was farther away and to the north in Istanbul. External differences – uniforms, flags, titles of officials – were obvious. As will be discussed below, peasants also seemed to have absorbed formal Ottoman rhetoric about safeguarding the peasantry as a source of wealth for the state.

Moreover, the peasants were directly affected by the increasingly emphasized Muslim ideology of the Ottomans under Süleyman and Ebu's-Su'ud Efendi, his *şeyhülislam*. Süleyman's reign marked the institutionalization of the *şeyhülislam* as head of the judicial-religious hierarchy of the empire. Ebu's-Su'ud emphasized Süleyman's title as Caliph, while others in the sultan's entourage of ministers and scholars reiterated his status as divinely designated ruler of the world.[20] Imperial ideology was translated and realized for the peasants of the empire in a decree of 1537 to construct mosques in all villages, in order to ensure the regular performance of prescribed prayers.[21] In fact, local surveys of Palestine from 1537 are unique among the Palestine surveys in listing an imam for *every* village; they are largely absent in previous and subsequent surveys.[22] Surely this marked a change from the Mamluk expression of adherence to Islam which largely consisted in the construction of mosques and religious schools.[23]

By the middle of the sixteenth century the *beylerbeylik* of Damascus, including the *sancak* of Jerusalem, was well integrated into the traditional Ottoman administrative framework. The forms of government had stabilized and the movement of peoples which accompanied the conquest and the first years of Ottoman rule had slowed. The major cities of the region – Cairo, Aleppo, and Damascus – grew and thrived as the far-reaching economic unity and security of the Ottoman empire encouraged trade from East to West and throughout the empire, while the households of wealthy officials fueled the local economies. Imperial building projects and new pious foundations contributed as well to various sectors of the local economy and society.[24]

Süleyman's successors were challenged by new problems towards the end of the sixteenth century. After two centuries of confronting relatively weak or weakening states, the Ottoman empire competed increasingly with large and strong political units like itself. The army had more mixed fortunes as the earlier era of expansion and conquest ended; the impact of international monetary mercantile trends grew although it was imperfectly perceived at the time; the balance of European power interests was shifting; and internal disruptions to the Ottoman state – the "Celali revolts" – spread through Anatolia and the Balkans.

Within the province of Damascus, the later years of the sixteenth century were, by comparison with the earlier period, similarly troubled. Reports of administrative abuses and Bedouin attacks increased and the income from Damascus declined, while central government control over the apportionment of revenues weakened.[25] Local powers began to reassert themselves. By the early seventeenth century, the rule of the southern Damascus *sancak*s was vested in the hands of a few chiefs: the Circassian Farrukh in Jerusalem, the Bedouin families of Raḍwān and Ṭurabay in Gaza and Lajjūn, and the Druze Fakhr al-Dīn Maʿn in Safad and Mount Lebanon. The sultan maintained control over them by playing them off against each other in different combinations.

Yet in the mid-sixteenth century, Palestine was still most influenced by the regulation, reorganization, and restorations undertaken by the new Ottoman rulers. The districts were focused inland, towards Jerusalem, Damascus, Cairo, the *ḥajj*, and Istanbul. Southern Syria was part of a huge thriving Islamic empire.

Peasants and peasant studies

In the classical theoretical formulation of good government adopted by the Ottomans, the *reʿaya* occupied one of the essential arcs of the "circle of equity":

> There is no *mulk* [sovereignty] and no *devlet* [state] without the military and without man-power.
> Men are to be found only by means of wealth (*mal*).
> Wealth is only to be garnered from the peasantry [*reʿaya*].
> The peasantry is to be maintained in prosperity only through justice.
> And without *mulk* and *devlet* there can be no justice.[26]

Ottoman provincial administration according to this abstract scheme promised prosperity and equity. Historians have generally described the empire as a thriving and well-governed state during the reign of Süleyman (1520–66). Numerous works have concentrated on the glory of his era. They point to the effectiveness of Ottoman administration, the successes of a well-trained and motivated military force, economic stability with flourishing international trade and internal markets, grand building projects and superb achievements in arts and literature.

In such a prosperous age, one might also expect the functioning of government at the most fundamental level of society, among the vast majority of the population, to be at its most effective and least obnoxious. It was crucial to the well-being of the empire that this be the case, for as Fernand Braudel has observed:

> the Mediterranean in the sixteenth century was overwhelmingly a world of peasants, of tenant farmers and landowners; crops and harvest were the vital matters of this world and anything else was superstructure, the result of accumulation and of

unnatural diversion towards the towns. Peasants and crops, in other words food supplies and the size of the population, silently determined the destiny of the age. In both the long and the short term, agricultural life was all-important.[27]

Braudel's mid-twentieth-century European analysis of the sixteenth-century Mediterranean agrees with the Ottoman insistence on the vital role of the peasants and their product. Did the peasants of the *sancak* of Jerusalem actually fit into the organic explanation of the "circle of equity" or Braudel's Mediterranean world?

We know relatively little about the workings of Ottoman provincial administration at the village level for this or any other period, until perhaps the nineteenth century. Studies have concentrated on different aspects of provincial administration, but almost invariably the peasants are seen in an aggregate blur or as inanimate stick figures hung with labels and numbers. If they constituted the underpinnings of the entire Ottoman empire, as the circle of equity, Inalcik, and Braudel suggest, then we cannot pretend to a firm understanding of that empire unless we investigate carefully the role of the peasants therein.

The economic foundations of pre-modern empires depended on agricultural production. The Ottoman government's calculation and distribution of revenues from resources proceeded according to estimates of annual yields. Yet these estimates had to be economically realistic and to this end the agrarian populace had to have a say, whether overt or implied, in fixing them so as to be able to meet imperial expectations. On the other hand, they had to meet imperial expectations to an extent which sufficiently satisfied the responsible officials. The resulting tension between estimates and actual tax revenues produced a shifting equilibrium which normally prevented either the bankruptcy of the empire or the complete penury of the peasant.

The Ottoman state, in the person of the reigning sultan, set the course of Ottoman policy. Its aims shaped various aspects of administration, including provincial administration as it touched the peasants. Simultaneously, policies were (re)defined by the people whom they affected. Peasants responded, as Inalcik's "compromise" suggests, with their cooperation, ambivalent acquiescence, or rebellion. And, because the peasants constituted the basis of imperial wealth, their participation in the imperial endeavor, however oblivious they were to it, was implicit in and fundamental to the success or mere survival of that endeavor.

"Peasant," as used in this work, is a translation of the Arabic word *fallāḥ*, plural *fallāḥūn*. The word comes from the Arabic root *flḥ*, meaning to split or cleave, as a cultivator or farmer does when plowing; "*fallāḥ*" passed into Ottoman usage as well. Ottoman *ferman*s often used the terms *reʿaya* and *raʿiyyet* to mean the peasants, although these words referred more precisely to the entire taxpaying population which included urban craftsmen, merchants, and others. The *ʿaskeri* (military) class in the Ottoman empire was exempt from taxes, and included not only the spectrum of military forces, but also the administrative officers of the state and the entire religious organization of scholars and judges.

In the Arabic documents from the Muslim court of Jerusalem (*al-maḥkama al-sharʿiyya*), villagers are referred to as "the peasants of village x" or "the people (*ahālī*) of village y" with equal frequency. And, it is the village identification which seems to attach most strongly to the individual. Even when people moved, whether to another village or into a town such as Jerusalem or Gaza or Ramle, they continued to be identified in official documents as "of the village x."[28] The underlying reason for this from an official perspective was their continued liability for certain taxes despite their changed residence.

The peasants around Jerusalem included Muslims and Christians, although the great majority was Muslim. Not all were long-settled agriculturalists. In some places, the cultivators were identified as members of a Bedouin tribe, and some tribes resided in the area for at least part of the year. The majority of villagers were probably sedentary cultivators, though how many Bedouins may have settled in villages, when they did so, or to what extent they maintained their tribal affiliations are questions still unexplored for this period. These observations should serve to prevent us from drawing fixed boundaries around the peasants, from defining them too narrowly.

Because most peasant studies refer to people outside Islamic history or the Ottoman empire, it is perhaps useful to state briefly what "peasant" does *not* mean in the present context. Peasant does not refer to an independent small landowner who possessed unconditionally the lands he worked. Peasants had the right to live on, work, and enjoy the fruits of certain lands (*tasarruf*) and could transfer this right to their children, but they could not sell these lands or endow them as *vakıf*. Peasants could own outright personal movable property, or nonmovables like vegetable plots, vineyards, or fruit trees, but the sultan was the actual owner of most agricultural land. Privately owned property was denoted *mülk* while the sultan's lands were labeled *miri*.

Neither does peasant mean serf. Peasants in the Ottoman empire, except in very rare and particular circumstances, did not belong to anyone.[29] They were attached to a particular place, not a person. Peasants could be restricted in their movements, but they seem to have been tied to the land practically as a function of the dearth or plenitude of agricultural labor, not absolutely.[30] In the eyes of the sultan, the peasants were subjects of the Ottoman state as embodied in himself. Moreover, while the *sipahi*s and other officials could sue individual peasants for tax debts, their own authority over villagers was limited largely to the fiscal sphere and keeping the peace for the duration of their *tımar* appointment, renewed annually, and potentially with a change of venue. Formal adjudication over *both* the officials and the peasants was the sole task and privilege of the kadi, a scholar trained in

Islamic law, and authorized to make decisions regarding sultanic decrees and local customary practice as well.

The Ottoman empire has been called feudal and non-feudal with equal vehemence.[31] In part, the specific debate over the feudal nature of the empire derives from the larger debate over the nature of feudalism and its most proper defining characteristics. I am here less concerned to take a conclusive stance for or against labeling the Ottoman empire as feudal. The fluid definition of the terms in the feudalism debate becomes especially problematic when applied to the limited empirical foundations of our understanding of the nature of Ottoman agrarian societies. However, the terms of the debate highlight a series of relationships which are not completely understood in the Ottoman context. One purpose of this book is to expand the empirical basis for understanding these relationships in the Ottoman empire.[32]

In the political-military sense, feudalism defines the relationship between sovereign authority and its military supporters. Loyalty and service of the latter were rewarded with grants of revenues. The juridical aspect of feudal societies in Europe emphasized the position of the serf vis-à-vis the master, who not only collected revenues from him but could judge and sentence him as well. Peasants in Ottoman Palestine were not subject in this way to their masters (*ustādh* or *sahib-i arz*, as the person holding revenue rights was called). Their relationship to the two independent lines of Ottoman authority – religious-judicial and military-administrative – was sketched above and will be further explicated in succeeding chapters. Moreover, the "master" or revenue holder in the Ottoman empire received his grant for only a year at a time, and in principle was reassigned to a different revenue source each year. The underpinnings of the political-juridical relationship, however, were economic, and thus the debate on the nature of feudalism focuses more often on "the rent extraction relationships intrinsic to all pre-capitalist landlordship."[33]

In its economic sense, feudalism defines a relationship between the sovereign power and the producers of agricultural revenues. It focuses on the means by which revenues are extracted from the peasantry: who collects them and are they collected as tax or as rent? One dividing line in the feudalism debate is between those who maintain that rent and tax modes of surplus extraction define two distinct modes of production, where only rent indicates a feudal mode; and those who find that tax and rent modes are different aspects of one feudal mode of production.[34] The question is whether *tax* and *rent* constitute two different modes of extracting agricultural revenues from the peasants. Does each define a distinct relationship between the sovereign and the peasantry, or only between the sovereign and the revenue collectors? And then, one must ask if the peasants have an appreciation for these different forms, such that they may prefer one to the other.

In either case, there exists a group of revenue collectors who derive their right to collect from the sovereign power. The relationship between the collectors and the sovereign power needs to be defined, as does their relationship to the peasants. It is important to determine to what extent the sovereign can control the revenue collectors and how they are able to usurp his authority. Further, their power over the peasants is a crucial factor, whether it extends beyond the mere collection of revenues to include various labor services.

In the Ottoman empire, there existed different kinds of revenue collectors, including salaried tax collectors (*emin*s), revenue-grantees (military *tımar* holders, members of the imperial family, and high-ranking administrators), and tax farmers. The managers of pious foundations (*vakıf*s) also controlled enormous revenues throughout the empire. Each group of revenue collectors stood in a different relationship to the sultan and to the producing peasants.

Most problematic in a discussion of the feudal nature of the Ottoman empire is the variety of landholding arrangements. They were intertwined with revenue-holding rights and taxpaying obligations. When one observes the Ottoman administrative system from the imperial perspective, as has been most often the case, local differences are minimized in favor of an apparent overriding uniformity. In fact, these local variations may be far more meaningful in trying to understand the nature and longevity of the Ottoman state. To a large extent, the elasticity of the Ottoman system was its great virtue. It allowed a multiplicity of relationships – between peasants and authorities, between people and land – to co-exist.

The "Gordian Knot" of Ottoman history, then, is the essential and practical meaning of landholding to each of the persons called a "landholder". The sultan had absolute ownership (*rakabe*) over virtually all open farmland. Peasants had rights of possession, tenancy, and use (*tasarruf*) of the farmlands, provided they worked them and paid their taxes. Revenue collectors acquired temporary income rights over these same lands, assigned to them by the sultan. Those who were not salaried collectors, but remitted a fixed portion or sum of the crops, were also said to possess the *tasarruf* of their lands, in the sense of "usufruct."

The chief rivals of the sultan for *rakabe* were the pious endowments (*evkaf*). The act of endowment required the transfer of the *rakabe* to God in perpetuity and the dedication of the *tasarruf* to pious purposes. Only the sultan, however, could legally transfer the *rakabe* of open farmlands to someone else. Each endowment was managed by a person (*nazır*) who collected and distributed the revenues produced by the endowed properties. The *nazır*, however, usually drew his salary from these revenues as well. Peasants on lands endowed as *evkaf* had the same status as peasants on *miri* lands, and sometimes some additional exemption privileges.

No thorough understanding exists of the way these rights were interpreted, used, and manipulated in different areas of the empire and at different times. It is clear, however, that their interpretation, use, and manipulation were subject to modification – both legitimate and abusive. Not only did revenue collectors, *nazır*s, and peasants usurp and misrepresent landholding rights, but the sultan confiscated lands wholesale. The ability of each to act defined in part the strength or weakness of the sultan and his regime. More empirical evidence about landholding and revenue rights as they functioned – and not only as formally defined – must be set out and interpreted, therefore, before one can engage the debate on the feudal nature of the Ottoman empire.[35]

"Peasant studies" as a separate field of investigation has been in existence since just after the turn of the twentieth century. It was born in Eastern and Central Europe as an intellectual and political attempt to analyze the movements of reform and revolution sweeping the huge peasant populations of those regions. Obscured during the 1930s and 1940s, the discipline advanced rapidly after World War II in the decolonizing and developing world.[36] Peasant studies of the Middle East and Islamic societies generally, developed, expanded, and swept forward in the general wave of attention turned to the "third world" and "underdeveloped societies." In the spirit of the times, however, most research concentrated on contemporary subjects. Peasants were little a focus for historical studies of periods prior to the nineteenth century, traditionally identified as the beginning of the modern era in the Middle East.

The study of peasants in classical and medieval Islamic history is in its infancy. Few works focus on peasants; those which address the subject at all do so primarily in the context of empirical research on agriculture or irrigation, or more theoretical discussions of feudalism, modernization, and revolution. Claude Cahen rather pessimistically assesses the subject as one "... almost virgin, which is largely condemned to remain so for lack of adequate documentation, but which, to the extent that something could be found, has almost never been the focus of serious inquiry."[37] To explain this lacuna, Cahen underlines the urban character of Islamic civilization and the overwhelming focus of literary works, composed by urban dwellers, on the cities. As a remedy to this imbalance, he suggests re-examining the texts of histories, geographies, legal writings, and literature, for references to rural life, as well as expanding the researcher's bibliography to include miniatures, archaeology, and architecture.

Humphreys echoes Cahen's thinking on the absence of peasant studies in the classical and medieval periods when he says:

> This neglect in part reflects the neglect of our sources, to be sure; illiterate and politically marginal, the peasant could not speak for himself, while the literate citied classes who lived from his labors were too preoccupied with the service of God and the heroics or antics of kings to pay him much heed. In medieval Islamic culture, the peasant seems both voiceless and invisible.[38]

In his proposed program for research Humphreys then looks at peasant studies carried out by European medievalists, in search of possible models to use with the source material available. Ultimately, he passes the chronological boundary of 1500 set for his essay, in order to discuss all the extant material on peasants in Islamic history, speculating on the possibilities for peasant studies in Ottoman history and the likelihood of backward extrapolation from them to earlier periods.

Humphreys, however, hints in his choice of the word "seems" that the medieval peasants may not be entirely dumb. Cahen's suggestion to re-examine classical sources of all kinds points in the same direction. Few peasant speeches or first-hand chronicles are likely to be uncovered. However, the experience of peasant studies, and the multiple methodologies developed in other fields, such as economic and social history, the Annales school, sociology, and anthropology, all provide tools for (re)reading and (re)interpreting texts.

Sheer common sense demands that we never depict to ourselves societies in which peasants were neither heard nor seen. This is science fiction, not sound historical insight. Peasants may appear politically marginal because they do not ride through literary chronicles as generals, governors, and scholars. But any moderately sensible political sovereign recognized that they were his immediate source of subsistence and wealth, and as such occupied some place in his political calculations. The dearth of research on peasants in Islamic societies, then, must be ascribed to a previous lack of scholarly interest combined with an apparent, and partly real, lack of source material.

Peasant studies of the Ottoman era are considerably more advanced as a result of the rich source material preserved in the Ottoman archives in Turkey and in the former provinces of the empire.[39] However, as far as concerns peasants, Ottomanists have mostly concentrated on one particular source – the survey registers (*tapu tahrir defterleri*). These registers have constituted the principal source for almost every work on peasants and agrarian society in the Ottoman empire prior to the nineteenth century. Now that scholars have resolved many of the difficulties of paleography and diplomatics presented by these documents, they may be examined with new questions in mind. Suraiya Faroqhi addresses this issue, commenting: "there is not really much point in continuing to publish lists of villages, taxpayers, taxes, and pious foundations without any well-thought-out problem to which these data are to provide an answer."[40]

Faroqhi, the Ottomanist, like Humphreys the medievalist, then turns to European history as a source of "*problématiques*," research questions by which to guide the nascent field of Ottoman peasant studies. Both scholars insist that new approaches must be utilized for peasant studies in Islamic history, and both point towards new source materials which should be exploited in the endeavor. As Humphreys puts it, "There is doubtless an enormous amount of information buried in the *sharīʿa*-court records and *awqāf* registers for anyone prepared to face the frightful task of ferreting it out."[41]

Humphreys is right on both counts: the *sijill*s are overflowing with material on peasants and reading them can be as tedious as it is rewarding. Using the judicial records of the kadi from one region of the Ottoman empire – the *sancak* of Jerusalem – I have tried to capture some echo of the voices of the peasants from the myriad disparate details the *sijill*s contain on the local population. Although the kadi sat in a city, peasants came regularly to his seat from the surrounding villages in order to record transactions, inheritances, debts, or complaints, and they were brought before him by their urban-based creditors and claimants.

Contacts between peasants and officials were largely defined by the fiscal expectations and obligations of either side, but their interactions were far more complicated than the simple remittance of goods and money. Through a description and interpretation of these contacts, the peasants acquire a voice, many voices, and their historical presence as individuals becomes more comprehensible, more vivid.

Sources

The villagers around Jerusalem did not leave memoirs or letters to open a window onto their personal world or to shed light on their sentiments towards the current regime and its agents. No early parish records have been found for Christian villages, listing births, baptisms, marriages, and deaths. And the Muslim Mediterranean knew no parallel to Europe's Inquisition, whose meticulous catalogues of peasant heresies have provided so much raw material for studies of European peasantry. Other kinds of sources, however, typically Ottoman or Islamic, furnish material on peasants in the Ottoman empire and their lives. These documents were composed for different purposes, from different perspectives. In combination, they become valuable sources about the peasants' roles, and their relationships and attitudes to the Ottoman government and its local officials. Used alone, however, each may prompt a distorted interpretation of the regime and the peasants.

Tapu tahrir defterleri

Tapu tahrir defterleri are survey registers listing population, estimated tax revenue, and the prescribed distribution of revenues in particular administrative areas. They were compiled periodically at the order of the imperial government to determine the income available from all taxable sources, including agricultural production, market taxes, tolls, fines, personal taxes on the *reʿaya* (the taxpaying population), and the *cizye* (poll tax) on Christians and Jews. According to the information in the registers, some of the revenues were then assigned to military and administrative officials as annual income in exchange for their services to the state. This was the basis of the Ottoman *tımar* system.

The detailed registers in the survey series (*mufassal defterleri*) listed the names of the adult males (and occasionally widows) by town quarter and by village, the different taxes levied, the estimated income from each, and whether the revenues calculated from each source were destined for the sultan's treasury, for the revenue grants (*tımar*s) of his cavalry officers (*sipahi*s), district and provincial governors (*sancakbeyi*s and *beylerbeyi*s), for individual owners of private property (*mülk*), or for the upkeep of a particular pious foundation (*vakıf*). They occasionally included marginal notes penned in later to explain some special circumstance or change.[42]

The survey registers are prescriptive documents as they relate to taxation, estimates of anticipated revenues, not statistics of collected revenues. The figures recorded represented a three-year average and there was a minimum lag of one to two years between collection and the final recording of data. Therefore the compilation of the survey register produced a systematic estimate of revenue based on past performance. And, under the best possible circumstances, the register was always slightly out-of-date.

Research based on the survey registers has tended to produce stereotypical pictures of both town and rural situations. The greater detail which exists in the surveys of the towns offers a relatively more diverse picture there, while the villages are more often than not reduced to lists of standard characteristics.[43] Moreover, the quantity of information from other sources on the towns makes it easier to evaluate the survey information with some perspective. No indicators exist in the surveys which distinguish between villages on the basis of their proximity to chief towns, principal products, tax category, population size or character, or outstanding topographic attributes, other than merely to note the existence of such. No distinctions appear within a village or a town pointing out the distribution of wealth or local power.[44]

The registers are understood to define the expectations of the imperial government concerning the tax yields of the province of Jerusalem. Ottoman rural administration was designed in this period primarily to support Ottoman cavalry troops and was based on certain assumptions about revenue production. On the basis of these assumptions, defined as revenues, *tımar*s were assigned to *sipahi*s. But, as the evidence of the Jerusalem *sijill*s reveals, rarely did a *sipahi* collect exactly what was assigned to him. Through their lists of villages and basic crops, the *tapu tahrir defterleri* set out the physical map and tell us what should have been, "in the best of all possible worlds." In order to utilize their contents best to describe an imperfect world, the reliability of the five registers which record information about the *sancak* of Jerusalem may be assessed critically by comparing the information in them with that gleaned from the *sijill*s.[45]

Many of the *defters* also included a *kanunname*, a codification of the schedule of tax rates for a specific province, based on a combination of imperial decree and local practice.[46] The *kanunname* served as a guide to the survey register, explaining on what basis the taxes were assessed, making it clear why certain information was recorded. Each local codification was an amalgam of Islamic law (*sharīʿa*), Ottoman decrees (*kanun*), and local customary law and practice (*ʿörf*).[47]

Despite the limitations described, the *tapu tahrir defterleri* are the foundation of our knowledge of rural society and economy in this period. Used serially, and in conjunction with narrative sources, these registers provide the basic framework of rural administration. Initially, the registers of southern Syria were studied by Lewis, who published parts of some of them and generally worked to explicate their basic form, language, and content. Hütteroth and Abdulfattah created a map of the whole of Syria, Palestine, and Transjordan, which displays graphically the distribution of population, production, and revenue recipients. The picture given is static, based on a single survey, yet it is the only comprehensive view available.[48] For the province of Jerusalem, the registers have been used to produce studies of the towns, the local rural population structure, and the character of local agriculture.[49]

In the present work, I have used the five extant *mufassal* registers for the province of Jerusalem in the sixteenth century. The first three are located in the *Başbakanlık Arşivi* (Prime Minister's Archives) in Istanbul;[50] the latter two are housed in the *Tapu ve Kadastro Umum Müdürlüğü* (General Bureau of Deeds and Cadastral Surveys) in Ankara.[51] The data in these registers are dated to:

I	TTD	427	924–5/1518–19
II	TTD	1015	937/1531
III	TTD	289	952/1545
IV	TTD	516	967/1560
V	TTD	515	1004/1595–6[52]

Of the Jerusalem registers, the first is the most brief and incomplete. Compiled soon after the conquest, this survey reflects the unsettled state of the province and its unfamiliarity to the Ottoman officials. Population and revenue figures appear without the listings of names of heads of households and breakdown of revenue sources generally found in the later registers. Missing entirely are the names of the *tımar* holders to whom the revenues were assigned. Only the general categories of beneficiaries are listed – *vakıf*, *mülk*, or *tımar* – without the more usual details. The second register contains many more particulars for each village, but it is not until the third and fourth surveys that the lists of crops, tax percentages, and other information are consistently provided for each village. The last register is the most problematic, as it shows signs of copying from its predecessor. Thus, the chronological framework of this study encompasses the period stretching roughly from the third to the fourth register; while being the most complete, the changes recorded from one to the next seem more to reflect actual changes locally.

Qāḍī sijillāt

The *qāḍī sijillāt* (s. *sijill*) of Jerusalem exist in complete series from almost the beginning of Ottoman rule to the present day.[53] A vast array of information is to be found in these volumes concerning imperial administration, city government, the affairs of townspeople, villagers, and Bedouin tribes, minority Christians and Jews, and dealing with almost every aspect of their lives be it personal status, taxes, loans, sales, price regulations, complaints, flight, or theft. Any matter requiring official resolution, registration, verification, or adjudication was potentially the domain of the kadi. In addition, imperial orders and decrees received from Istanbul were copied into the *sijill*s.

Qāḍī sijillāt provide enormous detail on the subject, frequency, location, and manner of official–peasant interactions. Disputes brought before the kadi, wherein either party could be the claimant, were primarily suits for unpaid taxes by Ottoman officials against local villagers. However, the *sijill*s also detail abuses by officials or misdemeanors by villagers, as well as the settlements of these cases. Unfortunately, they do not always record explicitly what the penalty was or whether the judgment or penalty was carried out. The latter task was not in the domain of the kadi's authority. After sentencing, responsibility for the matter passed to the *sancakbeyi*.[54] He, or one of his officers, was in charge of executing the sentence. Only the recurrence of a case fortuitously sheds light on its development after the original incident was recorded. In the case of fines or debts, very often payment or a postponement of the due date was stated.

As discussed above, the theory of classical Ottoman statecraft recognized the crucial place of the peasantry in maintaining a flourishing empire. The *sijill*s show the level of local and daily control necessary to maintain a relatively stable and secure society, and reflect something of the attitudes of Palestinian peasants towards their Ottoman rulers, how they conceived of authority and how it was imposed. They record how a symbiosis between ruler and ruled operated at the most basic level of interaction between the peasant population and the local officials, and the hierarchy of responsibility and authority among the officials and the peasants.

The attraction of the *sijill*s in connection with the *tapu tahrir defterleri* stems from two chief characteristics: copious references to rural matters and the local rather than imperial perspective they provide. One must assume that not all rural affairs reached the kadi for registration or resolution; many financial arrangements and disputes were probably settled without recourse to the official legal system. This is significant should one wish to draw conclusions based on the aggregate appearance of types of cases in the registers.[55] The tendency or willingness of peasants to take their internal disputes to a kadi may also have been a function of a village's proximity to the town, or of the ability of the persons involved to pay the required fee. Yet when a case involved a local person and an Ottoman official, the kadi seems more often than not to have acted as the arbiter between them. In his work on seventeenth-century Egypt, El-Nahal surmises that disputes within the community group were taken to the kadi only as a last resort, whereas in a case involving the state and the people, the latter were either forced to turn to the kadi, or better served by doing so.[56]

Data elicited from the *sijill* can serve to confirm, deny, refine, and elaborate on the assessments set out in the survey registers. While the *tapu tahrir defterleri* list the sums estimated to be paid, the *sijill* records some actual payments and affords a picture of how they were executed, as well as provisions for deferment or cancellation or penalization. Many villages or villagers appeared only when there was a delay or other difficulty involved in the annual remittances.[57] In other cases, where the surveys only state broad groups of produce, the *sijill*s specify particular crops. The *sijill*s also contain cases where money is stated in several currency equivalents, thus enabling one to assess the current value of coins used in the *tapu* as money-of-account.

The numerous entries provide through their very language a far more detailed picture of rural administration than the survey registers. The sheer quantity of entries in the *sijill* which touch on the countryside reveals many common and accepted practices. Repeated use of standard terminology identifies responsible individuals among the peasants, jurisdictions of officials, and the delegation of authority. Repeated, formulaic records of tax payments and deferrals are suggestive of normal usage. The more infrequent entries concerning special problems such as desertion of a village or over-collection of taxes fill out the variegated tableau of rural life.

Although the province of Jerusalem as defined by the survey registers included the districts of Jerusalem and Hebron, the scope and emphasis of the *sijill*s are somewhat different. Entries range over the entire district of Jerusalem, including the town itself, but less frequently touch on Hebron and its surrounding villages. Hebron had its own kadi and its own *sijill*s and so most local affairs were probably handled there.[58] Only matters which were of wider import, such as the management of the huge *vakıf*s of Hebron, general administrative affairs or general provincial problems such as Bedouin disturbances were taken up by the Jerusalem kadi. On the other hand, the Jerusalem *sijill*s sometimes record matters from beyond the borders of the *sancak* of Jerusalem, when a particular affair affected the city and its institutions.

Mühimme defterleri

The third major source utilized here is the series of registers called *mühimme defterleri* and the similar *ahkâm defterleri*.[59] *Mühimme* registers contain the file copies of *ferman*s (imperial orders and decrees) and replies to reports from all over the empire, including a summary of the incoming report or complaint with the text of the outgoing response. These specific orders, as well as the general imperial decrees, were dispatched to provincial officials and judges, addressing many aspects of administrative detail.[60]

Mühimme entries touch on questions of law and order, imperial revenues, military arrangements, foreign relations, administrative assignments, and any other matter which was submitted for the sultan's consideration. Although the orders more often refer to towns or provinces, they do include information on villages when relevant, or in the rare instance when a petition from a specific village arrived in Istanbul. Affairs of villages which formed part of imperial *vakıf*s or the endowments of the Muslim holy places were sometimes treated in these orders.

As a source, the *mühimme* and *ahkâm* entries are less problematic than the survey registers, perhaps because their limitations are more readily apparent. Although these registers, by their nature, offer records of extraordinary circumstances or very general imperial orders, by doing so they help define the expected norms. They provide further details on the workings of provincial administration, and their contents add substance to the outline drawn by the survey information. Like the survey registers, these are imperial rather than local sources; they reflect more the concerns of the central administration in Istanbul than those of the peasants in the villages. However, they describe the circumstances of imperial concern and intervention in provincial administration even as regards specific villages and administrators. The difficulty lies in discovering to what extent these orders were implemented. No follow-up notes were made on the copy of the original order, but subsequent *ferman*s may indicate where a chronic problem existed.

Travel accounts were not used as a major source for this work. On the one hand, they tend to concentrate exclusively on the towns and religious sites. More importantly, however, they impose a foreign framework and expectations on the societies they observe. One purpose of the present work is to discover the framework and expectations of the peasants, in their own terms as far as possible. Thus, the travelers potentially mislead more than they inform.

For similar reasons, the work does not borrow any one theoretical approach from European history, despite the suggestion that such a strategy will help scholars of Ottoman history to pose new questions and develop new *problématiques*. Until recently, the documents which reflect the imperial perspective have been the empirical basis for understanding the peasantry. They focus on "the peasant's obligations, which of course lay at the centre of the relationship between the state and the peasant. In other words, it was with the state's view and perception of the peasantry that peasant reality was overlaid."[61] Now, one must attempt to strip away the state's view, and reckon that of the peasants.

Peasants around Jerusalem, or anywhere else in the Ottoman empire, comprised societies which developed from their own political, economic, religious, cultural, and legal experiences and expectations. These should be the starting point for any theoretical conceptualization of the societies themselves.

CHAPTER 2

Aspects of authority

Authority for the efficient and effective governance of the Ottoman dominions was vested in the military and judicial officials appointed from Istanbul to the provinces and districts of the empire. The beylerbeyi (provincial governor) of the province of Damascus controlled ten *sancak*s (districts), including Jerusalem. At the district level, the officials included the *sancakbeyi* (district governor), *sipahi*s (cavalry officers), *subaşı*s (soldiers with police functions), a local garrison of janissaries, and the kadi(s). In turn, senior officials were assisted by subordinates and support staffs drawn either from their accompanying households or from the local population.

Rural administration focused on the collection of taxes and ensuring peasant production. Among the peasants, immediate authority over the community and responsibility to the government lay with the village leader(s), the *ra'īs al-fallāḥīn*. He was the principal channel of official communication to the village population, and the mouthpiece of the villagers before Ottoman authorities. Moreover, the village leaders assumed a legal obligation for the payment of local taxes, making them liable for the sum due from their entire community.

This chapter examines the structure of authority at the district level. It tries to define the functions of the various officials and the village leaders in the routines of annual taxpaying and collecting. The relationship between the local peasants and the Ottoman administrators was not a bilateral one; it rested on a triangular balance between the military-bureaucratic officials of the *sancakbeyi*'s staff, the kadi as judge of all and sundry matters for arbitration, and the peasants who produced food and agricultural revenues.

Officials

In the mid-sixteenth century, the combined urban and rural taxes of the *sancak* of Jerusalem supported the local Ottoman military administration: the *sancakbeyi*, fifty-six *tımar* holders, of whom most were *sipahi*s, and the janissary garrison. The local revenues of the *sancakbeyi* were designated *hass-i mir-i liva*, while those reserved for the sultan were labelled *hass-i şahi*.

*Sipahi*s were assigned *tımar*s (revenue grants) or *ze'amet*s (large *tımar*s) which were usually made up of the tax revenues due from local villages.[1] The *sipahi*s (cavalry officers) and janissaries were recruited either as slaves captured in war, through the *devşirme* (the periodic Ottoman levy of Christian boys from the Balkans as slaves) or from the sons of Ottoman officials. Occasionally, a *sipahi* may have originally been a Muslim of non-military status, a peasant or modest city dweller, who had volunteered for service and distinguished himself on campaign. *Sipahi*s and janissaries alike received rigorous training as servants of the sultan before being posted to the provinces.

In exchange for the income grants, by which they supported themselves and varying numbers of retainers and equipment, the *sipahi*s served on imperial campaigns and kept the peace locally. Each town and the fortresses built or restored by the Ottomans to safeguard the major routes had a garrison of janissaries to provide additional military manpower. They were primarily meant to be a military force, whereas the *sipahi*s combined military and administrative-bureaucratic functions. The Jerusalem garrison comprised 104 soldiers and other employees, including sixty-four janissaries, five gunners (*topçu*), twelve gatekeepers (*bawwāb*), two gatekeepers for the citadel, ten groomsmen and storekeepers, a jailer, carpenter, baker, men to maintain the moat and aqueduct, an *imam*, and a *müezzin*. This force in the citadel was commanded by the *dizdar*, aided by an adjutant (*kethüda*), secretary (*katip*), and servant.[2]

The lion's share of the revenues in the *sancak* of Jerusalem supported pious foundations (*vakıf*s), most of them local. These were the Dome of the Rock and al-Aqṣā mosque in Jerusalem, the "*vakıf* of Abraham" in Hebron,[3] and the *vakıf*s for various *medrese*s (religious colleges) and *ribat*s (hospices) founded by the Mamluks and their predecessors; some endowments also contributed to the maintenance of pious foundations in Mecca, Medina, and Cairo. The Ottomans also established several new *vakıf*s, including the large complex of *medrese*-caravansaray-soup kitchen called Hasseki Sultan *'imaret*; the sufi convent of Shaykh Aḥmad al-Dajjānī; and a fund to maintain the local water supply system.[4]

The *sancakbeyi* was the chief military-bureaucratic authority in the district of Jerusalem. In keeping with the norms of Ottoman provincial administration of the mid-sixteenth century, he would be a career military man, making his way through a progression of appointments around the Ottoman domains as a *tımar*-holding cavalry officer, then as a *sancakbeyi* in various districts, then to a post as provincial governor and one day perhaps to the office of vizier (minister) or even grand vizier. Appointments as *sancakbeyi*, as for other offices, were formally for one year, though they could be renewed immediately or after a tour of duty elsewhere. The *sancakbeyi* was responsible for general security inside his town seat and in the surrounding countryside; for the regular collection of urban and rural duties; for the correct conduct of commercial activity; for regular and sufficient food supply to the town; and for the condition of the local military force which he was required to lead on campaign when called. His main antagonists in the *sancak* of Jerusalem were Bedouin tribes passing through or seasonally resident, and unruly peasants. Orders reached the *sancakbeyi* from his immediate superior, the *beylerbeyi* of Damascus, and from the sultan in Istanbul.

Overall, the *sancakbeyi* probably had relatively little personal contact with the peasants. His own income was composed largely of urban-generated revenues in Jerusalem (market taxes and fines) and of agricultural revenues. All of these were collected for him by appointed deputies (*vekil*, *mandub*) who might be from among the local *sipahi*s, *subaşı*s, or janissaries assigned to the citadel.

It was the *sipahi*s, the *subaşı*s, and the janissaries who had the most to do with the peasants. The *sipahi*s were assigned the revenues of villages, or fractions of them, as *tımar*s. When not away on campaign, fulfilling their military obligations to the empire, the *sipahi*s had to spend some time and effort seeing to the proper cultivation and harvesting of their villages and plots. This they could do best by actually visiting their village(s), to make sure that the peasants were there, working as expected. Alternatively, these supervisory tasks could be assigned to a subordinate, or leased to a local person.

The *subaşı* was in charge of subdivisions within a *sancak*. He lived in town and constituted a kind of police authority or town commander, although he did not belong to a separate police corps. Assigned generally from Istanbul, the *subaşı*s served under the *sancakbeyi*, conducting investigations in military, commercial, and criminal cases, making arrests when necessary and presenting the facts of a case before the kadi. On campaign, *subaşı*s commanded the *sipahi*s of their subdistrict. They might also act as tax-collecting agents for the imperial *hass* and the *sancakbeyi*. In both the town and the countryside, their duties included keeping the peace and protecting the population. While the salaries of some *subaşı*s were paid as *zeʿamet*s, it is not clear that this was the rule.[5] There were *subaşı*s serving in the district who were not listed among the *zeʿamet* holders in the survey register. Finally, the number of *subaşı*s serving at one time and the length of their appointments are unknown.

Some of the *subaşı*s were drawn from the ranks of the *sipahi*s and janissaries stationed in the city. *Subaşı*s in the *sancak* of Jerusalem were assigned to specific jurisdictions, which included the town itself with the villages immediately surrounding it, and the regions called Banī Zayd, Banī Ḥārith, Bayt Natīf, Bayt Laḥm, and Bayt Jālā. A *subaşı* was also assigned to the villages whose revenues were part of the endowment of the imperial *ʿimaret* (complex) in Jerusalem, which took him outside the immediate district of Jerusalem.[6] For example, Husayn b. Ahmad Harj al-Layl was named *subaşı* of Bayt Natīf and its dependencies and Bayt Laḥm and Bayt Jālā, for which he collected 55 *sultani* per month and was responsible for his own men and horses.[7] ʿAli Bali b. Sinan, a *sipahi* who prompted complaints from the villagers of ʿInab because of his abuses, was also a *subaşı*, and served as one throughout much of his posting to Jerusalem.[8] For at least part of his tour as a janissary in the Jerusalem citadel, El-Hac ʿAli b. ʿAbdallah served as the *subaşı* of the ʿ*imaret* villages.

In and around Jerusalem, the *subaşı*s came into contact with the peasants quite regularly. They managed the villages of their own *tımar*s (when they had them) and also collected taxes acting as agents for others. For example, Ferhad *subaşı* of Bayt Laḥm collected 125 gold *sultani* from the village leaders for Farruh the *sancakbeyi*, whose *hass* was partly in that village; and Masih *subaşı*, acting for Ridwan *sancakbeyi*, collected 75 *sultani* from the people of Bayt Rīmā.[9] The *subaşı*s themselves also leased the right to collect taxes from other revenue holders, as when Murad *subaşı* leased the tithe of ʿAyn Kārim from the *sipahi* El-Hac ʿAli b. Yusuf.[10] This kind of leasing was called *iltizam*, and became widespread, the standard form of tax-farming found in provincial administration during later periods. While the kadi's records contain numerous entries in which this practice is mentioned, in none of them was it criticized as such.

Often one finds the *subaşı* escorting the parties in a dispute to the kadi, like Khalīl, his son Ibrāhīm, and a third man of the village of Jīb, who were all brought in bleeding from the blows they had given one another.[11] When Yūsuf b. Ṣalāḥ of Bayt Ṣafāfā refused the summons to appear before the kadi, it was ʿAşur *subaşı* who was sent to haul in the recalcitrant.[12] Or, it might be the *subaşı* who was sent off to investigate the circumstances of some wrongdoing. In the case of a break in a water pipe leading to Jerusalem, the *subaşı* accompanied the kadi himself to inspect the damage.[13] At other times, the *subaşı* might delegate this responsibility, as did Hasan *subaşı* in the investigation of the night-time assault on Ḥasan of Dayr Abū Thawr while he slept in his vineyard.[14] In the kadi's adjudications, *subaşı*s were frequently called to give evidence on the basis of their investigations. The peasants coming to Jerusalem met *subaşı*s in various capacities, including the people of Abū Dīs, who when caught selling their beans in the city, claimed it was the *subaşı* who had given them permission to do so.[15]

The men called *subaşı*s moved extensively around the province. From the list of attacks reported against them, the investigations or arrests to which they were assigned, and some of the complaints filed against them, it is clear that these officials spent much time on the district's rural paths. One further task they performed was escorting pilgrim groups along the routes to Jerusalem.[16] They must, therefore, have been familiar figures to the peasants, perhaps the most routine representatives of Ottoman authority in the countryside.

Among the Ottoman military personnel in the province of Jerusalem, no other group appears to have had as much regular direct contact with the rural population. However, it is not clear that the *subaşıs* constituted a group entirely distinct from the *sipahi*s and the janissaries, as noted above. Moreover, one of the janissaries occasionally acted as the deputy of a *sipahi* or other tax collector,[17] although outside the walls of the city the janissaries were engaged primarily in containing the Bedouin threat or guarding the *ḥajj* caravan. While the janissaries as a group had little official business in the villages, their companies were probably a familiar, if not common, sight on the local roads.

As the chief judicial official of the province, the kadi was a separate and complementary authority to the *sancakbeyi*. His role in provincial administration was as great as that of his military counterpart, and broader than the title "judge" would imply. Like the *sancakbeyi*, he was the recipient of a regular flow of imperial orders relating to good government and its abuse in the province. In many ways, however, the authority of the kadi exceeded that of the *sancakbeyi*, for the kadi could investigate and pass judgment against the *sancakbeyi* or any other member of the military administration. He judged matters covered both by Islamic law (*sharīʿa*) and by Ottoman imperial regulations (*kanun*), the latter being defined in sultanic decrees and derived from local and customary usage (*ʿörf*) as well as administrative exigencies.[18]

There were kadis in Jerusalem belonging to the four schools of Islamic law, although the chief kadi was a Ḥanafī, representing the official school of the Ottoman state. He was appointed annually from Istanbul, a senior member of the official hierarchy of religious scholar-teachers and judges, the *ʿilmiye*.[19] The subordinate kadis – Shāfiʿī, Mālikī, and Ḥanbalī – could be nominated from among the local learned religious men (*ʿulamāʾ*). The presence of kadis from more than one school of law in one town much predated the Ottomans, but in Jerusalem the presence of all four signalled the religious preeminence of this otherwise modest provincial town, which drew people from all over the Islamic world. The kadis of Jerusalem came under the supervision of the chief Ḥanafī kadi of Damascus, himself a member of the *ʿilmiye*.[20]

The jurisdiction of the Jerusalem kadi extended well beyond the borders of the province. He was described in the *sijill* as being "the master of the judicial district of Jerusalem and the town of Hebron and the fort of Bayt Jibrīn and its dependencies."[21] Despite the fact that towns and some large villages like Hebron, Bayt Jibrīn, Ramle, Gaza, and Nablus all had their own kadis, people from these places brought some of their cases to the kadi of Jerusalem. These might involve endowment (*vakıf*) properties located in Jerusalem, local endowments for holy places in Jerusalem, the behavior of the *sancakbeyi* and his men, or peasants who had abandoned their lands and moved to a location within the kadi's defined jurisdiction.

Unlike the military officials, the kadi did not hold a *tımar* grant. He received a daily stipend determined by his status in the Ottoman judicial hierarchy and fees from clients for the various functions of his office: marriage contracts, inheritance settlements, manumission decrees, property sales, or any other of the routine decisions the kadi was called upon to make. A copy of any decision could be obtained for a fee,[22] but copies of imperial decrees of the type of the *adâletnâmeler*, issued to elucidate specific points in the *kanunname* or redress abuses, were obtainable free of charge.[23] In order to increase their incomes, kadis were known to raise fees arbitrarily, or insist on a formal judicial proceeding where none was required. Further, unauthorized deputy kadis were sometimes appointed for money, a corrupt but profitable practice.[24]

Various functionaries were attached to the kadi to carry out auxiliary tasks. As mentioned, a *subaşı* could be sent to arrest someone and bring that person before the kadi, or to investigate the circumstances of a case. Normally, the *muhzir* was the arresting officer. There were a head scribe, the *başkatip*, and his subordinates, who penned the *sijill* records and made copies of documents for people who wanted to pay for them.[25]

Although the kadi was an Ottoman appointee, part of the religious judicial hierarchy, and therefore part of the corps of Ottoman provincial officials, he cannot be seen as being unambiguously partial to the Ottoman military officials. In a schematic image of provincial authorities, we might best envisage a triangle whose three sides were occupied by the military officials, the kadi and his assistants, and the local population. One essential role of the kadi was as an arbitrator between the military administration and the peasants; he was the official who heard the complaints of both the tax collectors and the taxpayers. Sultanic *ferman*s addressed to the kadi ordered him to investigate administrative irregularities which had come to the imperial ear. As evidenced in the *sijill*, the kadi was clearly not a puppet of the governor, for he found sometimes in favor of the administrators, sometimes for the peasants in their grievances against the Ottoman officials.

Finally, in the constellation of interests identifiable in the province of Jerusalem, there were the administrators (*nazır*s) and trustees (*mütevelli*s) of the numerous *vakıf*s in Jerusalem and Hebron.[26] They or their deputies went out regularly like the military officials to collect revenues due to the *vakıf*. The foundations drew their incomes from urban and rural sources alike, and all or part of the revenues from a village might form part of one or more *vakıf*s. Here too, the right to collect the revenues could be sub-leased.

The *nazır*s and their staffs stood in a somewhat different relationship to the peasants than did the *tımar* holders, the other military officials, or the kadis. More often than not, the *vakıf* employees were local persons. Unlike the *tımar* holders, they did not draw their own income as a direct percentage of the agricultural revenues, but were generally paid a fixed salary, established in the endowment deed. Yet they were responsible for collecting the *vakıf* revenues, and so shared the routine duties and difficulties to be discussed below with all those who collected agricultural revenues. Because employees' salaries were ultimately dependant on successful management of the *vakıf* properties, including agricultural revenues, the *nazır* did have an interest in promoting the welfare of the endowed villages. However, he served no policing function, as did some of the military officials. The job of the *nazır* was also unlike that of the kadi, in that the *nazır* had no formal power to adjudicate. Yet he did at times receive complaints about the behavior of military officials from the villagers who cultivated *vakıf* lands. Moreover, in some instances a kadi could hold a position as the *nazır* of a *vakıf*.

Peasants

The third official Ottoman survey of the *sancak* of Jerusalem, dated to 952/1545, shows a fairly homogeneous collection of 174 villages distributed along the mountain ridge from Hebron to Nablus. Between and beyond the villages, around the city of Jerusalem and scattered across the province, were *mezraʿa*s, cultivated areas which might be inhabited seasonally, as well as smaller plots (sing. *kıta-i arz*).[27] Since the Ottoman conquest of the region almost thirty years earlier, the population and agricultural output had steadily increased. The latest figures showed a continuous rise in the number of adult males, and in the production of each village. Some of the population increase resulted from the improvement in rural conditions. More villages were inhabited as the population grew and rural security improved. However, the increase also reflected the more efficient registration of population in the third register; in the two previous surveys often only the village name and the types of taxes were noted. Separating the effects of improved registration from the actual population and revenue rises is virtually impossible. We must be content only to observe the increase here.

This third register did, however, include enough information on each village to indicate more clearly what the whole province was worth. In the survey register of 952/1545, a village population of some 5,813 adult males was recorded in the *sancak* of Jerusalem (Table 2.1). Eighty-seven percent of the rural population was Muslim; Christian villagers were concentrated in two clusters of villages, one along the road north from Jerusalem around Rāmallāh, the other to the south towards Bayt Laḥm.[28] There were no Jews recorded in the villages of the *sancak* of Jerusalem, nor elsewhere in rural Palestine except near Safad, where they were prominent in the local wool industry. Most people lived in villages of ten to fifty households.[29] In the district of Hebron, the villages were fewer and more spread out, with people tending to concentrate more in larger villages.[30] Nomads and semi-nomadic groups, mostly Arab Bedouin, also inhabited the *sancak* of Jerusalem. Sometimes they appeared as part of a village population, but more often the names of the tribes and sub-tribes were listed in the surveys with a general sum due in taxes. Tribal populations were not listed.

When the *defterdar*'s office (the Ottoman finance ministry) examined the fourth register of Jerusalem dated to 967/1560, it found the villages around the province to be much the same as in the previous survey (Table 2.1). The rate of population increase had apparently slowed: the rural population rose just over ten percent, while that of the city of Jerusalem actually dropped six percent. (The quality of the third and fourth surveys is comparable, so that the changes between them are more definable and meaningful than those between the second and third surveys.) Eight new villages were recorded in 967/1560 which previously were *mezra'a*s attached to a particular village. In the intervening years, people had settled in them permanently so that they were now registered as separate settlements.[31]

The final survey, dated to 1004/1595–6, indicates that the rural population remained stable until the end of the century, while that of the city continued

Table 2.1 *Population of the Sancak of Jerusalem according to the* Tapu Tahrir Defterleri *(Ottoman Surveys) #289 (952/1545) and #516 (967/1560)*
Figures are numbers of: heads of households/bachelors/religious figures/handicapped.[32]

Survey:	*#289*	*#516*
Jerusalem (town)		
Muslims	1,987/141/15/1	1,933/ 95/109/4
Christians	303/135/ /3	281/142/ /2
Jews	324/ 13/ /1	237/ 12/ /
total:	2,614/289/15/5	2,451/249/109/6
Jerusalem (*nahiye*)		
Muslims	4,177/ 84/ 6/	4,550/198/ 4/
Christians	641/ 38/ 1/	598/ 64/
Jews	————	————
total:	4,818/122/ 7/	5,148/262/ 4/
Hebron (town)		
Muslims	969/ / 1	983/129/ 3/9
Christians	————	————
Jews	8/	11/
total:	977/ / 1	994/129/ 3/9
Hebron (*nahiye*)		
Muslims	782/ / 2	1,043/ 86
Christians	91/	112/ 7
Jews	————	————
total:	873/ / 2	1,155/ 93
TOTAL:	9,282/411/25/5	9,748/733/116/15

to drop.[33] The countryside here did not share in the gradual decline of population recorded for the towns of Palestine,[34] nor was the situation comparable to that in the countryside of Ramle, just to the west along the coastal plain. There, the rural population declined by sixteen percent from 964/1557 to 1004/1595–6, reflecting renewed insecure conditions in the coastal regions.[35]

Once again, Bedouin incursions became a prominent theme in the history of Palestinian settlement. Like the Mamluk emirs before them, the Ottoman *sancakbeyi*s were challenged to protect the settled village population from Bedouin raids. From the end of the sixteenth century until the late eighteenth century, the entire region of southern Syria was controlled by prominent Bedouin chiefs, who were officially recognized by the Ottomans as local governors.[36] While unable to overcome or break the power of these tribes, the Ottomans nonetheless were able to establish and maintain a tenuous balance of power among them. From Istanbul, they were reasonably successful at playing off one against the other, thereby preserving Ottoman sovereignty and ensuring a moderate annual income from this region to the imperial treasury. Most importantly, the Ottomans were usually able to rely on one or another of the Bedouin chiefs to bring the *ḥajj* caravan from Damascus to the Hejaz and back again in safety.

The *ra'īs al-fallāḥīn*

Every village had one or more leaders, men who by virtue of their age, experience, and local prominence were designated as heads of the village. They represented their fellow-villagers before the Ottoman authorities with regard to taxpaying, and acted as their spokesmen in matters brought before the kadi. This did not mean that no one but the leaders ever went to the kadi. In the numerous cases involving individuals – such as sales, marriage contracts, inheritance settlements, or criminal offenses – the person(s) concerned was often present, with the *ra'īs* there acting as a witness or guarantor. The leaders appeared most often in connection with the fiscal obligations of their communities, or when the security and well-being of the village or the province was at issue.

The leaders were known as *ra'īs al-fallāḥīn* or *ra'īs ahālī qaryat*...[37] Often they were cited in the *sijill* in pairs (*ra'īsān*) or groups (*ru'asā*). The leaders were clearly identified in the *sijill*, as for example: "al-Asad b. Shu'ayb, Mūsā b. Mus'ad and 'Abd al-'Azīz b. Basīṭa, all from the leaders of the peasants of Abū Dīs," or "Ma'ālī b. 'Ulyān and Tūba b. Aḥmad, leaders of the peasants of Bayt Laḥm."[38] Over the course of years, one can identify persons who repeatedly acted as leaders, or brothers and sons who stepped into this office. In Abū Dīs, one Muḥammad b. 'Alī b. al-Basīṭa, a relative of 'Abd al-'Azīz, was *ra'īs* in 963/1555–6; in 'Ayn Silwān, Muḥammad Abū Ra's was followed by his son Suleymān b. Muḥammad Abū Ra's;[39] various members of the Baṣbūṣ family served as leaders in Bayt Laḥm.[40]

In addition to the appellation "*ra'īs*," other important people in the village were known as *mashā'ikh*, *akābir*, or *a'yān*, "elders" or "notables."[41] Persons with any of the four titles appeared at times labeled "*mutakallimīn*" or "spokesmen" for their communities.[42] While the leaders were demonstrably drawn from these groups, not all the elders and notables were automatically leaders. Hence, Mūsā b. Mus'ad, Jibrān b. 'Alī al-Ba'jī, 'Abd al-'Azīz b. Ibrāhīm Basīṭa, and Nimr b. Abū Dahīm were said to be "of the *ru'asā* of the people of Abū Dīs and *a'yān* of their community,"[43] while three *akābir* of the peasants of al-Aṭrūn (Latrun) were "now the leaders in the village."[44] However, we cannot assume that the sixteen "elders (*akābir*) of the villagers of Bayt Laḥm" who came to testify about having broken the water-line into Jerusalem all served as *ru'asā* as well.[45]

Elders and notables were not always plainly separable. The five men from Naḥḥālīn who reported the impoverishment of their village to the kadi in 968/1561 were called "*akābir* and *mashā'ikh* of the people," while the four peasants from Gaza who made a similar deposition in 962/1555 were called "*akābir* of the peasants of the village and *a'yān* of their community."[46] The same person, such as Mūsā b. Mus'ad or Jibrān b. 'Alī al-Ba'jī of Abū Dīs, appeared now as *ra'īs*, now as from the *a'yān*, but we cannot automatically assume that in the latter instance he was still an official "leader."

To confuse the matter just a little further, the scribes who copied the *sijill* documents did not always insert the titles of various people, perhaps because the titles were not formally awarded. Thus, we find Mūsā b. Mus'ad and Jibrān b. al-Ba'jī of Abū Dīs referred to in one document from 960/1553 as leaders, but not so designated in another entry from the same year.[47] Khalīl b. Ibrāhīm and Bashīr b. 'Abd al-'Azīz of Liftā were cited in one year both as leaders and without that title.[48] Often persons who can be identified as leaders from previous years or subsequently were referred to without titles.

The distinction between the position of *ra'īs* and the various titles of prominence is not artificial. Unlike the elders or notables, the leader or leaders received official compensation for the duties they performed. From the taxes assessed annually, a portion was earmarked for them. In Abū Dīs, the leaders gave an account of the revenues to be delivered to the *vakıf*, after which "the *nazır* must undertake [to give] to them their *muṭlaq* and their robes, according to their previous custom."[49] *Muṭlaq*, "the part released or given," seems to refer to an accepted proportion or sum to which the *ru'asā* were entitled. The robes were a recognized symbol of official standing from the early Islamic and Mamluk eras, adopted by the Ottomans at every level of administrative office.[50]

Frequently, the portion of the leaders was calculated as a sum, either in cash or in kind, which was "the equivalent of the price of their robes."[51] In fact, the sum was not tied to the price of an actual garment, but seems to have been fixed at a percentage of the taxes due. Percentages generally ranged up to ten percent. The leaders of ʿAyn Kārim received 100 *akçe* from the 1,900 *akçe* due in taxes; in Bittīr 400 *akçe* were set aside from the 4,000 *akçe* assessed for the *vakıf*.[52] Occasionally, the portion of the leaders was more substantial, as in Siʿīr, where 3 gold *sultani* out of 15 were earmarked for the robes of the *ru'asā*. Notably, no mention was ever made of compensation to the *akābir*, *mashā'ikh*, or *aʿyān*; this difference would seem to prove the distinction between them and the *ra'īs*.

It is difficult to determine the number of leaders in any village at one time. More than one leader might serve at the same time even in smaller villages like Bayt Fāsīn and Bīr Zayt, with twenty-six and twenty-four adult males, respectively, registered at mid-century.[53] In the larger villages like Abū Dīs and Bayt Jālā, ten leaders and perhaps more held the title together. However, no statement exists of how many leaders were needed for each village, nor any formula for calculating the ratio of leaders to villagers. In the Ottoman survey register, leaders were not specifically identified as such, nor was there a list found in the *sijill* of all the leaders in one village at a particular time. The following examples caution against drawing any fixed conclusions about the numbers of leaders relative to the size of the village population. In ʿAyn Silwān, with thirty-one adult males registered in 952/1545 and fifty-nine in 967/1560, nine leaders were found listed for the year 960/1552–3.[54] In contrast, seven and ten leaders were found for the years 960/1552–3 and 963/1555–6 in Bayt Laḥm, which had a far greater population. Neither of these lists is necessarily complete.[55]

A comparison with what is known about the office of the *shaykh al-yahūd* may shed some light on the rural situation. In the town of Jerusalem, the *shaykh al-yahūd* – the leader of the Jewish community – was a figure comparable to the *ra'īs* in the villages.[56] Because the Jewish community lived in town, constituted a religious minority liable for the annual poll tax, and was active in numerous commercial spheres, its internal activities were better documented than those of the peasants. Each official, however, stood at the head of a taxpaying community and served primarily as an intermediary fiscal authority for the Ottoman officials. It was they who apportioned collectively-imposed taxes, made up the shortfall for some individuals of the community, and provided guarantees for others.

The *shaykh al-yahūd*, though publicly confirmed by the Ottoman authorities, was appointed from within the community. We have no indications about how the village leaders were chosen, but it seems likely that had the appointment been an officially managed procedure, evidence would emerge from the *sijill*s or from other Ottoman documents, since so much other material relating to the fiscal administration of the villages is found there. However, no mention is made anywhere, either of nomination or of confirmation of the *ra'īs*.[57] In the survey registers, no designation identified the leader(s) in the lists of names of heads of households.

The motivations for choosing a man of some economic and social position to serve as head of the Jewish community probably applied in the village as well. "It was the combination of wealth and a large, highly influential family that invested the shaykh al-yahūd with authority, both in the community and in the eyes of the rulers."[58] The *ra'īs*, as we have seen, came from among those people called elders and notables, indicating a certain status. Since one of his chief functions was to guarantee and supplement the payments of his villagers, the *ra'īs* must also have been among the wealthier peasants, or have had access to considerable resources, in rural terms. One significant contrast between the two offices, however, was the origin of their remuneration. The salary and expenses of the *shaykh al-yahūd* were arranged within the Jewish community, whereas the village leaders were compensated from the tax money itself.

Tenure in the office of *shaykh al-yahūd* was indefinite. It seems to have been dependent on personal willingness to serve and the general approval of the community. As such, the *shaykh* was appointed for an unspecified term, and might leave the post only to return to it in some future year. The arrangement in the villages may have been very similar, as the shifting titles of the prominent villagers suggest.[59] Leaders in both communities came from a recognized elite of elders and notables. Presumably chosen for their ability – real or perceived – to deal with the Ottoman officials and arrange the community's economic affairs, the *ra'īs* or the *shaykh* might choose to remain in office if successful, or to leave in the face of overwhelming economic pressures or popular dissatisfaction.

In general, the local Ottoman administration seems to have organized the subject population according to existing communities, recognizing within each a responsible person or persons who would serve as a channel of communication and a buffer between the authorities and the larger taxpaying population. Among the several Christian sects of Jerusalem, each had its own *ra'īs*. Within the villages where the population was mixed, like Bayt Jālā and Bayt Laḥm, separate leaders existed among the Christians and Muslims.[60] In the northern area of the district, the villages of Banī Zayd constituted a defined group, recognized partly by the existence of a "shaykh of the region of Banī Zayd."[61]

Was the *ra'īs al-fallāḥīn* (or the *shaykh al-yahūd*) an office introduced by the Ottomans or did they find it in place when they conquered the area? If we consider the area of Syria-Palestine, there is considerable evidence for the existence of formal village leaders prior to the Ottoman conquest. The position of *ra'īs* was an important office in cities from at least the time of Seljuq rule in Syria. Claude Cahen speaks of the *ra'īs* in rural Syria under the Franks, and identifies him as a notable who was in principle named by the *seigneur* (lord), and who presided over the administration of justice based on customary practice within his group, be it social, professional, confessional, urban quarter, or village.[62]

The fourteenth-century jurist Ibn Taymiyya mentions the *ru'asā al-qurā*, the heads of the villages, in an enumeration of persons in responsible positions, and says they are the *dahāqīn* (s. *dihqān*), property holders.[63] The encyclopedist Nuwayrī (d.1332) listed the duties of the *ru'asā al-bilād* which included closing off the cultivated lands in order to assess them for taxes, and overseeing the various stages of the harvest.[64] These are precisely the kinds of fiscal duties which occupied the *ra'īs al-fallāḥīn* under the Ottomans. As noted above, the recompense received by the village leader was his "according to previous custom." Many disputes discussed in the *sijill* were resolved in favor of "previous custom" or "customary practice." There is no certainty that this implied a pre-Ottoman usage. On the other hand, "previous custom" from the vantage of a single generation of Ottoman rule may well refer to regular practice under their Mamluk predecessors.

Additional evidence that the *ra'īs* was a common element of the village population comes from the Mamluk documents from the Ḥarām al-Sharīf of Jerusalem.[65] Documents from the early fourteenth century mention village headmen who undertook to cultivate the lands of their villages, to refrain from causing trouble, and others who acknowledged debts both in kind and in cash.[66] A late fourteenth-century deposition lists the names of three villagers, each called "*ra'īs*," together labeled "ar'ru'asā in the village of Nūbā [in the sub-district of Hebron]."[67]

In the case of the *ra'īs*, the argument from silence also has some force. Judging from the entries in the *sijill*, the kadis frequently took up matters of village administration. If the official organization of village leadership (*riyāsa*) had been established by the Ottomans, some evidence of this would be expected to appear in the *sijill*, perhaps in the form of appointment confirmations. Instead, the only Ottoman treatment of the subject was the habitual mention of the leaders as they were engaged in their various functions. Nowhere was the system itself discussed, either with regard to its structure, the apportionment of offices or the appointment and removal of persons from the office itself.

The same is true regarding the urban *shaykh al-ḥāra* (shaykh of the quarter) and *shaykh al-zuqaq* (shaykh of the lane) in the town of Jerusalem. Such an office existed in Mamluk times, and the Jerusalem *sijill* contains clear evidence that it continued under the Ottomans. Yet nowhere in the survey registers of local population are these functionaries mentioned, though the town surveys are divided into quarters, specifying the *imam* of the quarter. Cohen and Lewis speculate that:

> about the middle of the century [sixteenth], this office [*shaykh al-ḥāra*] probably lost its importance, as the Ottomans became increasingly acquainted with the details of conditions under their rule, and the decreasing population of the cities made it possible to dispense with the services of *Shaykh al-Ḥāra*. This change is probably part

of a larger process, in which the officialdom of local origin and authority declined, and was supplanted by the increasingly effective imperial service.[68]

One possibility is that the *shaykh al-ḥāra*, like the *ra'īs al-fallāḥīn*, still served as local spokesman to the authorities and as their intermediary before the local population, though he was not part of the normal ranks of Ottoman officialdom. Certainly the *shaykh al-yahūd* operated in this capacity, and like the other local leaders, it is in the *sijill* that we find him frequently enough to understand his position and role within his community.

Among the large corpus of imperial Ottoman edicts touching on administrative issues large and small, no treatment of the position of village leader is known. The *ru'asā* were sometimes mentioned in the text of an outgoing order, but it was only repeating the gist of the incoming petition. In this way, a *ferman* about the role of "the priests and leaders of each [town] quarter and village" in keeping the *cizye* rolls up to date used the term *ra'īs*.[69] The text of another order implied more clearly that the position of *ra'īs* was not an Ottoman institution, because the organizational principle had to be explained to the sultan by the local officials. In this case, the sultan had sent an order concerning the rebellious peasants of Nablus, to say that their chiefs (*mukaddem*) should be captured. In reply, the *sancakbeyi* of Nablus wrote that the rebels "have no established chiefs, [but] every village has a headman (*re'īs*) or two..."[70]

In comparison, for the town of Bursa, in the heart of Ottoman Anatolia, Gerber has stated that despite the communality of the villages, a "wide measure of communal independence and autonomy was not reinforced by any single, strong, formal or informal leader. Such officeholders were still in the misty future."[71]

Finally, although the *tımar* system was instituted soon after the conquest in Syria-Palestine, initially the Ottomans seem to have implemented few changes at the village level ("from below") other than to regularize and secure rural cultivation and taxation. Aiming at the untroubled functioning of the fiscal order, it is unlikely that they attempted to institute an entirely novel administrative structure within the village. An episode from the beginning of Ramaḍān 937 (mid-April 1531) demonstrates that even fifteen years after the conquest, Ottoman officials encountered resistance to their presence and methods. While attempting to register in the tax rolls the number of grapevines in the village of Bayt Jālā, south of Jerusalem, the Ottoman official charged with making the survey met a group of villagers who refused to answer his queries seriously. The men mocked the sultan's authority and the official's record-making, saying: "your writing down (*kitābatukum*) is like the wind from a donkey."[72] This was not the first, but at least the second Ottoman survey to be conducted in the area. Yet even this somewhat familiar procedure elicited a scoffing and uncooperative response from the peasants.

The Ottomans probably incorporated the existing village organization into their own larger administrative system, as they did certain forms of taxation. Local forms of rural communal organization in Greece seem to have persisted into Ottoman times as well. Authority within these communities was vested in notables chosen from within the community, by its members.[73] Even the practice of recompensing the leaders for their services probably predated the Ottoman regime, for it seems the village leaders would have had difficulty persuading the new rulers to initiate a system of compensation where it had not before existed. Nor were the Ottomans likely to have introduced payments to these local officials which did not exist before, and for which there was no precedent in the older provinces of the empire.

As Cohen and Lewis have suggested, some positions in the local officialdom may have lost prominence under the Ottomans, but they did so to different extents and at a varied pace. In the villages, the *ra'īs al-fallāḥīn* is found named as such in the *sijill* approximately to the end of the sixteenth century. However, the title is absent in the seventeenth-century *sijill*s, suggesting that either the office itself disappeared, or else it was subsumed in the role of another person.[74] The latter seems to be more likely, based on the evidence of later centuries. In the *sancak* of Damascus in the eighteenth century:

> The shaykh of the village [*shaykh al-qariya*] usually deputized for the villagers in transacting business with the authorities, such as transporting pilgrims or provisions to the Hijaz, or accompanied them to the law-court to defend a common cause. The shaykh, or shaykhs, of the village also collected money from the villagers for the payment of taxes and impositions due on the village. When the villagers wanted to depose their shaykh, they usually had recourse to influential persons in Damascus to help them achieve this goal.[75]

Though the title *ra'īs* is gone, the functions enumerated for the *shaykh al-qarya* clearly establish the connection and identity between the two offices. The *shaykh al-qarya* is found in eighteenth-century Palestine as well, as an unofficial representative of the lowest-ranking Ottoman functionary, the *shaykh al-nāḥiya*. In the Galilee and the Nablus regions, the shaykhs increased their power and independence, mirroring the empire-wide decentralization of imperial authority.[76]

Under Muhammed 'Ali of Egypt, the position of *shaykh al-qarya* changed fundamentally, becoming a government post of the lowest rank. This *nātūr* became the *mukhtār* established by the Ottoman Law of Vilayets of 1864, a functionary whose interests were more defined from above by the government than by his fellow-villagers.[77]

Thus, the *ra'īs al-fallāḥīn* appears to have been a constant figure in the basic organization of village life in this region. His role as liaison and representative to the ruling authority was of focal importance in rural administration, for he constituted the most common point of intersection and interaction between the Ottoman authorities and the local rural population.

The ra'īs *at work*

The village leaders earned their robes. Their routine duties, dictated by the fiscal rhythms of the various harvests, gave these men a pivotal position in the relationship between the Ottoman administrators and the peasants. However, a year's routine was predictably interrupted by unforeseen crises. These too often fell to the leaders to arbitrate and resolve. Below, we examine the regular activities of the *ra'īs*. The role of the *ra'īs* in more extraordinary events and unusual circumstances will be considered later. Because the leader was so central to village relations with the authorities, this discussion elaborates the general pattern of rural life in its interactions with the Ottoman administration.

The village leaders were responsible for the payment of annual taxes to the *tımar* holders or the *vakıf* administrators. However, they were not collectively responsible for the entire levy. The burden was divided and assigned. Below are two lists of leaders from Abū Dīs:

I. al-Asad b. Shuʿayb
Ramaḍān b. Saʿd
Kisya b. ʿAbd al-Dā'im
ʿAbd al-ʿAzīz b. Ibrāhīm Basīṭa

II. Khalīl b. Ḥaḍāra
Mūsā b. Abū ʿUlyān
Jibrān b. al-Baʿjī

Each group was obliged to pay one-half of the grains due to the *vakıf* for the year 960 (1552–3).[78] In 963 (1555–6), the leaders of half the people of Abū Dīs – al-Asad b. Shuʿayb, Mūsā b. Musʿad, and Muḥammad b. ʿAlī b. al-Basīṭa – were listed as owing back payments to the *vakıf*.[79] In the *sijill* they were described as leaders of one-half of the peasants, not as specifically responsible for one-half of the revenues due in 963. In 964, the leaders were again split into two groups, each responsible for one-half the revenues:[80]

I. al-Asad b. Shuʿayb
Mūsā b. Musʿad
Shaykh ʿAbd al-ʿAzīz b. Ibrāhīm [Basīṭa]

II. Jibrān b. ʿAlī al-Baʿjī
Masīf b. Abū Dahīm Nāmir
Nimr b. Abū Dahīm.

The division of responsibility was not always in halves. In the village of Rammūn, the three leaders – Jumʿa b. ʿAbd al-Sā'ir, Nāṣir al-Dīn b. ʿAbd al-Ḥāfiẓ, ʿImrān b. ʿAmmār – split the debt of olive oil to their master Nasuh *çavuş* equally three ways.[81] And the proportion was not fixed, for eighteen months later a new debt owed to Nasuh was divided equally among four leaders.[82] Perhaps this meant that the number of groups for which there were leaders, or the number of leaders in a village, was not constant. In ʿAyn Kārim, the leaders Dibyān b. ʿAlī (and his son Zaʿn), Aḥmad al-Fahl,

Muḥammad b. Khalīl, and Aḥmad b. Dīb owed 44 gold *sultani* to the *vakıf*. The amount was to be paid in three installments, each leader being responsible for one-quarter of the total, making a total of twelve different payments to be accounted for and collected.[83]

Thus, the burden of payments could be split, though it need not be in half, and it could also be shared by a pair or group of leaders for a given fraction of the village. Remittances were spread over the course of several months, allowing time for the sale of crops and the collection of monies by the leaders. Finally, the shares apportioned to different leaders were not always equal. Two hundred *mudd* of wheat and barley due from the people of ʿAyn Kārim to the *vakıf* were divided among Dibyān b. ʿAlī – 84.5 *mudd*, Muḥammad b. Khalīl – 50 *mudd*, and Khiṭāb b. Ghānim – 65.5 *mudd*.[84] In the village of Dayr ʿAmmār, the two leaders ʿAlī b. Ṣarṣūr and ʿAbd al-ʿAlī b. Ismāʿīl owed Farrukh the *sancakbeyi* 51 *sultani* from the tithe: ʿAlī owed 31.5 *sultani* and ʿAbd al-ʿAlī 19.5.[85]

Muslims and Christians in the same village had separate leaders, and the burden of the taxes was shared between them. In one case where the shares were specified, three Muslim leaders of Bayt Laḥm were responsible for one-third of the revenues due to Kurd *sancakbeyi*, while two Christian leaders were assigned the remaining two-thirds.[86] According to the survey registers, the Muslim and Christian populations were roughly equal in 952/1545, while by 967/1560 the Christian population was almost forty percent larger than the Muslim, though both had shrunk in the meantime.[87] The proportional division of the revenues due could indicate that the population shift had occurred well before the survey which documented it. Or, the disparity between the Christian and Muslim shares may reflect greater prosperity among the Christians of Bayt Laḥm.

A leader was responsible to or for a specific group of people in the village, frequently described as "his group" (*jamāʿatihi*). Perhaps these people constituted a relatively permanent group – a family, tribe, religious grouping, or quarter – which was eligible to choose one or more leaders for itself. The leaders do not appear to have been generally selected by the entire village, unless perhaps in a very small place. However, before the kadi, they were mostly identified as "leaders of the village," without any particular group-affiliation, unless that was germane to the case being heard.

In the normal course of things, the leaders probably collected the revenues due (in kind or cash) from the villagers, then passed them on to the *sancakbeyi*, the *tımar* holder, the *vakıf* manager, or their representatives. They confirmed that the amount due was correct, and guaranteed the villagers who were in arrears with their payments. In Shaʿbān 963/July 1556, four leaders of the village of Māliḥa agreed that they owed Murad *sipahi* 25 *sultani*, which was the remainder of the revenues of 961 (1553–4). They confirmed that the money was their debt and that of "their community, the people of the village."[88] Sāliḥ b. Khaṣīb, *raʾīs* of the people of Kafr Naʿma, acknowledged in the winter of 964/1557 that he owed Mustafa *za'im* 15 *kintar* and 78 *ratl* olive oil "which is the equivalent of his share of the revenues of his olive trees and the olive trees of his relations in the village." At the same time, Ba'lūj b. Suwaylim, another *ra'īs* from the same village, acknowledged his debt as 16 *kintar* and 5.5 *ratl*, "being the equivalent of his share of the dividing [of the shares] of his olive trees and those of his group."[89]

Whether the revenues due were from grains, olive oil or were even the *cizye* (poll tax on Christians and Jews), the role of the *ra'īs* between those paying and the recipients was the same. Sāliḥ b. 'Īsā, leader of the Christians of Dayr Abān, was confirmed in his payment of the poll tax due from his community of twenty-three persons for the year 963 (1555–6).[90] In Bayt Jālā, four leaders of the Christian villagers were confirmed as having delivered the poll tax from 131 persons for the same year.[91] It is curious that the Ottoman survey conducted four years later recorded the same number – twenty-three – of Christian adult males in Dayr Abān, but for Bayt Jālā the survey shows 218 adult males – more than a sixty percent increase.[92] Yet there was no quarrel recorded in the *sijill* that the payment for the Christians of Bayt Jālā was perhaps low.[93] In the winter of 964/1557 the leaders of each village in the region of Ramle which was endowed to the *vakıf* of the *'imaret* appeared before the kadi to give an account of their outstanding debts.[94]

Responsibility for guaranteeing the tax payments devolved upon the leaders because they possessed some financial means. It is not hard to imagine that opportunities for enhancing their own economic position presented themselves to the leaders as they collected crops and money from a community of villagers. In Ṣafar 963/December 1555, three notables (*akābir*) of al-Aṭrūn (Latrun) came before the kadi to complain about one Ja'wān b. Ḥamīda, a former leader in the village, during whose tenure conditions there deteriorated so greatly that not only the villagers were harmed by his abusive behavior, but the officials as well. Ja'wān was arrested at the request of the clerk of the *vakıf* supported by the village, for fear that he would ruin the village. The three elders who originally filed the complaint were then appointed to be leaders, and Ja'wān was removed from the position of leadership (*riyāsa*). These new leaders then guaranteed the cultivation of the village and proper remission of taxes.[95]

Though this appointment by the clerk would seem to contradict the idea presented earlier, that the leaders were not chosen by the Ottoman officials, it seems more likely to result from the special circumstances here. Being most immediately worried for the prosperity of "his" village, the clerk wanted to be confident of the character of the men in charge of it. These three were in any case among the prominent villagers, and had demonstrated their concern by complaining to the officials about their fellow. The very fact that they reported him, requesting some action from the kadi, indicates that the situation of the village had become truly intolerable under Ja'wān's leadership. Of the *sijill*s examined, this is the only such case found. In general, internal problems probably remained within the village, settled through local mediation if at all possible, avoiding the cost and complication of involving the Ottoman authorities.

While possibilities for abuse or self-enrichment surely existed for village leaders, the risks of impoverishment or financial duress in the same office were at least as great. The leaders were the ones to acknowledge and confirm the taxes due or in arrears. Most entries mentioning the leader(s) had to do with debts. Some portion of the debt was the individual share of the leader, but more often the sum mentioned as due was from the whole village. In ʿAyn Silwān, two leaders owed 30 gold *sultani*, which was the equivalent of the share due to Ilyas *sipahi* from the tithe of the village garden for one year.[96] Likewise, four leaders of Rāmallāh owed the *vakıf* sustained by the village its share of grains from the village yield.[97] These are only two of many such examples. Ultimately, the leaders were liable for the taxes. The peasants who had not initially paid their share would be expected to make good their obligations to the leader, but meanwhile he was out of pocket. As we have seen, debt fragments remained outstanding for months and longer. Perhaps as in the Jewish community of Jerusalem where the *shaykh al-yahūd* laid out any shortfall in the *cizye*, the village *raʾīs* got help from the kadi later in collecting what he had advanced to other villagers.[98]

Guarantees

Basically, the village leader was a guarantor, a *kāfil*, for the rest of the village population. In a variety of circumstances, he formally accepted a legal obligation of *kafāla* (surety), either for the actions of "his group," or for the payments owed by the community. Surety and the terms of liability in these instances were principally a financial arrangement, called *kafāla bi'l-māl*. As opposed to surety for a person (*kafāla bi'l-nafs*), the guarantor here was liable for the specific claim he undertook to ensure, not for producing the original debtor.[99] As a guarantor in the village, the *raʾīs* was liable for the payments and fines owing from "his group." However, since the *kafāla* was recorded with the kadi, the *raʾīs* could then also call upon him to help enforce the collection of debts owing from his fellow villagers.

Because of the uncertainty about who exactly was a *raʾīs* at any given time, it is difficult to declare that guarantees were provided only by leaders. For example, Saʿīd b. Saʿāda of Ḥūbin, as guarantor for the rest of the people in his village, was sued for the remainder of the taxes for 961 (1553–4).[100] Saʿīd was listed as a *raʾīs* in 970 (1562–3), but there is no certainty that he was one in 961. However, in the village of Māliḥa in 962 (1554–5), Muḥammad b. Jumʿa and Ismāʿīl b. Abū Bakr owed their *sipahi* money and olive oil from his share of the village revenues from 961. They were guaranteed by ʿAlī b. Muḥammad al-Kābūlī and Dīmūs b. Samarī who were both listed as *raʾīs* in that year.[101] Finally, in a case from Bayt Laḥm, five men, all described as *mashāʾikh*, provided mutual guarantees for the good condition of the village.[102] That they were all also called *ru'asā* in the same year, 962, is evident only from other documents. It stands to reason that any of the village notables might stand surety for another villager, or the entire village, as long as they possessed sufficient resources. And, since the guarantors were not specifically identified as *ra'īs*, even when they were, there may not have been a necessary correlation between the two functions.

Not everyone was eager to be a guarantor. When two shaykhs responsible for the *vakıf* income from the village of Dayr 'Ammār tried to impose the role of guarantor on one 'Abd al-'Azīz of that village, he successfully resisted. They insisted that he owed them his own portion and that of two other men as their guarantor [*fī dhimmatihi... iṣālatan wa-bi-ṭarīq al-kafāla 'an...*]. 'Abd al-'Azīz acknowledged his personal liability but denied any obligations beyond that, swearing an oath that this was the case. As the shaykhs were unable to produce written proof of their claim, 'Abd al-'Azīz was exonerated.[103]

Guarantees were also made by a leader or notable from one village for the condition of another, or for the liability of another village's leader(s). For example, Ṣadīq b. Battīkh and Muḥammad b. Ḥamīda, leaders of Naḥḥālīn, were entrusted with a certain amount of grain belonging to their *tımar* holder from the share of the year 960 (1552–3). The surety for them was provided by Aḥmad b. al-Afra', a notable of Bayt Laḥm.[104] Two notables from the villages of Sāris and Qulūnya guaranteed a man from 'Inab.[105]

In addition to providing purely financial guarantees for the villagers to the Ottoman officials, the leaders (and prominent men) were also called upon to ensure the regular cultivation and settlement of their villages. The most basic form of guarantee was given for the "cultivation and population of their village, and an absence of wrongdoing and evil in it, and the [delivery] of the rightful due of their master."[106] The leaders of al-Aṭrūn mentioned above made this sort of pledge when they were installed. The guarantee of the prominent Muslim and Christian men[107] of Bayt Laḥm elaborated a more detailed obligation. They committed themselves to "the peopling and cultivation and settledness of the said region, on the condition that anyone of them who was absent, should it be requested of the others that they produce him, when it was requested of them, they would all or one bring him forward."[108] This is *kafāla bi'l-nafs* as well as the usual *kafāla bi'l-māl*. Two notables of Fāghūr attested that hereafter they would guarantee their village, work its lands, and not incite any mischief. They accepted joint liability (*taḍāmanū wa-takāfalū*) in these matters, and for paying the money due annually to the *vakıf*.[109] Guarantees such as this one appeared frequently in the *sijill*, but not systematically or annually. They seem to have been an implicit part of the leaders' duties, specifically articulated before the kadi only when some previous incident – peasant absence, gross tax arrears, rebellious disruption – imposed the need to extract a commitment with greater liability attached.

In some cases, the guarantee of the leaders contained an explicit pledge not to cultivate the lands outside the village before they had finished working the lands within the village. The lands "within the village" were presumably those assessed for tax purposes. The external lands could have been not only immediately outside the village, but also farther away. In either case, the implication is that such activity took the peasants away from their primary obligations on the registered village lands. Even though some of the external lands may have included uninhabited plots (*mezraʿa* or *kıtʿa-i arz*) which were assessed in the survey registers, the quality of the land may have been poorer, and the ability of the officials to supervise tax assessments weaker. Stiff fines were imposed on the villagers if they were caught flouting the commitment to work the "internal" lands first. The leaders and other peasants of Fāghūr were liable for a penalty of 100 gold *sultani*. Likewise, in Bayt Ḥanīna, the leaders gave their guarantee to cultivate first the lands of the village – and to make sure that the villagers did likewise – or else pay 1,000 *akçe*.[110]

Arrest was a common tool for resolving debt claims and enforcing the fulfilment of guarantees undertaken. It required that the person arrested either arrange for immediate payment, or find another guarantor acceptable to the claimant. Should some peasant fail to pay his tax debts, the leader responsible for him could be arrested. So it was for one ʿAbd al-ʿAlī b. Ismāʿīl of Dayr ʿAmmār, the *raʾīs* who had stood surety for two villagers' debt of olive oil. In 961/1554, ʿAbd al-ʿAlī was arrested for an unpaid debt from the years 954–6/1547–9 which he had guaranteed.[111] Leader(s) could also be arrested for the debt of the entire village. Ṣalāḥ b. Zayn and Kāmil b. al-Faqīh ʿAbd al-Karīm, leaders of ʿAllār, were arrested in Ramaḍān 960/August 1553 on account of the taxes due to Nasuh bey, none of which had been paid.[112]

Though arrest may appear a harsh action, it pointed to the fundamental rights of the peasants to work their lands and the basic landholding–revenue distribution system of the Ottoman empire. A person might be penalized for not cultivating or jailed for debts, but as long as he worked the lands, debts or no, the *tasarruf*, the right to work a given area, was secure. In general, the peasant's claim on a particular piece of land was far more secure than that of the *sipahi* who held it as *tımar*, or the *vakıf* administrator collecting the foundation's dues. Either of these officials could be and was rotated or reassigned on an annual basis.

In Jerusalem or in the countryside, the various military-administrative and judicial officials regularly crossed paths with the local peasants. Yet while they were a familiar sight to each other, most formal interactions occurred between the village leaders and the officials. These *ruʾasā* played a crucial role as mediators, communicating demands and complaints between the peasants and the officials, representing each to the other. Most often the issue was revenues due.

While the portrait of a strong village leader emerges from the court records, he did not have a monopoly on contact with the Ottoman officials, for there were also individual peasants who arrived to settle personal business – marriage, divorce, inheritance, property transfers – with the kadi. Purely commercial transactions, unrelated to tax issues, may also have taken place between individual peasants and the various officials, either in town or in the villages, but of this there is no record, for they needed no official document.

Nevertheless, the peasants appear to have been dependant on their *ru'asā* to represent and protect their interests to a large extent, and this intermediary role probably reinforced the dominant position of the *ra'īs* within the village. On the other hand, the Ottoman officials relied on him to help organize an effective local administration. The *ra'īs* knew his fellow villagers and their assets far better than any Ottoman official, and so could plead with or pressure them to pay their debts or otherwise conform. He was also liable for their failures and shortfalls in producing revenues demanded. The officials, however, were never dependent on the village leaders in the same way as the peasants. As representatives of the sovereign authority, they always had the option to use force to obtain what they wanted. This use of force was supposed to be authorized by the kadi and carried out by the *sancakbeyi* and/or his men. While the normative procedure is often indicated in the kadi's records, complaints of arbitrary actions also appear in these same records and in the official decrees which replied to petitions sent to Istanbul.

Neither the military-bureaucratic nor judicial administration was a mystery to peasants. *Subaşı*s had frequent business throughout the countryside. The regular movement of *sipahi*s in and out of the region as they set off for the summer campaign season and the sorties of the janissaries against Bedouin or other troublemakers made the Ottoman military force visible to the local villagers. And everyone knew the way to the *maḥkama* where the kadi sat. The Muslim judge was probably the most approachable official figure for the peasants. He was supposed to represent a source of redress against the Ottoman officials or anyone else, including their fellow villagers, who abused them. Moreover, the kadi was a recognized authority from well before the Ottoman conquest. Under the Ottomans, the basis of his adjudications had been expanded to include the decrees of the sultan and he was appointed through the centralized religious institution. As such, he was plainly an Ottoman official, but one whose legitimacy was tied to a much older authority, the *sharī'a*. Although the administration and its agents remained foreign in many ways, they were not unfamiliar, especially after thirty or forty years in the region.

CHAPTER 3

The rules of local administration

I have ordered that you [*sancakbeyi* and kadi of Jerusalem] look into this: whether from olden times in this region these aforementioned matters [taxes] were habitually taken in the manner mentioned; whether noble orders were not given contrary to it; and whether they [persons deputized to collect taxes from the villages] take more [than habitually due] contrary to the *şer'*, the *kanun*, and the *defter*; [if so, then] prevent [this]. In these matters henceforward let [the taxes] be taken according to the *defter*, let nothing extra be taken contrary to *şer'*, *kanan*, and the *defter*... [1]

Relations between the Ottoman officials and the local peasantry were governed by the statutes of the Muslim holy law (*sharī'a*), Ottoman regulations (*kanun*), and local customary practices (*'örf*). The three sources of law did not govern entirely discrete areas. All together served as the basis for decisions by the kadi, especially in regard to administrative practices. The *sharī'a* laid down rules about tithes on agricultural produce and the poll tax on non-Muslim subjects (*zimmi*s). The more general guidelines of the *sharī'a* were often supplemented by the detailed provisions of *kanun*s. And the *kanun*s were typically informed by local practice as discovered by the Ottoman officials who carried out the initial provincial surveys and those who governed in the numerous provinces of the empire. The Ottoman administrative regime, therefore, did not impose a rigid code of laws uniformly on all conquered populations of the empire. It shaped itself to fit each province, and was continually being adjusted as a result of repeated problems and repeated encounters with specific and particular local practices.

The most regular application of Ottoman authority in provincial administration was in the realm of tax assessment and collection. For this reason, the present chapter examines the laws and practices which governed taxation in the district of Jerusalem. The bases of the discussion are the third and fourth Ottoman *tapu tahrir defter*s of the series extant for Jerusalem. The first, second, and fifth surveys are included in considering the longer-range development of administrative practices and agricultural production during the sixteenth century.[2]

Taxation

How were taxes assessed? The blueprint for this operation was the *kanunname*, a codification of tax rates and regulations, which was found at the beginning of many survey registers.[3] In the case of Jerusalem, the earliest surviving *kanunname* is found in the fourth survey (#516, 967/1560), and it was copied unamended into the fifth (#515, 1004/1595–6). However, we find quotations from something called the "new *kanunname*" in Jerusalem court records dated well before the fourth survey. These suggest, as one should expect, that there was already a *kanunname* in effect at the time of the third survey (#289, 952/1545),[4] although the extant copy of that survey does not contain a *kanunname* text. Furthermore, this earlier document, as the qualification "new" suggests, was probably a revised version of a still older *kanunname*.

Around the middle of the sixteenth century, an empire-wide review of landholding and taxation policies was initiated. Ebu's-Su'ud Efendi, *şeyhülislam* from 1548 to 1575, was the chief instrument of these reforms and his *fetva*s, cited in numerous subsequent *kanunname*s, document the revisions implemented. One impetus for these revisions appears to have come with the conquest of Hungary in 1541, when Sultan Süleyman was apparently anxious to set up an agrarian regime which adhered rigorously to Islamic law.[5] However, the review of landholdings and taxation appears to have been prompted also by the noticeable loss of lands from the holdings of the state. By various devices, state lands became private holdings; private holdings could subsequently be endowed to pious foundations as *vakıf*. In either case, the public treasury lost a measure of revenue, since neither private nor *vakıf* lands were eligible for the full range of levies imposed on state lands.

All cultivated fields among the lands conquered by the Ottomans became the property of the public treasury and were known as *arz-ı memleke*, or *miri* land. When Ebu's-Su'ud drew up the *kanunname*s for Skopje and Salonika at the accession of Selim II in 976/1568, he analyzed the problem facing the government:

> In the former registers no attempt was made to determine the true nature of various forms of landholding in the well-protected territories of the Ottoman state. Since it was not scrutinized and clearly stated whether the lands are *'öşrī* or *harācī*, and whether they are the freehold property (*mülk*) of their possessors, the peasant *re'āyā*, considering the lands in their possession as *'öşrī* (private property subject to tithe), dispute paying as much as one-eighth of their produce, and also buy and sell land among themselves like the rest of their property; some even think they can make *evḳāf*. And the judges, being unaware of the true *mīrī* status of the land, deliver certifying documents for their buying and selling, and draw up *vaḳf* deeds contrary to the sacred Shari'a. Since this situation has caused a substantial deterioration in the orderly functioning of state affairs, and confusion in the transactions made among

the people, the present Sultan [on his accession to the throne] ordered that, in the introductions to the imperial survey registers, the true nature of land and the possession rights of their owners in the well-protected territories be thoroughly investigated and specified.[6]

This passage explicitly summarizes the rationale for changes observed in Syria and Egypt. The *kanunname* of Damascus was reissued in 955/1548.[7] In Aleppo, changes in the agricultural tithe were apparent around 959/1551–2, when a new tithe (*ʿöşr-i cedid*) was recorded.[8] The *kanunname* of Egypt was issued in 960/1553, in an effort to recover revenues for the imperial treasury which otherwise were being sheltered in *vakıf* endowments.[9] Certain recording practices and tithe assessments around Jerusalem changed noticeably in the third survey (952/1545) when compared with its predecessor.

The conquest of the vast Muslim territories of the Fertile Crescent and Egypt probably added to the need to clarify Ottoman policy, as was eventually undertaken by Ebu's-Suʿud Efendi. Particularly in Egypt and southern Syria, large amounts of land were protected from full taxation because they were endowed to support the very numerous *vakıf*s of these regions. Further, the *defter*s of southern Syria clearly show that the classic Ottoman *çift resmi*, the basic farm tax paid by peasants in Anatolia and the Balkans, was not levied in Bilād al-Shām.[10]

Two processes were thus initiated by Ebu's-Suʿud and Sultan Süleyman: (1) an attempt to ensure the status of *miri* land, perhaps even reclaiming *miri* land improperly assimilated to private holdings; and (2) the imposition of taxes as tithes on existing *vakıf*s, in an attempt to regain some revenues to the treasury from these lands whose principal fruits supported private endowments. And thus, the "new *kanunname*" of Jerusalem was part of a more widespread reform of provincial administration.

The Jerusalem Kanunname

The *kanunname* was a catalogue of both urban and rural levies. The portions which applied to the rural areas of the district read as follows:

In this district, because the *kısm*[11] of each village is different, each [*kısm* rate] is written separately [for each village].

Rumani olive trees:[12] the *fellah* (peasant) has the *tasarruf* (usufruct) of half the produce as his recompense for attending to it; and the other half is the usufruct of the *sahib-i arz*.[13]

Islami olive trees: one *akçe* per two trees;

Fruit-bearing walnut trees: two *akçe* per mature tree, one *akçe* per young tree;

Date trees: two *akçe* per tree;

Mulberry and fig trees: one *akçe* per four trees;

Various other fruit trees: one *akçe* per five trees.

It was recorded that *haraç* be paid at ten *akçe* for every hundred trellis of young vine shoots;

And some places, which in the old register paid *kısm*, and then afterwards were assigned as gardens from which *kısm* was not taken [but] formerly used to pay *kısm* and in the old register were recorded as "*kısm* from the *dibs* [grape syrup]," in these places, *kısm* should be recorded in the new register according to the old register;

And each trellis of vines in the districts of Jerusalem and Hebron: one *akçe* is recorded for every ten trellis of which every trellis is [mature enough to be] able to bear fruit (*hasıla mütehammil olmağın*).

And in those places where the tithe is recorded as being "from all the produce," (*'an cümlet el-mütehassıl*), the tithe is taken "from all the produce" from grain, and from the *haraç* "from the money of the *vakıf*." (*'an mal ul-vakıf*).[14]

And from places which did not formerly pay *haraç* but paid *kısm*, and were afterwards assigned as vineyards and which moreover were recorded as *kısm* according to the old customs in the register, *haraç* should not be recorded; in these places, it should be recorded again in the new register that the tithe be taken "from all the produce."[15]

Rumani olive trees in this *sancak* are recorded: half the produce is the usufruct of the *sahib-i arz*, and the other half is the usufruct of the *fellah* as his recompense for attending to it. In some places, half the revenue does not belong to the *sahib-i arz*, but perhaps (*belki*) they are accustomed to take one *akçe haraç* for every *rumani* olive tree;[16] they take one *akçe* every year whether the olive tree is prosperous or suffering scarcity; but it was recorded that those who do not take [a fixed sum of] *akçe*, but take *kısm* from olive oil in prosperous times, not take *haraç* again in scarce times at [a rate of] one *akçe* each [tree per year] and on the other hand take *kısm* in prosperous times.

And *Islami* olive trees are thus as well: in those places where formerly olive oil was [taxed according to] *kısm* and the price of the olive oil was recorded in the register, in those kind of places in prosperous times olive oil is [taxed according to] *kısm*; in scarce times *haraç* is not to be taken; and from a place which is recorded as *haraç* which from olden times used to pay *haraç*, that place pays *haraç* in prosperous and scarce times.[17]

For every two sheep or goats, one *akçe*; and for lambs which are considered fit for the flock, taxes are calculated as for sheep.

For every hive, one *akçe*; but if a person sends his hive to someone else's land, the owner of the land and the owner of the hive share the tax in halves.

And the tax on winter quarters and pasturage [of sheep] is taken [at a rate of] one sheep per hundred, or its equivalent price from those who come from elsewhere and spend the winter. And the pasturage tax is taken also if someone comes from elsewhere and keeps his sheep in a sheepfold and they lamb, likewise [at a rate of] one sheep per hundred or its equivalent price.

For every water buffalo being milked, 6 *akçe*.

[There follows here a list of taxes collected in the Jerusalem market, as well as various city tolls.]

And as the *vakıf*s of the *Haremeyn ül-Şerifeyn*[18] and Jerusalem and Hebron were exempt from extraordinary taxes and the tithe in the old register, they were likewise recorded to be thus in the new register.

[A list of toll rates for Christians and Jews coming on pilgrimage to the holy places in and around Jerusalem.][19]

What did these complicated clauses mean in practice? The first paragraph says that the *kısm* varied, so that it was recorded individually for each village. In fact, *kısm* rates around Jerusalem varied very little. The majority of villages were taxed at a rate of 1/3 and a minority at a rate of 1/4. Although these latter villages tended to be smaller and to produce less, there was no absolute distinction in *kısm* rates along these lines.[20] *Kısm* crops included cereals, most often wheat and barley, and sometimes olive oil, grape syrup (*dibs*), and/or summer crops (*mal-i seyfi*) as mentioned in the *kanunname*.[21] Exceptionally, the village of Qūfīn paid *kısm* at a rate of one-tenth, because it was assigned the special task of protecting pilgrims from plunderers along the road to Hebron.[22]

According to the *kanunname*, olives and olive oil fell under different regimens depending upon whether they were *rumani* or *islami* for the former, or their tax history for the latter. Makovsky has pointed out that *rumani* and *islami* mean very little to anyone examining the details of the survey registers, and one can only note that the *rumani* assessment was higher.[23] However, Cohen says that *rumani* trees were generally thought to be over one thousand years old, while the *islami* trees had been bearing fruit for only a few hundred years, therefore bearing less. The difference between the trees was most probably evident to the knowledgeable resident observer, most especially, the local peasants.[24]

What merits consideration here is that if something was not written in the register, it was unlikely that someone in Istanbul would know the distinctions on the ground. The *sipahi* who was assigned a *tımar* which included the taxes on some particular olive trees would be equally uninformed when he first arrived at the village. He probably depended on his predecessor, the kadi, some local official, or the villagers themselves to explain the situation.

Who *did* know the local situation? Each villager certainly knew about his or her own trees, and some villagers probably knew about the status of many trees in the village and beyond. Cases in the *sijill* demonstrate that peasants had quite a precise knowledge of their own holdings. Furthermore, the kadi continually called on a group of local experts, the *ehl-i ʿörf*, to investigate in different cases that came before him. One can speculate that it was these kinds of complexities which encouraged *sipahi*s and other "foreign" revenue holders to sub-lease the right to collect their revenues to local persons who knew far better than they what revenues could be expected from each producer and product.

Due to the complexities of the law, the collection of olive and olive oil revenues demanded extensive knowledge of the local situation. One wonders how effectively the Ottoman officials could acquire and record such information. Perhaps herein lies part of the explanation for the sudden appearance of neat accounts of olive oil in the third survey register of 952/1545. After twenty-five years of collecting, or trying to collect, taxes according to three or four different types of assessment, someone made a decision to standardize collection in oil, as far as possible.

Grapevines were also taxed in more than one manner, depending on their maturity if *haraç* was levied, and on their tax history if taxed according to *kısm*. Note, too, that like olives, grapes could also be taxed in the derivative form of grape syrup (*dibs*). The *haraç* rates on the other fruit trees were more straightforward, listed at fixed rates of *akçe*/trees. As before, their collective registration makes them indistinguishable to the *defter* reader.

The last category of taxable rural produce was animals. Goats and sheep were the principal and ubiquitous livestock of the region. Goats were omnipresent in the registers after the first survey, but the rubric "goats" probably hid the presence of sheep, which were taxed at the same rate. Bees, and the implied production of honey for sweetening, were listed with the goats from the third survey on. Because of the collective category "tax on goats and bees," it is impossible to deduce whether a particular village was a major honey producer or had huge herds of goats or sheep. Goats and sheep provided milk, wool for yarn, and meat for local consumption, with some surplus to be sold in the towns, and meat to celebrate local festivals or to host Ottoman officials who passed through.

The Jerusalem villages did not maintain very large herds, that much is clear from the survey registers. Yet meat was a vital commodity for the city of Jerusalem and always in short supply. The butchers guild was responsible not only for slaughtering but for ensuring the regular provisioning of meat to the city. It purchased sheep and goats mostly from Turcoman and Bedouin tribesmen in Syria and Anatolia. Local meat, *baladī*, was least in demand, as it was of the lowest quality.[25]

Water buffalo were registered only in three villages in the Jerusalem district, all of which were located in the Jordan River valley.[26] These heavy beasts were unsuited to work on the steeper mountain slopes, and they were too costly for most peasants. They were more often found in the coastal plain, in the districts of Ramle and Gaza.

Unlike other areas of southern Syria, especially the coastal district of Gaza or the areas north of Jerusalem, we find no textile crops such as flax, cotton or silk recorded here. They may have been grown in small quantities, but were not regularly of enough substance to interest the tax assessors.

Tithes

The *'öşr*, or tithe, was calculated as a percentage of the total estimated value of agricultural production for many *vakıf* villages in the Jerusalem survey registers. It constituted another levy in addition to the *kısm* or the *haraç*. According to the *kanunname* of 967/1560 and internal evidence from the surveys, villages endowed to *vakıf*s of the *Haremeyn-i Şerifeyn* and Jerusalem and Hebron were exempted from the tithe if they had been registered thus in previous surveys.[27] These *vakıf*s included the endowments for the Dome of the Rock and al-Aqṣā mosque in Jerusalem, the *vakıf* of Abraham (*sayyidunā Khalīl*)[28] in Hebron and the tombs of the prophets Moses, Jonah, and Lot (Mūsā, Yūnus, and Lūṭ) and the Hasseki Sultan *'imaret* in Jerusalem.[29] In the district of Jerusalem, twenty-two percent (37 out of 166) of the villages were tithe-exempt. While not all of these villages were very large or "wealthy,"[30] the largest and most revenue-yielding villages in the district such as Bayt Laḥm (Bethlehem), ʿAzariyya,[31] Dayr Ghassāna, Rīḥā (Jericho), and Ṭurmus ʿAyyā were among them.

Villages which were part of *vakıf*s for the numerous *medrese*s, *ribat*s, inns, tombs, and other private foundations around Jerusalem were not exempt from the tithe. Many of these *vakıf*s had been established under the Mamluks. When the Ottomans took over, they preserved the *vakıf*s, but taxed their income by imposing a tithe.[32] This group included fifty-three villages, thirty-two percent of the district total. Among them were villages which were part tithe-exempt *vakıf* and part tithe-paying *vakıf* such as Bayt Saqāyā, where fourteen *kırat*[33] of the village revenues went to the *vakıf* of the Dome of the Rock, while the other ten *kırat* were split among three smaller foundations. The register explicitly said that "the tithe is to be taken from all the revenue except from the share of the Dome of the Rock."[34]

Villages which were not part of any *vakıf* or which were part of tithe-exempt *vakıf*s did not pay any tithe. This group included seventy-six villages, forty-six percent of the district of Jerusalem. Most of the villages which were not part of any *vakıf* were relatively small, with fewer than twenty-five households, and they were among the poorer villages of the district. Thus it appears that tithes here were taken only from *vakıf* lands, reinforcing the conclusion that the Ottomans used this levy to tax what was otherwise untaxable.

How was the tithe calculated, once it was established from which body of revenue it was to be drawn? The *kanunname* offers two possibilities: either the tithe was calculated "from all the revenue," or "from the money of the *vakıf*."[35] The latter was the less complicated of the two. Whether the village was entirely or partly *vakıf*,[36] ten percent was levied as tithe from that portion designated for the *vakıf*. For example: the village of ʿAyn Qinyā paid 8 *kırat* of its revenue to the *vakıf* of the Medrese-i Tankiziyye in Jerusalem; the remaining 16 *kırat* were part of a *tımar*. In the third register the share of the *vakıf* was 600 *akçe* and the tithe was 60 *akçe*; in the next survey the *vakıf* revenue was 1,300 *akçe* and the tithe 130.[37] Sixty percent of the villages paying tithes were assessed in this manner throughout the century.

However, where the tithe was calculated "from all the revenue" the situation was more complicated. Until the third survey, this tithe was calculated as a percentage of the total revenue due (*hasıl*) recorded from the village. Looking at the second survey one finds the following: (a)in Abū Dīs the total was 3,500 *akçe*, and the tithe 350 *akçe* (ten percent), and (b)in ʿAyn Kārim the total was 2,500, and the tithe 500 (twenty percent).[38]

Beginning from the third survey of 952/1545, the tithe "from all the produce" was calculated differently. Now, ten percent was calculated from the total produced in the village *before* it was divided according to the *kısm* in figuring the total revenue due (*hasıl*). This was roughly equal to a tithe of thirty-three percent of the *vakıf* portion, but the tithe was calculated from the total at ten percent, and not from the *vakıf* portion at thirty-three percent. This becomes clear when one recalculates the tithe.

Abū Dīs was one example of such a village. In the third survey its *hasıl* was 6,250 *akçe*, and the village paid *kısm* at the rate of one-third. It paid 2,084 *akçe* as tithe. The *hasıl* multiplied by the *kısm* gives the total value produced (6,250 × 3 = 18,750). This total plus the tithe gives a number, ten percent of which equals the tithe: (18,750 + 2,084 = 20,834).[39] The same was true in ʿAyn Kārim: *hasıl* = 3,990; *kısm* = 1/3; tithe = 1,328. (3,990 × 3 = 11,970) + 1,328 = 13,298 × 0.10 = 1,329.[40]

Bayt Saqāyā was a village where the tithe was taken "from all the revenue," excluding the revenue of the *vakıf* of the Dome of the Rock. In the third survey, the *hasıl* of Bayt Saqāyā was recorded as 6,000 *akçe* of which 14 *kırat* was tithe-exempt *vakıf*. The total value produced in the village, whose *kısm* rate was one-third, was thus 18,000 *akçe*. 10/24 of 18,000 (the share of the tithable *vakıf*s) equals 7,500, of which ten percent is 750. The tithe in the third survey was, in fact, recorded as 750 *akçe*.[41]

The crux of the matter here is that when the tithe was calculated "from the money of the *vakıf*," approximately thirty-three percent of the total village revenues were taken (where the *kısm* was one-third). The tithe here reduced the share received by the *vakıf* and did not increase the total amount taken from the total village revenues. But the tithe "from all the produce" was assessed *before* the *kısm* was calculated and thereby constituted an additional levy from the peasants, as well as reducing the share of the *vakıf*. In this way about forty percent of the total value of village production was taken.[42] This latter system imposed a heavier burden on the peasants. The *fallāḥīn* were aware of the difference. They complained when someone tried wrongly to collect "from all the revenues," and on occasion even lied that the tithe was "from the money of the *vakıf*" in their village when they thought they might pay the lower rate unchallenged.[43]

The regime described above was a vehicle for the state to gain access to otherwise untouchable revenues, those endowed for *vakıf*s, or held in freehold (*mülk*). As discussed, the change in the manner of assessing the tithe which took place at mid-century served to increase the yields from that tax by a substantial amount. As revenues were simultaneously rising, this implied an absolute as well as a relative gain in revenues for the recipient of the tithe income, be it the imperial treasury or a *tımar* holder.[44] One further aspect of tithe assessment and collection must be considered. According to Ottoman *kanun*, the tithe on grains was to be taken in kind from the peasants. Only the garden and orchard tithes could rightly be demanded in cash. However, numerous complaints sent to Istanbul from around the empire made it clear that both tithes were regularly levied in cash, sometimes calculated according to an inflated price per measure of grain.[45]

In the area around Jerusalem, tithes discussed in the *sijill* are repeatedly stated in cash.[46] No complaint was found to have been leveled against this practice by the local peasants. If cash tithes had been customary under the Mamluks, then perhaps the practice was not perceived by the peasants as irregular. Yet the absence of complaint is curious, particularly since the Ottoman government clearly considered cash tithes to be noxious and improper. Moreover, this official attitude seems to have remained consistent over a long period, for in the second half of the nineteenth century the cash tithe was still considered abusive and was discouraged around Jerusalem. At that time the peasants were forced to realize their crop at a low price or else borrow money and risk indebtedness in order to pay in cash.[47]

As we will see below, peasant tax debts were regularly stated in cash terms in the sixteenth century. They may have been accustomed to translate their produce into its cash value. In addition, an important consideration here is the fact that not all villages paid tithes. Only villages which were part of a pious endowment were recorded as owing the tithe, and only in some cases did the tithe affect the peasants directly. Where it was calculated "from the money of the *vakıf*," the manager had to forfeit part of the endowment's share; this was probably irrelevant to the peasants.

Non-agricultural taxes

All of the revenues discussed above were derived from taxes on agricultural produce and livestock. Other non-agricultural or irregular taxes were also collected from the peasants. These taxes, although not mentioned in the *kanunname* of Jerusalem, were recorded in the survey registers and are known from other Ottoman records. They included the *resm-i ʿarus* (the marriage tax)[48] and the assorted fines and levies collectively called *bad-i hava*.[49] The sums recorded under these categories in the registers were irregular and small, thus they probably just served to sweeten the regular income of various revenue holders. Although no complaints were filed during this period, officials later found these taxes easy to abuse, inflate or even invent. A portion of these taxes belonged to the revenues of the *sancakbeyi* of Jerusalem.[50]

In addition, the *resm-i ʿavariz*, an accidental or occasional tax, could be assessed. This rubric covered a range of levies used by the Ottomans to raise cash, services or supplies, generally for military campaigns.[51] It was calculated according to a unit called *ʿavarizhane*, which was not necessarily a single household, but more often a group of households. An imperial *ferman* of 976/1568, while confirming that the townspeople of Jerusalem were excused from these extraordinary taxes, indicated that there was no blanket exemption for the surrounding villages.[52] The *kanunname* of Jerusalem says that villages exempt from the tithe were also exempt from the *ʿavariz*, but does not provide any details about the tax itself. The survey registers are not very informative in this regard either; they recorded no *'avariz* taxes. None of these taxes was included in the revenue from which the tithe was calculated.

Christians living in the villages around Jerusalem also paid the *cizye*, the poll tax on non-Muslims. Although according to *sharī'a* the *cizye* could be assessed at three different rates – high, medium, and low – in Ottoman Palestine it was listed at the lowest rate of one gold coin, and collected per household, not per person. In the first survey the *cizye* was listed at 60 or 70 *akçe* per household, then at 80 *akçe* per household until the final survey at the end of the century when it rose to 90 *akçe*, reflecting the devaluation of Ottoman coinage during the sixteenth century.[53] The *kanunname* of Jerusalem listed a detailed schedule of taxes to be paid by Christian pilgrims to Jerusalem, but did not mention the *cizye*. In the *kanunnames* of Gaza, Nablus, and Damascus, an increase in the *cizye* by 5 *akçe* for Christians and 10 *akçe* for Jews was decreed sometime after the death of Sultan Süleyman, probably at the accession of his son Selim in 974/1566.[54] It might also have been the case in Jerusalem, but if so then the *kanunname* was not followed in the villages, as a 10 *akçe* increase per Christian household was recorded.

The Ottoman system of taxation as it applied to Jerusalem does not appear very complex on paper. Taxation in the countryside was far less involved than in the city, due to the limited number of taxes and products. Nonetheless, the realities of computation and collection were much more involved than the regulations themselves indicate. The main point regarding the *kanunname*, however, is that the Ottomans did not introduce a whole new tax regime with many new levies. They largely maintained the existing system, concentrating instead on improving security and administrative effectiveness during their initial period of rule.

Production

The production of the Jerusalem region expanded tremendously through 1560, according to the tax assessments made in the first four surveys. This was accompanied by rapid population growth. Production and population growth may have begun even before the Ottoman conquest. Both continued more slowly after 1560, as reflected in the fifth survey of 1595–6 when compared with the fourth survey thirty-five years earlier. There is no survey after that of 1595–6 to indicate the pace and direction of growth in the seventeenth century.

From 1531 to 1545, wheat production rose thirty-six percent and barley seventy-four percent according to Makovsky's calculations based on the survey registers.[55] However, the figures from the second survey were not as complete as those from the third and the fourth. In the second survey, several villages, such as Jīb, Fāghūr, and Bittīr, still recorded one lump tax sum as *maktu'*, undifferentiated according to crops. In villages where *kısm* was

Table 3.1 *Gross changes in tax revenues, Survey II to III*

	Old	*New*	*% Change*
Wheat	36,963 *kile*	39,854 *kile*	8%
Mixed grains	30,258 *kile*	39,694 *kile*	31%
Olive oil	30.5 *kintar*[58]	276.5 *kintar*	807%
Mukata'at,[59] *rusum,*			
Bad-i hava	701,610 *akçe*	725,077 *akçe*	3%
Cizye	814 persons	1244 persons	
	65,120 *akçe*	99,520 *akçe*	53%

recorded, the breakdown according to crops not always given.[56] Thus the second survey is problematic as a basis of comparison.

Figures from the *icmal defteri*, a summary register which covered the second and third surveys, are given in Table 3.1. If the same changes which Makovsky calculated are computed based on these totals, the percentage changes were eight percent and thirty-one percent respectively for wheat and barley revenues as opposed to the thirty-six percent and seventy-four percent he found. *Mezra'a* production was likely included in the *icmal* calculations, as the numbers of cultivated and abandoned *mezra'a*s were carefully recorded at the beginning of the summary register.[57] There is no surviving *icmal* register which covers the changes between the third and fourth surveys.

The deviations between Makovsky's calculations and those based on the *icmal* suggest that figures in the detailed survey registers should be quoted as given, rather than converting them according to uncertain contemporary equivalents. Such discrepancies also discourage estimations, however tempting it might be to fill out the incomplete series of numbers. In citing the *icmal* figures, one is likewise faced with the difficulty of translating them into Jerusalem measures, as they were listed in Istanbul *kile*.[60] A further problem is to assess whether such gross totals were adjusted at any stage, and if so, why and by whom. I believe that by the time this information reached Istanbul, it was well beyond the scope of anyone who could benefit from its distortion. Such adjusting, if it existed, would be expected from those who were immediate taxpayers and revenue recipients.

The years at mid-century were the most prosperous since the Ottoman conquest, based on the increase in taxes assessed in kind and in cash[61] on the major grain crops of wheat and barley from 1545 to 1560. This was also the peak period of the entire century. Between the third and fourth surveys, expected wheat yields rose approximately twenty-two percent and barley fifteen percent. Thereafter expected tax yields stabilized and that of barley even declined towards the end of the sixteenth century.

In the registers for the district of Jerusalem, measures of area cultivated were not recorded until the fourth survey. Therefore, unlike studies of Anatolia or the Balkans, one cannot measure the expansion or contraction of lands under cultivation.[62] Was the rise in production due, therefore, to an extension of existing cultivation or to its intensification through improvements in agricultural techniques? Scant evidence can be marshalled by observing the location of *mezra'as* which became villages between the third and fourth surveys. The eighteen such sites were found scattered across the district. The summary register listed 283 *mezra'as* in use, and 149 ruined at the time of the third survey. This represented an increase of sixty-eight in the number of cultivated *mezra'as* from the second survey. Under the heading "ruined *mezra'as*" the *icmal* listed a decrease from 246 to 149, and labeled the difference of 77 [sic. 97] "*mamur*" (cultivated). These appeared in addition to the *mezra'as* listed first, but it is unclear whether the two were actually separate groups.[63] Amiran's observation that the villages on the eastern flank of the Judean mountains extended their cultivation eastwards and down as far as the Jordan River valley in secure periods is pertinent, but unconfirmable for this case.[64] The evidence, on balance, points toward an expansion of sown area rather than a change in cultivation methods to explain the rise in production.

Olive oil yields rose along with those of grain, and became a particular concern to the Ottoman survey makers around the middle of the sixteenth century. The increase in olive oil recorded from the second to the third survey is completely out of proportion to the rise in wheat and barley production. Total recorded output rose more than 800 percent![65] In part, it reflects a change in recording conventions. The registers had two rather broad categories for non-cereal agricultural produce: *mal-i seyfi* (summer crops)[66] and *harac-i aşcar* (tax on trees).[67] Under these headings might come olives, olive oil, grapes, carob, indigo, and the vague "other things" (*wa-gayrihi*). The latter heading was used in all the registers, so that it is impossible to assess each of these crops individually. One can only repeat what was listed in any particular instance and the sum given. Few details, therefore, are available on olive oil production from the earlier surveys. However, beginning with the third register, olive oil, grapes, trees, and grape syrup frequently were each recorded separately.[68] The separate recording of the *harac-i zeytun*, the tax on olives or olive trees, practically disappeared after the second survey, although it did recur sporadically under the general headings along with olive oil, grapes, and grape syrup.[69]

Production of olive oil also increased in response to the growing demands for oil as the basic raw material for soap, as well as being one staple in every local diet. Olive oil kept well, thus making it an attractive investment. And soap brought a handsome and consistent return on the initial investment in oil, adding to the popularity of oil purchases. The price of both commodities fluctuated within any year and from year to year, but over the course of the century prices rose steadily.[70] In the surveys, the price of olive oil in money-of-account rose from 4 *akçe* per *mann* in the first survey, to 8 *akçe* per *mann* in the second, and then dropped to 6 *akçe* per *mann* for the rest of the century.[71]

The customs tariffs due on locally produced soap exported to Egypt from Jerusalem were only recorded beginning from the third survey so that a direct comparison with the earlier period is impossible. But the newly recorded tariff is itself an indication of the growing importance of soap-making and export to the local economy. Revenues from taxes on the scales used to weigh olive oil also showed a threefold increase from the second to the third survey, and a further forty percent increase from the third to the fourth.[72]

Grape harvests were the object of more diligent assessments in the third survey and afterwards, though not at the level of olive oil. They were still recorded in some instances under the collective heading of "summer crops" or "tax on trees." Grape syrup also began to appear separately in significant quantities at this period.[73] Did the two items together reflect an expansion in grape cultivation? Beginning at the same time, summer crops and trees themselves were also more consistently recorded, though it remains impossible to distinguish exactly what these categories included. Whatever it was, however, there was more of it, and it was worth recording more carefully.

The weight of taxation

One question which remains to be considered following the discussions of taxation and production is: what kind of a burden did Ottoman levies on the peasants constitute, and did the increases in production and population in the period under consideration offset each other or did one factor outdistance the other?

The following table (Table 3.2) shows the average amount of the tax burden per adult male (including both heads of households and bachelors) according to the third and fourth survey registers. This was computed by dividing the total tax estimate for the village as recorded in the survey registers by the number of adult males in the village. The purpose of such a chart is to give a sense of the relative prosperity of villages and the variations possible from village to village, as opposed to observing simply their absolute population or estimated tax, figures which may mislead due to their size. The villages chosen are those discussed in the next chapter.

In the far right column, the percentage change from one survey to the next is computed. The majority of villages experienced an increase in the average estimate per adult male from the third to the fourth survey. Where the population rose, the rise in the average tax was thus due to increased production. In about half the villages, however, a decline in population

Table 3.2 *Average tax per adult male (in* akçe*)*

Village	*Survey III*	*Survey IV*	*% Change*	
Abū Dīs	53	135	[15%]	155%
'Ayn Kārim	87	121		39
Bittīr	44	98	[17%]	122
Bayt Laḥm	57	124	[22%]	117
Bayt Jālā	34	110	[20%]	224
'Inab	150	144		−4
Rīḥā	302	731	[21%]	142
Fāghūr	81	118		46
Jīb	74	168		127
Some Villages of the Banī Zayd region:[74]				
'Abwīn	169	147		−13
'Ajjūl	66	89		35
'Arūrā	151	182		21
'Aṭṭāra	58	60		03
Dayr Dibwān	132	178	[8%]	35
Dayr Ghassānā	101	274	[14%]	171
Jaljilya	266	316		19
Kafr 'Ana	165	97		−41
Kafr 'Aqab	32	67		109
Mazāri'	273	467	[9%]	71
Qarāwā	327	673	[6%]	106
Rammūn	147	140		−5

accounted for some of the increased average estimate. These places are noted with the percentage decrease in adult males in square brackets.

As the taxes were calculated as a fixed proportion of agricultural production and/or a fixed rate per tree, sheep, etc., the rise in the average estimate per adult male is understood to mean an overall rise in production which continued through the fourth survey.[75]

What magnitude of additional burden did the *cizye* constitute for the Christian villagers? If one assumes that they participated equally with the Muslims in paying the agricultural taxes in their villages,[76] then the table below (Table 3.3) shows an approximation of how many *akçe* per household were due, calculated by dividing the total revenues due (*hasıl*) by the number of adult males (Muslims and Christians) in the village.

In villages such as Dayr Abān, Naḥḥālīn, and Taqū' where there was a mixed Muslim–Christian population of moderate size, the *cizye* of 80 *akçe* in the third survey of 952/1545 was equal to or even greater than the average tax burden per adult male based on agricultural production: 59 *akçe*, 109

Table 3.3 *Computation of tax burden*

Village	*Survey III*	*Survey IV*
Dayr Abān		
Muslims (households & bachelors)	20	23
Christians (households & bachelors)	22	23
Total[77] (*akçe*)	2500	9145
Per household (*akçe*)	**59.5**	**198.8**
Cizye (*akçe*)	80	80
Naḥḥālīn		
Muslims (households & bachelors)	27	24
Christians (households & bachelors)	7	7
Total (*akçe*)	3706	5231
Per household (akçe)	**109**	**169**
Cizye (*akçe*)	80	80
Taqūʿ		
Muslims (households & bachelors)	115	105
Christians (households & bachelors)	14	5
Total (*akçe*)	11188	29318
Per household (*akçe*)	**87**	**267**
Cizye (*akçe*)	80	80

akçe, and 87 *akçe* for the three villages, respectively. Fifteen years later, at the time of the fourth survey, production had increased so that the 80-*akçe cizye* represented at most half the amount of the other levy: now 198 *akçe*, 169 *akçe*, and 267 *akçe*, respectively (Table 3.3). From even this casual computation, it is clear that the *cizye* was not a negligible tax for the Christian households, but its rate did not rise as fast as the increase in production, so that its relative burden gradually declined.

Other evidence of increased production is to be found in the changing distribution of revenues over the course of the sixteenth century. In the first survey, no assignments to the imperial domain, the *sancakbeyi*, or to *zeʿamet*s were recorded. This was a natural consequence of the low revenue yields which appeared in the register, and perhaps of the somewhat unpredictable flow of revenues in the earliest period as well. A few *tımar*s were awarded, but the bulk of local rural income went to support the *vakıf*s, or was not specifically assigned in the registers. By the second survey, many of the villages had been assigned as *tımar*s, or portions of *tımar*s. As shown by the figures in Table 3.4, the distribution of grain revenues remained relatively constant through the middle of the century. The most significant change was in the assignment of olive oil revenues, which decreased for the imperial

Table 3.4 *Changes in revenue distribution, Survey II to III*[79]

	Wheat	*Mixed Grains*	*Olive Oil*	*Mukata'at, Rusum, Bad-i hava*	*Cizye*
Hass-i şahi					
Old	12%	7%	33%	11%	83%
New	12	6	0.3	13	68
Hass mir-i liva					
Old	2	3	24	9	–
New	4	4	4	10	–
Ze'amet/tımar					
Old	36	39	5	20	–
New	35	39	18.6	23	–
Vakıfs[80]					
Old	48	50	38	–	17[81]
New	48	50	77	–	32
Mülk					
Old	0.4	0.1	–	–	–
New	0.5	0.5	–	–	–

domain but rose enormously for *tımar*s and *vakıf*s. However, this must also reflect the change in olive oil recording noted above. A greater share of the *cizye* was also directed to *vakıf*s at this time.

Beginning from the fourth survey, the *hass-i şahi* and *hass-i mir-i liva* portion gradually took over village revenues which had earlier belonged to *tımar*s.[78]

Another change in revenue distribution was brought about in the third *defter* with the change in tithe assessments. The additional revenues which the higher tithes yielded were in turn assigned as parts of the imperial domain, the share of the *sancakbeyi*, *ze'amet*s, *tımar*s, and even to other *vakıf*s. By dividing off the tithe from otherwise untouchable *vakıf* monies, the government managed to get into what was seemingly a "locked chest" of revenues.[82]

Further shifts in revenue assignments were brought about by the endowment of a large new foundation in Jerusalem by Süleyman's wife, Hurrem Sultan. The *vakıf* took over some agricultural revenues in the district of Jerusalem, most of which had belonged to the share of the Jerusalem *sancakbeyi*, as well as village revenues in other districts.[83] Founded in the early 1550s, the *vakıf* appears first in the fourth survey. Other small *vakıf*s were established during the sixteenth century, but these were made generally from the private holdings of the local endowers.[84]

Revenue increases from expanding production point perhaps to a general improvement in local conditions through the mid-sixteenth century. The burgeoning soap industry mentioned above demanded larger and larger quantities of olive oil to maintain and boost production levels, quantities which were available for an affordable price. Grain exports from Palestine to neighboring areas of the Ottoman empire, such as Egypt and Rhodes (conquered 1522), were apparently common by mid-century, made possible by increased yields. Merchants from as far away as Ragusa also came to buy grain in the eastern Mediterranean, though imperial *ferman*s explicitly prohibited commerce in grains with infidels, except in cases where specific orders were issued.[85]

Looking at the long-term trends of population growth, and extension of cultivation which LeRoy Ladurie described for sixteenth-century Languedoc, we can see the same basic trend described by the figures of the *tapu tahrir defterleri*.[86] The recovery of population and cultivation in Palestine, and the provinces of Ottoman Syria, during the first fifty years of Ottoman rule there may have been as much part of a natural convalescence after the weakness of population and cultivation engendered by the effects of the Black Death as it was a result of the benefits of Ottoman rule. Certainly, the Ottomans did offer a new measure of political stability and economic regulation, but these may have coincided with other, natural processes at work in the sixteenth century.

However, our interest here lies with the local peasants. Their obligations were clearly laid out in the *kanunname*. This records the local assessment practices and names the taxes collected. Most notably, the *çift resmi* is absent and does not appear in the *sijill* either. Presumably there was no precedent here for this tax. In Anatolia and the Balkans, it represented a monetary substitute for services once owed by the peasants to the *sipahi*s or *tımar* holders.[87] If these were a vestige of Byzantine rule in those areas, then they had disappeared in Palestine under the Arabs, Crusaders, Ayyubids, and Mamluks who had ruled there since the Byzantines.

The *kanunname* appears very precise and meticulous when its provisions are explicated. However, the extent to which they presume an extensive knowledge of local conditions suggests that the enforcement of its stipulations was not easy for the Ottoman officials. This points to one of the paradoxes of Ottoman provincial administration, especially in periods immediately following the conquest of an area. The external structure or superstructure of Ottoman administration was Ottoman and common features were shared by most provinces: a *sancakbeyi*, *sipahi*s, a *kanunname*, agricultural taxes, urban taxes, commercial tariffs, the *cizye*, *subaşıs*, kadis, janissaries, etc. Underneath or within this framework, however, the specific regulations and taxes and the functioning of the officials, were determined to some degree by local practice, as registered in the *kanunname*. Thus the complicated clauses of the *kanunname* forced the revenue holders to rely on the local population to a great extent. As long as the Ottoman sovereign was committed to a regime which respected the written statutes, and was able to enforce this commitment in his local provincial officials, then he had yielded some measure of power to local persons, including the peasants.

CHAPTER 4

Real accounts and accounting

"Fee fark bain Hhusâb es-serai wa-Hhusâb el kurai"[1]

(Palace and peasant calculations do not coincide.)

Relationships between the peasants and the Ottoman authorities were far more complex in operation than in structural outline. Taxpaying, the subject of the present chapter, was the nexus of peasant–official interactions; it defined and punctuated the agricultural routine of the year. The following discussion concentrates on tax payment and collection, using several cases to illustrate different aspects of this essential feature of rural administration. The disparities between the estimates of the survey registers and the annual assessments found in the *sijill*s illustrate more fully the character of the survey data. Charts containing data from the survey registers for the cases cited may be found in Appendix 1. The fluctuations recorded in the *sijill*s depict more realistically how the underlying agricultural rhythms affected each year separately. And, the difficulties of payment and collection show how tensions between peasants and officials were the product of more than numerical disparities.

Abū Dīs

The village of Abū Dīs is located three to four kilometers east-southeast of Jerusalem, probably on the same site as the contemporary village of Abū Dīs. Settlement in the mountains stretching between Hebron and Nablus has been relatively stable over time, and many of the villages here today may be identified with those listed in the Ottoman surveys.[2] Entirely Muslim, Abū Dīs was among the most populous villages in the *sancak* throughout the sixteenth century; with over one hundred adult males registered in the third and fourth surveys, it must have had a population of several hundred.[3] By the fourth survey, the population of Abū Dīs had started to decline while, in general, the rural population around Jerusalem was still growing. Even when the overall population of the province fell by the time of the fifth

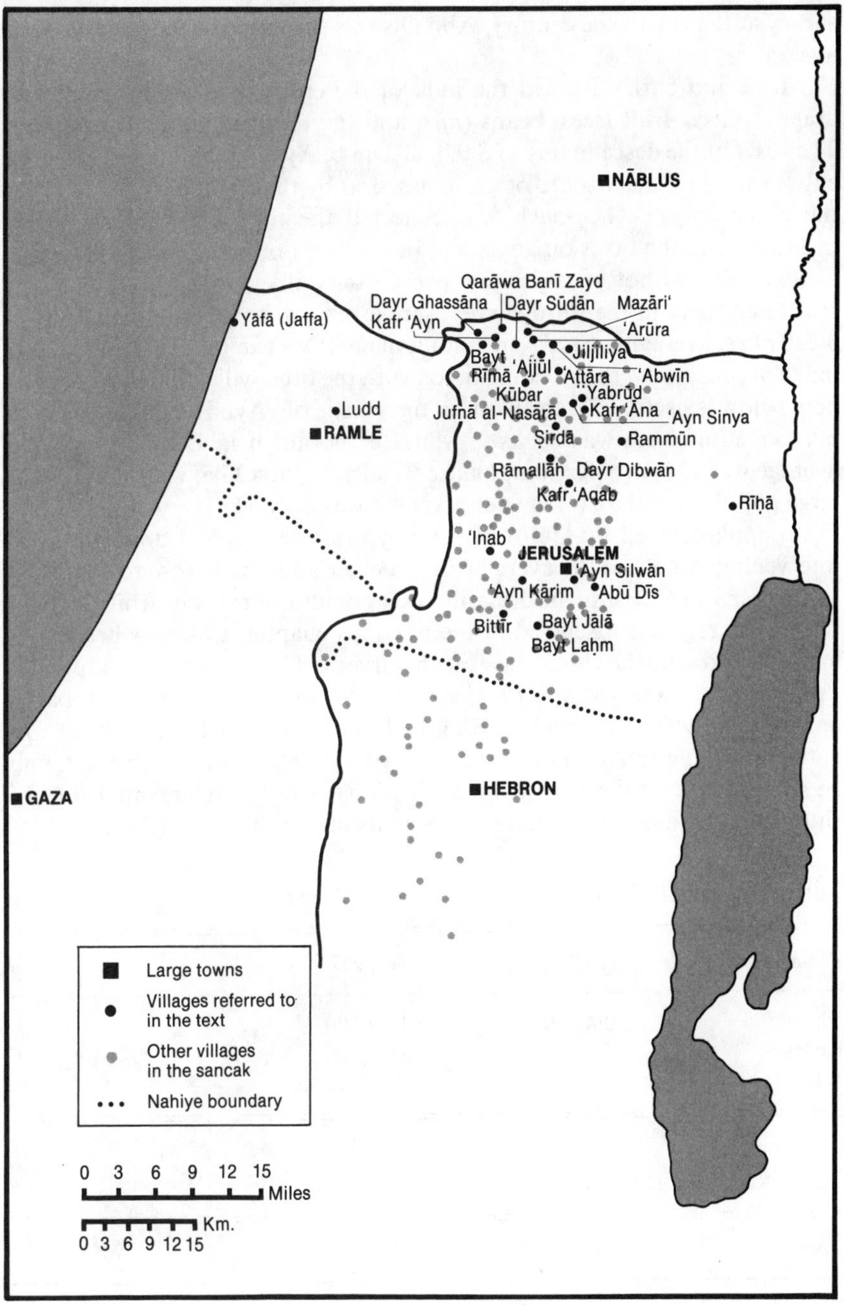

Map 3 Villages of the sancak of Jerusalem

survey at the end of the century, Abū Dīs was shrinking faster than the local average.[4]

Wheat and barley formed the bulk of the crops here, supplemented by grapes, olives, fruit trees, beans (*fūl*), and the products of goats and bees. The *vakıf* of the descendants of Salāḥ al-Dīn b. Ayyūb (Saladin) received the entire one-third *kısm* share of grain assessed by the state, plus the taxes on the other crops.[5] The *sancakbeyi* collected the tithe (*ʿöşr*) "from all the produce" and the taxes on goats and bees as part of his *zeʿamet*.

Abū Dīs was not an especially prosperous village; the 118 adult males registered there in the third survey were estimated to pay an annual tax of 6,250 *akçe*, averaging 53 *akçe* per adult male. If we can take this as a kind of index of prosperity, then a comparison with the other villages to be discussed here below is useful.[6] To the west, in the village of ʿAyn Kārim, the average tax per adult male was 87 *akçe* while to the north in Dayr Dibwān the average was 132 *akçe* per adult male.[7] Finally, in Bayt Jālā, which had a very large population, the average per taxpayer was only 34 *akçe*. Although Abū Dīs' population fell by the fourth survey, its revenues had doubled in the intervening years and the average estimate per adult male rose to 135 *akçe*.

Table 4.1 includes the information on agricultural taxes in Abū Dīs from the survey registers discussed in the previous chapter. Columns headed III and IV represent the third and fourth surveys. The third survey stipulated that Abū Dīs was to pay 10 *ghirāra* of wheat and 5 *ghirāra* of barley annually; by 967/1560 this had risen to 15 *ghirāra* of each. A series of *sijill* entries referring to Abū Dīs in the same period, collected in Table 4.2, may be compared with the survey figures in Table 4.1. The figures in Table 4.2 show the total amounts actually assessed as due in the years given.

Table 4.1 *Abū Dīs according to the survey registers*

ITEM	*III (952)*	*IV (967)*
wheat[8]	10/4,800	15/7,200
barley	5/1,300	15/3,900
tithe	2,084 akçe	4,537 akçe

Table 4.2 *Abū Dīs in the* sijill

Year	*959*	*960*	*961*	*962*	*963*	*969*
Wheat[9]		12		4	9	
Barley		12		10	13	18
Tithe[10]	8000		6000		10400	

Let us examine more closely the cases presented in the *sijill*, to see how the business of tax assessment and payment was carried out.

On April 14, 1554 (11 Jumādā I 961), it was established before the kadi that four leaders of the peasants of Abū Dīs (al-Asad b. Shu'ayb, Ramaḍān b. Sa'd, Kisya b. 'Abd al-Dā'im, and 'Abd al-'Azīz b. Ibrāhīm Basīṭa) owed 6 *ghirāra* of wheat and 6 *ghirāra* of barley, which was half the share of the *vakıf* from the grains, summer and winter crops, grapevines and cucumbers of the village for the previous year (960). Two weeks later, the *sijill* recorded that three other villagers from Abū Dīs (Khalīl b. Ḥaḍāra, Mūsā b. Abū 'Ulyān, and Jibrān b. al-Ba'jī) also owed the same amount from the village produce to the *vakıf*.[11] Since the entire tax share of grains from Abū Dīs was reserved for the *vakıf*, these two entries of half-shares together recorded the total assessment of grain for 960, which equaled 12 *ghirāra* each of wheat and barley.

Two years later, in the spring of 1556 (963), three leaders of half the peasants of Abū Dīs (al-Asad b. Shu'ayb, Mūsā b. Mus'ad, and Muḥammad b. 'Alī b. al-Basīṭa) owed 5 *ghirāra* of barley and 2 *ghirāra* of wheat, being the share of the *vakıf* of half the village taxes on grains, summer and winter crops, grapevines, cucumbers and other things, from 962. Two other men of Abū Dīs owed 1.62 *ghirāra* (116.5 *mudd*) of wheat and 3.84 *ghirāra* (276.5 *mudd*) of barley, which was 4/5 of one-half of the village taxes on grains, summer and winter crops, grapevines, cucumbers and other things from 962. The total amount due for the year 962 should thus be 4 *ghirāra* of wheat and 10 *ghirāra* of barley.[12]

One year more passed, and in May 1557 (Rajab 964) three leaders of the people of Abū Dīs (Mūsā b. Mus'ad, al-Asad b. Shu'ayb, and 'Abd al-'Azīz b. Ibrāhīm) owed 4.5 *ghirāra* of wheat and 6.5 *ghirāra* of barley, and 7 gold *sultani* in cash, the share of half the taxes on grains, summer and winter crops, grapevines and other things from 963. Four other leaders owed the same amount.[13] For the year 963, the total due was thus 9 *ghirāra* of wheat and 13 *ghirāra* of barley. Ten months after this record was made before the kadi, one of the leaders was sued for an outstanding debt of 11 *ghirāra* of wheat and barley, and 7 *sultani*. He claimed to have paid the money, and was excused from paying it, but still owed the grain.

Finally, a record from May 1563 (Ramaḍān 970) showed that five elders (*mashā'ikh*) of the people of Abū Dīs owed the *vakıf* 18 *ghirāra* of barley, which was the amount due from the taxes on summer and winter crops, grapevines, cucumbers and other things from 969. Two elders owed one half of the barley; three elders owed the other half.[14]

Entries from the *sijill*s thus record the actual assessments, which varied from the prescribed norm. The amounts of wheat and barley due from Abū Dīs changed from year to year. Wheat yields fluctuated, mostly below the expected figure in this period; barley seems to have been a hardier, more reliable crop, surpassing the fixed demand, perhaps compensating for lower wheat yields. The *sijill* documents which recorded these accounts did not refer to them as deviations, nor to the survey registers as the standard. The absence of a reference to the surveys in the entries dealing with specific tax payments suggests that annual assessment was not measured against the *tapu* sum. Rather, the tax yield of the crops was calculated in Abū Dīs at a rate of one-third as stated in the *tapu*; it varied annually, as expected, influenced by shifts in rainfall, seed quality, temperatures, or the invasion of pests.

Another indicator of yearly variations in the total village yield was the amount paid as tithe. The third survey recorded a tithe of 2,084 *akçe* from Abū Dīs; by the fourth survey, the estimated tithe had more than doubled to 4,537 *akçe*. The estimated grain yields in Abu Dīs between these two surveys had also doubled, from 15 to 30 *ghirāra* in total. The tithe as calculated in the registers here was to be "from all the revenues," i.e. based on the total yield before the portion due to the *vakıf* was set aside.

The amounts of the tithes recorded in the *sijill*s – like the grain taxes – differed considerably from the tithes estimated in the survey registers. Fluctuations in the tithes reinforce the picture of annual variance in yields and hence in taxes due. On May 26, 1553 (12 Jumādā II 960), eight leaders of Abū Dīs acknowledged that they owed Farrukh bey, *sancakbeyi* of Jerusalem, a tithe of 100 gold *sultani* for 959. One hundred *sultani* was equal to 8,000 *akçe*.[15] The village leaders had already paid 49 *sultani* to Fakhr al-Dīn, *kethüda*[16] of Farrukh bey, and deferred payment of the remaining 51 until the present date.[17]

The tithe recorded as due from a group of four elders for 961 was 75 *sultani*.[18] For the year 963, five leaders plus ʿĪsā b. Musʿad owed 130 *sultani* as tithe to the *sancakbeyi*.[19] In *akçe*, the tithes for 961 and 963 were 6,000 and 10,400 *akçe* respectively.

The disparity between the tithe as estimated in the surveys and as collected according to the *sijill* records is evident in Table 4.3 below:

Table 4.3 *Tithes in Abū Dīs (in* akçe*)*

Survey	*III (952)*				*IV (967)*
	2,084				4,537
Sijill		*959*	*961*	*963*	
		8,000	6,000	10,400	

Let us examine more closely the cases presented in the *sijill*, to see how the business of tax assessment and payment was carried out. The tithe was calculated on the value of grains estimated as due, a value computed using a notional price per *ghirāra*; this price remained unchanged for most of the sixteenth century.[20] According to the surveys, the notional price of 1 *ghirāra* of barley was 260 *akçe*. Yet in August 1556 (Shawwāl 963), the actual price of barley was 360 *akçe* per *ghirāra*, thirty-eight percent higher than the notional price.[21] This may represent a seasonal price movement, or a price change prompted by causes not explained in the *sijill*. It is of course possible that the higher price was the norm by this time. However, based on the amounts of wheat and barley due for 963 (see Table 4.2, above) equal to one-third of the total production plus the tithe, the tithe still seemed higher than the ten percent set in the survey register. In fact it was twenty percent "from all the revenue."[22]

The tithe levied on the peasants of Abū Dīs was thus much higher than the figure given by the survey register. In this village, moreover, since the tithe was "from all the revenues," it was taken from the total before other assessments were made, and so constituted a direct tax on the peasants, not on the share of the *vakıf*, as in some other places. Two explanations are possible for the higher value of the tithe: either it indicates that the yields were significantly larger than originally anticipated, or the inflated tithe taken by the *sancakbeyi* was more than was rightfully allowed him. If the latter was the case, the decreased population of Abū Dīs in the fourth survey may reflect a reaction to the weight of this levy.

Other disruptions to the accustomed routine may have contributed to the decline in population. The frequent change of adminstrators of the local *vakıf* may have provided an additional factor motivating the exodus from the village. The discontinuity probably disrupted the steady management of the *vakıf* and its assets.

In October 1553 (Shawwāl 960) Shaykh Sa'd al-Dīn al-Sharafī al-Mālikī was administrator *(nazır)* of the *vakıf*.[23] In July 1554 (Sha'bān 961), Muḥammad al-Fākhūrī was appointed *nazır* by the kadi at the request of three men who were the beneficiaries[24] of the *vakıf* of Salāḥ al-Dīn. These three had come to the kadi because the former *nazır* had been absent, and as a result they feared for the "loss and ruin of the capital of the *vakıf*."[25] As the new *nazır*, Muḥammad was given permission to seize and guard the grains and all the things attached to the *vakıf*.[26] Three months later, however, in a suit heard before the kadi in October 1554 (Dhū'l-Qa'da 961), Nūḥ al-Qādirī appeared as *nazır*. By the spring of 1555, Muḥammad al-Fākhūrī was again *nazır* of Abū Dīs, a function he retained at least through May 1563 (Ramaḍān 970).[27] Thus, four different people within two years served as *nazır* of the *vakıf* supported by the revenues of Abū Dīs.

An order sent from Istanbul dated early June 1555 (*evasıt* Receb 962) tells more about the troubles in Abū Dīs. Difficulties with the villagers had driven the *nazır* Muḥammad al-Fākhūrī to Istanbul where he petitioned the sultan as follows:

> In the *kaza*[28] of Jerusalem is the *vakıf* of my ancestors; in fact, the *re'aya* who are recorded [as living] in the villages of Abū Dīs and Ṭūr Zaytā[29] where I am *nazır*, cultivate other lands, and some of them have left their *çifts*,[30] and make their living from other trades, and some of them live in another village, and do not come to their own places, and they dispute [returning] (*niza' ederler imiş*).

The sultan ordered that there be an investigation of the circumstances reported in the petition. If they were found to be correct, the following actions were to be taken:

If the *re'aya* who were recorded [as living] there had entirely not cultivated the places which they previously used to cultivate, as they were cultivating other lands, it is the law (*kanundır*) to take two tithes from them, one tithe for it [the lands which they now cultivate] and one tithe for the *sahib-i arz* [the person entitled to the tithe from Abū Dīs]; and as for those *re'aya* who did not cultivate the places which they used to cultivate and had gone to live in other villages, moving their houses, since whichever year it has been, persons like this ought to be made to change their residence and brought back to their villages; but if the person had moved more than ten years earlier, it was impossible to force him [to move back]; the *raiyyet rüsūmu*[31] should be taken promptly according to the *kanun* and the *defter*.[32]

This petition was dated about one year prior to the *sijill* entry discussed above which recorded a tithe of twenty percent. In the years before that entry, the tithe figure also appeared to have exceeded the normal ten percent. Some peasants in this village, which was not among the most flourishing in the area, may have picked up and left as a reaction against the heavier tithe.[33] In the imperial *ferman*, the official response was to identify and return these peasants to their village as quickly as possible, although there was a statute of limitations which protected anyone who had been gone for more than ten years.[34] The threat of a double tithe seemed harsh enough to persuade people to return, provided that it could be enforced. But if the regular tithe on the village had become unbearable, then the penalty for desertion may not have seemed so grave. In this instance, we do not know if these villagers returned or were returned to Abū Dīs, but by the time of the fourth survey the overall population in the village had fallen from that in the previous register. Despite the overall rise in population throughout the century, there is no evidence of real population pressure on the land in Palestine. On the contrary, the close attention given to peasant movements suggests a potential or real shortage of labor.

The concern of the beneficiaries of the *vakıf* revenues of Abū Dīs, the frequent changes of the *nazır* within a few years, and the runaway or absent peasants were consistent signs of disrupted routine in the village. At the same time, the intense attention and the continual supervision demanded by one village, even one as close to the city of Jerusalem as Abū Dīs, demonstrate how tenuous were the links between the villagers and the local authorities.

Not only did Muḥammad the *nazır* have to keep close track of the villagers of Abū Dīs, but his authority over them was not as absolute as he pretended. In March–April 1555 (Jumādā I 962), Muḥammad testified before the kadi that several peasants from Abū Dīs had disposed freely (*taṣarrafū fī*)[35] of some green beans (*fūl*), selling them "without his permission or knowledge." The villagers were caught with the beans in the market of Jerusalem as they were selling them, and acknowledged their action, but claimed they had asked leave to do so from the *subaşı*, who had given his permission.[36] Although Muḥammad assumed that as *nazır* he had control over the disposition of goods legally included in the usufruct of the *vakıf*, in fact, within the city limits the authority of the *subaşı*, an Ottoman officer with local police authority, conflicted with his.

Certain features of local organization emerge as one begins to describe the administration of individual villages. The numerous persons connected with this one village represent the spectrum of authority which was delineated in Chapter Two. It began somewhere in the ranks of the Ottoman officials and continued into the local village population. The annual revenues due from Abū Dīs had to be gathered from the hands of several responsible individuals, each of whom in turn had to collect them from his immediate community. The fragmented bookkeeping needed to follow village accounts, and the other difficulties recounted above, belie the order and regularity suggested by the survey registers.

ʿAyn Kārim

Southwest of Jerusalem about seven kilometers lies the village of ʿAyn Kārim, where today terraced vineyards descend the slope of the small valley looking north to the deeper course of the *wādī* below. In the sixteenth century the village population was entirely Muslim although Christian tradition holds that this was the birthplace of John the Baptist. The village spring (*ʿayn*) is called St. Mary's Well (ʿAyn Sitt Miriam) because of a visit there by Mary. During the time of Louis XIV (1638–1715), ʿAyn Kārim was reputedly given to the Franciscans by the sultan.[37] According to the Ottoman surveys, the village grew from ten to thirty-nine households during the first twenty-five years of Ottoman rule; its production rose 50–60 percent over the same period, at which time both population and revenue seemed to stabilize for the remainder of the sixteenth century. A typical mix of wheat, barley, goats, grapes, olives, and carob trees was taxed at a rate of one-third to support the *vakıf* of the hospice (*zaviye*) of the Maghribīs in Jerusalem.[38] The tithe, collected "from all the revenues," was part of a *tımar* which also included the tithe of the village of Qulūnya a few kilometers north of ʿAyn Kārim.[39] Table 4.4 gives the tax figures for ʿAyn Kārim from the survey registers, and below them, some annual sums from the *sijill*.

On April 29, 1553 (15 Jumādā I 960), Shaykh Shihāb al-Dīn Aḥmad b. ʿAbd al-Razzāq, shaykh of the Maghribīs and *nazır* of the *vakıf* of the hospice, claimed that three leaders of ʿAyn Kārim (Aḥmad al-Fahl, Zaʿn b. Dibyān, and Muḥammad b. al-Aʿmā) were responsible for the payment of 1,900 *akçe*, which was the share of the *vakıf* from one-half of the produce for the year 959. One hundred *akçe* were deducted from this for the three men in remuneration for their position as village leaders. The remaining 1,800 *akçe*

Table 4.4 *Revenues of ʿAyn Kārim (in gold* sultani*)*

ʿAyn Kārim in the survey registers[40]					
Survey/Year	*III (952)*		*IV (967)*		
Total (*hasıl*)	50		62		
Tithe	17		21		
ʿAyn Kārim in the *sijill*					
Year	*959*	*962*	*963*	*966*	*968*
Total (*hasıl*) for *vakıf*	49[41]	44	40	33/40/41/45	30
Tithe			5		14

were due in three installments of 600 *akçe* each: on June 13 (1 Rajab), October 8 (the end of Shawwāl), and December 6 (the last day of the year). On the same day, Shaykh Shihāb al-Dīn likewise made two other men of ʿAyn Kārim responsible for the other half of the revenues.[42]

The following spring, three village leaders (Dibyān b. ʿAlī, Muḥammad b. Khalīl al-Aʿmā, and Khaṭṭāb b. Ghānim) were recorded as owing 100 *mudd* of wheat and 100 *mudd* of barley, which was the share of the *vakıf* from all the revenues from the wheat, barley, other grains and cucumbers, excluding the grapevines, olive trees and gardens, for the year 960. Dibyān owed 84.5 *mudd* (half wheat, half barley), Muḥammad 50 *mudd* and Khaṭṭāb owed the remaining 65.5 *mudd*. They were to deliver this to the hospice in Jerusalem.[43]

When compared with the figures in the third survey (952), the revenues of ʿAyn Kārim for the year 959 matched official estimates almost perfectly. One year later, grain yields appeared to have fallen dramatically as only 200 *mudd* were claimed as due. According to the survey, grains made up the bulk of ʿAyn Kārim's revenues, so that the overall income that year must have been very low, less than one-third of the survey estimate.[44] The yield of 959 seemed to represent a short-term high for *vakıf* revenues from ʿAyn Kārim. From 49 *sultani* assessed for that year, the figure declined during the next ten years to reach a low of 30 *sultani* in 968. The fourth survey, however, showed an increase of 1,000 *akçe* in estimated revenues from ʿAyn Kārim, from fruit trees and grape syrup.[45]

Not only was there a change in the amount of revenue collected, but the manner of its collection altered as well. According to the pattern described above, in May 1556 (Rajab 963), under the auspices of a new *nazır* and shaykh of the Maghribīs, five leaders of ʿAyn Kārim (Dibyān b. ʿAlī, his son Zaʿn, Aḥmad al-Fahl, Muḥammad b. Khalīl, and Aḥmad b. Dīb) were confirmed as owing 44 gold *sultani*. This sum was equivalent to the share of the *vakıf* from all the village revenues for the year 962. Of the 44 *sultani*, 2.5 were reserved to the leaders as their due portion. The remaining 41.5 *sultani* were split into three equal parts for payment by the end of the *hicri* year, as was the case with the revenues of 959. The debt itself was divided into four parts among the leaders.[46]

However, in the account recorded for the following year, it was Murad b. ʿAbdallah *subaşı*, one of the *sipahi*s, who acknowledged that he owed the *vakıf* 40 *sultani* from the revenues of ʿAyn Kārim from all crops for 963. By the time of his affirmation in May 1557 (Rajab 964), Murad had already paid 15 *sultani*, and owed the remaining 25 by the end of the *hicri* year (late October). Two *sultani* were given to the village leaders for their robes from the tithe which was taken "from the money of the *vakıf*."[47] Murad paid the tithe of 5 *sultani* to El-Hac ʿAli b. Yusuf *sipahi*.[48]

Murad had leased the right to collect the *vakıf* revenues of ʿAyn Kārim from the *nazır*. His lease was first effective for the revenues of 963 which were collected in 964. Murad was responsible for giving the *tımar* holder the tithe from the *vakıf* share and for paying the leaders of the village. So Murad, now, was the one to make arrangements with the leaders for the delivery of the sums and/or crops due for the *vakıf*. His own profit from this rental contract was not stipulated, but he certainly hoped to gain something. Whatever remained from the amount delivered by the peasants of ʿAyn Kārim for the *vakıf*, after the tithe had been paid, was his. If the year was a bad one, or not particularly profitable, Murad risked a net loss. The five *sultani* of the tithe paid to ʿAli *sipahi* were much less than the tithe estimated in the survey and again point to reduced yields. Or did Murad perhaps reduce his own losses at ʿAli's expense?

The competition between Murad and ʿAlī for the revenues of ʿAyn Kārim came out clearly towards the end of 967 (early September 1560). On August 30, 1560, Murad acknowledged before the kadi that he owed the *vakıf* 33 *sultani* from the village revenues for the year 966. Within a few days, this had been corrected to 40 *sultani*.[49] On September 7, however, the *nazır* was recorded as leasing the right to collect the *vakıf* revenues of ʿAyn Kārim for 966 to ʿAli *sipahi* for a sum of 41 gold *sultani*, "one *sultani* more than Murad *subaşı* the former leaseholder."[50] The "former leaseholder" had had his lease confirmed only a week earlier! However, ʿAli quickly lost his new privilege. Later that same day, Murad was again confirmed as the leaseholder of the 966 *vakıf* revenues of ʿAyn Kārim by the *nazır*, now for 45 gold *sultani*, "four *sultani* more than El-Hac ʿAli, the former leaseholder."[51] Murad had to pay 25 *sultani* on the spot, deferring the remaining 20 for two and a half months. His payment of this latter sum was delayed, for in the following summer we find him being dunned by the *nazır* for 9 *sultani* still due. Murad acknowledged that he owed the money, and then turned around to claim it from ʿAli, who confirmed his own debt.[52]

By that time, however, the actual lease had passed to someone else, for the revenues of 968 were paid in 969 to the *nazır* by two of the *mustaḥfiẓīn* (the garrison troops) of the Jerusalem citadel. Times were harder (or perhaps the leaseholders more aggressive,) for they paid the *nazır* only 30 *sultani*.[53] Meanwhile, 'Ali was still trying to collect his share of the tithe, bringing suit against a leader of 'Ayn Kārim for the tithe of the grains from 968 and 969. The man owed him 14 gold *sultani* and 80 *mudd* of barley, from himself and as guarantor of his community, of which he was able to pay only 4 *sultani* at the time.[54]

Although the struggle described here was between two officials, the prize they fought over was the right to collect the revenues of the peasants of 'Ayn Kārim. Ultimate authority over the disposition of the revenues remained with the *nazır* of the *vakıf*, but he had removed himself by one, if not two, levels from the actual collection. Murad, in this case, won the final bid for the lease on 'Ayn Kārim, but the hierarchy of debt for the outstanding 9 *sultani* indicated that Murad later sub-contracted his own lease to 'Ali, or hired him in some subordinate function. 'Ali held his *tımar* in the village, which entitled him to the tithe from the *vakıf* share. Yet he sought more direct access to the revenues by a lease of the right to collect the *vakıf* share itself as well.

In Abū Dīs, two basic groups active in the countryside – the officials and the peasants – emerged as two hierarchical networks of people. Further subdivisions appear in 'Ayn Kārim. Village revenues, instead of being directly collected, were sub-leased to a local Ottoman official by the person with a right to the revenues; the official made his profit on the difference between the actual yield and the predicted yield. As we saw, the person who took over the lease of revenues might be a *sipahi* with a claim to other revenues in the same village. In so doing, he consolidated his power over the village. Yet this was just the situation the Ottomans worked to prevent, by assigning *tımar*s for only one year at a time, and by splitting a man's *tımar* over two or more villages instead of assigning all the revenues from one place to a single person. Around Jerusalem, this policy was more easily instituted as many of the villages, like 'Ayn Kārim, had *vakıf*s claim part of their revenues. The *sipahi*s and other officials, however, managed to find ways to overcome this obstacle, as illustrated here.

Payment of revenues due was distributed in installments over several months, both when collected from the peasants by the *nazır*, and when paid over to him by the leaseholder. Finally, the responsibility for tax payments was divided among the leaders named; the amount of their remuneration was not fixed, but rather varied according to the extent of their obligation, since in the year 960 the same sum of 100 *akçe* was divided between three people in one case, and two in another.[55] The total emolument made to the leaders of 'Ayn Kārim, however, was consistently five percent of the total due the *vakıf*, in those cases where it was stated.

What first appeared in the survey registers to be a comprehensible arrangement of villages and administrators gradually reveals itself to be a morass of subordinate authorities and partial remittances. At the same time, the enormous detail recorded in the *sijill*s attests to the careful accounting of each payment, and the official supervision of revenue leasing.

Bittīr

Bittīr is about six kilometers southwest of ʿAyn Kārim near the railway line built from Jaffa to Jerusalem in 1892, assuming the village has not moved since the sixteenth century. Like Abū Dīs and ʿAyn Kārim, Bittīr paid one-third of its revenues to a *vakıf*; its tithe belonged to a *tımar*, then a *zeʿamet*. Like Abū Dīs, the village yielded a moderate quantity of produce, and its population was already falling by the time of the fourth survey. However, estimated revenues from wheat and barley doubled between the two surveys and revenues recorded in the *sijill*s rose between 960 and 970, as in Abū Dīs and ʿAyn Kārim.

There seems to have been nothing very extraordinary in the dealings of Shaykh Sharaf al-Dīn Mūsā al-Dabarī, the *nazır* of the *vakıf*,[56] with the people of Bittīr in 961 and 962. For two years in succession, three leaders of Bittīr were recorded as owing 50 *sultani* (4,000 *akçe*) to the *vakıf* from the revenues of the village for 960 and 961. From this, 400 *akçe* were deducted annually for the cost of their robes. Fifty *sultani* was considerably more than the 29 *sultani* (2,331 *akçe*) estimated in the third survey, but slightly less than the 54 *sultani* (4,299 *akçe*) in the fourth.[57]

In August 1556 (Shawwāl 963), the village leaders were involved in a serious dispute over the revenues of Bittīr and the payments due from them. The progress and resolution of this case demonstrate how the villagers could and did safeguard their interests with the help of the kadi. Although the suit was initiated by a complaint from the *nazır* of the *vakıf*, the final decision favored the villagers.

The deputy of the *nazır* brought suit against the three leaders (ʿAbd al-Laṭīf, Aḥmad al-Hatīmī, and ʿĪsā) claiming that they had acknowledged the revenues of their village for the year 962 to be 550 *sultani* (total), of which they had paid 55 *sultani* to the tithe collector, and owed 170 *sultani*[58] to the *vakıf*. He also demanded 15 *sultani* from each man as his own share of their debt, which they refused to pay. The three men claimed that the former *nazır* of the *vakıf*[59] had assessed the revenue due for 962 as 50 *sultani*, of which he had taken eight, but without the knowledge of the current *nazır* and with no record of the payment having been made in the *sijill*. The deputy *nazır* answered that the leaders' behavior was treacherous and accused them of conspiring against the *vakıf* monies, stating that the *nazır* had ordered his predecessor not to touch any part of the *vakıf* revenues except with his own knowledge. For their part, the village leaders were required to pay 15 *sultani* each. ʿAbd al-Laṭīf, one of the leaders, became furious, refused to pay, shouted at the employees of the kadi, behaved badly, and said, "even if you had passed 500 verdicts against me, I wouldn't have accepted it!"[60]

Nine months later, in late April 1557 (end of Jumādā II 964), the case was still unresolved, and again came before the kadi. The original suit was repeated. Now the leaders asked for an oath from the current *nazır* that he had not consented to the former *nazır*'s assessment of the revenues. Finally, the current *nazır* and the leaders agreed on a sum owing that was ten percent more than the original assessment.[61]

The former *nazır*, although he acted with no authority, had made what seemed to be the normal assessment for Bittīr. The 50 *sultani* he fixed as due equalled the sum paid in the two previous years. The original figure in the suit, 170 *sultani*, was reduced to the original amount, plus a negotiated addition of about 12.5 *sultani*. Did the yields of 962 reflect the ongoing rise in wheat and barley yields seen in the survey, such that the *nazır* and his deputy thought themselves justified in taking an extra sum from the peasants of Bittīr? The tithe of 55 *sultani* which the leaders apparently paid with no quarrel was equal to the entire sum paid previously by the village to the *vakıf*, but should have been a tithe of ten percent. It was correct if the gross yield for 962 was 550 *sultani* as the *nazır's* deputy originally claimed.

This case then remains an unsolved puzzle. If the total revenues were 550 *sultani*, then why did the *nazır* accept 62.5 *sultani* instead of the 170 *sultani* apparently due to the *vakıf*? The final compromise worked out suggests that the initial claim of 170 *sultani* was indeed exorbitant, but we do not know why it was made. Nor, finally, was there any complaint over the tithe of 55 *sultani*, which was also high. Returning to the 62.5 *sultani* finally paid in taxes for that year, we see that the peasants successfully intervened to negotiate a smaller increase in their obligations.

Did the former *nazır* knowingly try to steal from the current *nazır* by continuing to make and collect the annual assessment, playing on the confusion inherent in the transition from one administrator to another? Or was he acting to protect the villagers for some reason, by establishing the assessment at an artificially low level? Were they paying him to do so? Was the deputy of the current *nazır* acting for the good of the *vakıf* or for himself when he tried to impose such a high assessment on the village at a time when some increase seemed justified? These questions remain unanswered for lack of evidence, but they emphasize the complexities of the system which left much to the initiative of the individual officials. At the same time, the villagers were able to block or reduce excessive demands by bringing matters before the kadi.

Nāḥiyat Banī Zayd

According to the survey registers, the Ottoman *sancak* of Jerusalem was divided into the two sub-districts (*nahiyes*) of Jerusalem and Hebron. From the *sijill*, however, there were clearly further divisions of the area, defined by particular groups of villages. The Ottomans used these smaller local divisions to fix the appointment of officials in the rural areas although they ignored them in the surveys drawn up for Istanbul.[62] In the nineteenth century, the *sancak* was divided into eleven *nahiye*s whose boundaries within those of the *sancak* were not permanently fixed. The names of these divisions were either geographical, for a major town in the area, or tribal.[63]

Two principal divisions within the sixteenth-century sub-district of Jerusalem were Banī Zayd and Banī Ḥārith. The names were those of the Bedouin tribes prominent there at some earlier time or who may still have lived in or controlled parts of these areas.[64] Banī Zayd and Banī Ḥārith were both referred to in the *sijill*s as the jurisdictions of officials as in the case where Abū Bakr of Bayt Jālā said to ʿAli the scribe, "even if you become governor of all the villages of Banī Zayd, Banī Ḥārith and Banī ʿAmr... "[65] In the first survey of Jerusalem, Banī ʿAmr was listed as a third official *nahiye* with eight villages on the western edge of the province. These villages became part of the district of Gaza after that time, and the sub-district was no longer recognized as separate.[66] Banī Ḥārith was also listed in the first two surveys as a quarter (*mahalle*) of the town of Jerusalem, though it seems to have been outside the walls near the citadel.[67] The quarter of Banī Zayd, documented for the Mamluk period, was not mentioned in the *tapu*.[68]

Nāḥiyat Banī Zayd comprised a group of villages in the northern reach of the province: Dayr Dibwān, Dayr Ghassāna, Bayt Rīmā, Kafr ʿAyn, Qarāwā, ʿArūrā, ʿAbwīn, Mazāriʿ, Kafr ʿAqab, Rammūn, Dayr Sūdān, ʿAjjūl, Kūbar, ʿAṭṭāra, Jufnā, ʿAyn Sinya, Yābrūd, Kafrʿ Ana, Ṣirdā, and Jaljiliya.[69] In addition, three villages from the *sancak* of Nablus, north of Jerusalem, were also listed as part of Banī Zayd, a phenomenon which supports the idea that these divisions predated the Ottoman administration.[70]

While individually these villages were registered and organized like the other villages in the *sancak*, they were also treated as a group. In addition to the separate village leaders, a local person held the title "*shaykh* of the villages of Banī Zayd."[71] His position was one of "super-*raʾīs*": he was cited as owing the sums due from the villages, in much the same way that the *raʾīs* was named as responsible for his particular village. Shaykh Abū Riyān b. Shaykh Mannāʿ was shaykh of the *nahiye*[72] of Banī Zayd in July 1556 (Ramaḍān 963), when he guaranteed the leaders of the villages listed in Table 4.5 below for a total of 233 *kintars* of olive oil.[73]

The villages of Banī Zayd varied in the size of their populations from ʿAyn Sinya, Dayr Sūdān, and Jaljiliya, each with under ten households, to ʿAjjūl and Dayr Ghassāna with over eighty apiece in the third survey. Jufnā, sometimes called Jufnā al-Naṣārā, was entirely Christian, while Bayt Rīmā had a minority Christian population.[74] Tax revenues from these villages supported *tımar*s and *vakıf*s, especially the *vakıf* for the mosque of al-Aqṣā and the *vakıf* of Hebron.[75]

Revenues in Banī Zayd were generated from the usual list of agricultural crops, although in somewhat different proportions than the region south of

Table 4.5 *Olive oil due, in* kintars[79]

Year	*Survey* *III (952)*	*IV (967)*	*Sijill* *957*	*962*
Dayr Ghassāna	20	60	13	36
Bayt Rīmā	60	64	17	46
Kafr ʿAyn	40	52	16	36
Qarāwā	34	62	18	36
ʿArūrā	25	30	12	21
ʿAbwīn	19	24	10	16
Mazāriʿ	38	69	12	34

Jerusalem. Wheat and barley were omnipresent, but in much smaller quantities. Olive oil dominated the economy of the mountain villages between Jerusalem and Nablus. Of the twelve villages which the third and fourth surveys estimated as yielding over 1,000 *mann* (=20 *kintar*) per annum each in taxes, eight were from the Banī Zayd region.[76]

Olive oil had three basic uses at this time: it was the main ingredient in soap production; it was a cooking staple; and it was used for lighting.[77] Concomitant with the rise in olive oil production was a resurgence of the soap-making industry in Jerusalem. Old soap works (*maṣbanas*) were repaired and new ones built. Soap was used locally, but also exported to Egypt and Istanbul in significant quantities.[78]

Table 4.5 shows the amounts of olive oil assessed in the survey registers as compared with the quantities listed as due in the *sijill*. From both sets of figures, a large rise in olive oil yields in the mid-sixteenth century was evident. As described in Chapter Three, this rise was notable only from the third survey, when the separate recording of olive oil became common.

The discrepancies between the quantities of olive oil in the survey and *sijill* figures probably arose from a combination of factors. First, as with grains, annual yields varied. However, the difference between the estimate and the actual amount produced was greater in every case of olive oil than of grains. Second, one of the totals recorded in the two examples from the *sijill* may have been from an "off" year in the olive cycle. Olive trees bear fruit in an alternating cycle: one year there is a full crop; the following year there may be little or no fruit.[80] Neither of these explanations is fully satisfactory, however. It seems possible that a large amount of olive oil is unaccounted for here, perhaps as a category of payments unrecorded.

Olive oil was paid to *vakıf* agents and *tımar* holders as part of their rightful revenues. Although this was often called a "tax on olives" (*harac-i zeytun*), the assessment and delivery were made chiefly in oil.[81] The villagers sold oil to Ottoman officials, presumably for use in their own households, or to be resold by them in the town. They also supplied oil to the various soap manufacturers. When a sale was made, the *sipahi*, or other official, paid cash in advance and contracted with the peasants that the oil be delivered to him. Although one finds accounts of olive oil due from various villages throughout the year, transactions were mostly completed by the late summer when the olives had ripened sufficiently to predict the crop yield and before the oil was pressed. Deliveries were then arranged for a month or several months later.[82]

The notional price of olive oil in the survey was calculated at 6 *akçe* per *mann*, or 3.75 *sultani* per *kintar*. In the *sijill*s, however, olive oil was calculated at 10 *sultani* per *kintar* (16 *akçe* per *mann*), both in sales to individuals and in calculating the cash equivalent for tax purposes.[83] The implications of such a difference are numerous. If the *tımar* holder collected his olive oil in kind, then he could sell it, effectively raising his net income above what was assigned to him. If he took the cash equivalent from the villagers for the olive oil, then he had profited as well, as long as he could demand the market value of the oil and not the notional price written in the survey. Moreover, the oil was easy to store, thus allowing someone to wait for prices to rise. More often, one of the large *vakıf*s reaped the profits of this conversion, as the greatest quantities of olive oil belonged to them. Finally, the villagers were probably able to convert produce to cash easily, because the demand for oil came not only from private households but from the expanding local soap industry as well.

One must, then, wonder at the priorities of the Ottoman administration. Why did it not adjust the notional price of olive oil in the survey registers? The quantities of oil listed in the surveys reflect the increasing importance of the crop locally. Presumably, the greater net worth which could be calculated for a village would mean that the same area could have supported more *tımar*s. Why did the government not seem interested to take advantage of this? Did it not know? Or did it think that the predominance of the *vakıf*s as beneficiaries would minimize its own ability to tap into the olive oil as a money-maker? In this instance, the change in tithe calculations which came at mid-century is clearly understandable as it allowed the government to tax an extremely profitable commodity which was otherwise out of reach. Perhaps at the outset, the Arab provinces were less important economically, more a strategic asset and a symbol of the Ottoman empire as the guardian of the Islamic holy sites and preeminent Muslim power. Only after several years of occupation did the Istanbul regime also try to maximize its revenues from the region.

Olive oil and the transactions surrounding it reveal another point of contact and mode of interaction between the peasants and the local Ottoman officials. In addition to officials as tax collectors and keepers of the peace, they appeared in the countryside as consumers. Naturally, some of these officials came in all three guises, at the same moment or at different times during the year. If they did not come, they sent their agents. One can speculate, too, that in a bad year there might be competition for the scarce product, engendering rivalries among officials and alliances between officials and peasants and possible clashes over accusations of hoarding.

In Banī Zayd one can see the extended official organization of Ottoman administration reaching into the local regions of the province, while at the same time the region reveals a blurring of some lines which looked fixed, namely the provincial borders. The accounting of olive oil, the disparity between the imperial registers and local reality, all reinforce the image of the surveys as general, and provide a further example of the flexibility of the fiscal regime at work.

Bayt Laḥm and Bayt Jālā

Bayt Laḥm is eight kilometers south of Jerusalem and Bayt Jālā lies two kilometers west of Bayt Laḥm. Because of the sanctity of Bayt Laḥm as the birthplace of Jesus, we can be certain of its unchanged location. Bayt Jālā is described in the *sijill* as being next to it.[84] These two were the most populous villages in the district, based on the number of households. Both had a majority Christian population. Bayt Jālā only gained a few Muslim households in the latter part of the century, while Bayt Laḥm seemed to be equally Muslim and Christian for a period in the mid-sixteenth century, but completely Christian by the end (Table 4.6).[85]

Both villages were so large by the end of the century that in the final survey they had been sub-divided into quarters (*rubʿ*) like the towns. Bayt Jālā had four quarters and Bayt Laḥm seven, all but one named after the first person listed in each.[86] Neither, however, had any of the other characteristic features of towns found in the survey registers, such as the numerous market taxes or road tolls.

The Christian villagers, like non-Muslims throughout the Ottoman empire, were required to pay the *cizye*. In the second, third, and fourth

Table 4.6 *Populations (adult males) of Bayt Laḥm and Bayt Jālā*

Survey	*I*	*II*	*III*	*IV*	*V*
Bayt Laḥm					
Muslim	39	46	162	107	0
Christian	60	83	164	148	287
Bayt Jālā					
Muslim			36	2	6
Christian	129	157	240	218	239

empire, were required to pay the *cizye*. In the second, third, and fourth surveys, the *cizye* was stated to be 80 *akçe* per adult male. The calculation of the *cizye* for each village in the survey was written separately from the total of population or other taxes. "Two hundred and forty individuals, each one 80 *akçe*, the total being 19,200 *akçe*," was the entry for the *cizye* of Bayt Jālā in the third survey.[87] Yet when Mehmet bey, a *sipahi* from Damascus, was sent to collect the *cizye* from the Christians and Jews of Jerusalem, Gaza, Ramle, and their dependencies in 960, his deputy collected only 40 *sultani* from the people of Bayt Jālā. The deputy, in turn, delegated one Bayram *çavuş*[88] to collect the rest of the *cizye* from Bayt Laḥm, Bayt Jālā, Bayt Sāḥūr al-Naṣārā, Dayr Abān, Jufnā, Taqū', Kafr Shū', and Ludd (in the *nahiye* of Ramle), for which he paid the deputy 25 *sultani*.[89] Forty *sultani* was only 3,200 *akçe*, roughly one-sixth of the *cizye* estimated. Even accounting for the decline in the Christian population between the third and fourth surveys, 3,200 *akçe* did not exceed one-fifth of the total due. Bayram was left to collect what the deputy had not.

It was possible that Bayram never received the entire sum of the *cizye* as stated in the survey. Among the Jewish and Christian communities living in the town of Jerusalem, the *cizye* was a sum arrived at by a process of negotiation between the *ra'īs* of the Jews and the authorities.[90] The same could well have been true for the Christian communities in the villages. For example: Mehmet bey *sipahi* of Lajjūn (the province north of Nablus), acting as a deputy in the collection of the *cizye*, acknowledged on February 7, 1556 (25 Rabī' I 963) that he received from the leaders of the Christians in Bayt Jālā all the *cizye* for 131 persons. The leaders confirmed that this was all of them.[91] If the figure in the survey was even approximately correct – 240 adult males in the third survey, 218 in the fourth – then 131 was far lower than the number of eligible *cizye* payers. The *sijill* contained no accusation against the Christians of Bayt Jālā that they were concealing their true numbers, nor a complaint from the villagers that their numbers were overestimated. As with the taxes on agricultural produce, no reference was made to the figures in the survey registers as the "right" numbers.

The third and fourth surveys showed Christians from Bayt Jālā and Bayt Laḥm living and taxed in the city of Jerusalem.[92] Perhaps this was evidence of a more widespread migration. Although Christians from these villages did not appear in the other towns of Palestine, Christians from Bayt Rīmā, north of Jerusalem, were recorded in Gaza, Ramle, and Ludd.[93]

Apportioning the *cizye* within the community itself, moreover, may not have been as simple as asking for 80 *akçe* from each man liable to pay it. 'Īsā, a Christian of Bayt Jālā and his blind son Ghanā'im came to the kadi to complain that the people of the village increased the *cizye* they took from Ghanā'im. 'Īsā claimed that Ghanā'im was dependent on him for his subsistence. Ghanā'im was confirmed by witnesses to be truly blind, and 'Īsā produced a formal legal opinion (*fetva*) stating that legally no *cizye* was due from a blind man.[94] On the strength of this evidence, the kadi ordered the village people not to demand the *cizye* from Ghanā'im at all.[95]

Ghanā'im's exemption was a matter of Muslim law, upheld by the kadi. Moreover, the case demonstrates how the total *cizye* for each village was left to the villagers to assign and collect among themselves. In fact, this was the situation among the Jews living in Jerusalem; religious figures were exempted, but more of the burden could presumably be placed on wealthier members of the community.[96] Finally, 'Īsā's procurement of a *fetva* to justify his claim of Ghanā'im's exemption from the *cizye* illustrates the degree to which Christian villagers were integrated into the Muslim legal-religious culture. We have seen Christians and Jews coming to the kadi for the adjudication of their own intercommunal affairs. Here, a Christian man went to the proper Muslim religious-legal authority to receive a formal opinion based on Muslim religious law by which to justify his plea before the kadi. Christians, like Jews, were legally handicapped, but the law also limited the handicap and the kadi enforced the law.

As might be expected from large populous villages, Bayt Laḥm and Bayt Jālā produced greater quantities of wheat and barley than found elsewhere. However, these villages also had very low ratios of tax revenues to adult males, making them among the poorer villages of the sub-district in this regard. Grapes predominated over olives as the major fruit crop in the area south of Jerusalem. When the *sancakbeyi*'s deputy received an acknowledgement of their debt from the leaders of Bayt Laḥm, it was for 125 *sultani*, 120 from the grapevines and 5 from the olive trees.[97] In Bayt Jālā, a four-year agreement by the villagers to pay 180 *sultani* annually from the olives, grapevines, figs, and other trees, was broken down as 150 *sultani* from the grapevines and 30 from the olives.[98] Higher amounts of taxes estimated from goats and bees also indicated that these two villages were extraordinarily large.

Presses in the Jerusalem area were used for making grape syrup or olive oil.[99] The surveys of the towns of Jerusalem and Hebron listed presses, but it was unlikely that all villagers brought their grapes and/or olives to town to be processed.[100] Among the villages of the district, only six were recorded with presses at any time in the century, none throughout. Bayt Jālā was to be taxed 80 *akçe* for one press (*ma'ṣara*) according to the fourth and fifth surveys. Yet based on the surveys and the *sijill*s, it was clearly customary to pay taxes in the form of olive oil, not olives. Each village or close grouping of villages probably had its own press, powered by animals or people, which produced grape syrup or olive oil from the local crop. These small operations apparently were not worth taxing, perhaps because they were locally maintained and because the final product was regularly taxed in any case. In Bayt Jālā, the tax on the press may have been prompted by the size of the grape harvests.[101]

Who enjoyed the large tax revenues generated from these two villages? At the time of the first and second surveys, both paid one-fourth of their assessed dues to the *vakıf* of the Haremeyn-i Şerifeyn, while the remainder was part of the imperial domain. The imperial domain had become the grant of the *sancakbeyi* in the third survey. In the fourth survey, a complete shift occurred, when the shares which had been the *sancakbeyi*'s grant became part of the endowment for the new *'imaret*. The remaining one-fourth portion was thereafter recorded as part of the *vakıf* of Sultan Qaitbay for the *deshīshe* ("porridge") of the Haremeyn.[102] This may simply be a fuller recording of the details of the *vakıf* than in previous surveys.

The fourth survey listed the obligations of Bayt Jālā and Bayt Laḥm exactly as the final endowment deed of the *'imaret* stipulated. However, the actual transfer of revenues from the *sancakbeyi* to the new *vakıf* took place sometime *between* the third and fourth surveys. The *vakıf* was officially founded in mid-June 1557 (mid-Sha'bān 964), but a draft of the endowment deed dated May 24, 1552 (30 Jumādā 959) showed that the planning began several years earlier.[103] Beside the entry for the village of Jīb in the third survey was a note, dated mid-February 1554 (mid-Rabī' I 961), which stated that the 2,500-*akçe* share of this village which had been a *tımar*, was now transferred to the mother of Sultan Selim (Süleyman's wife).[104] This was three years before the official founding of the *vakıf*.

Disentangling the *sancakbeyi* from the financial affairs of Bayt Jālā and Bayt Laḥm required more complex calculations. On August 18, 1557 (22 Shawwāl 964), the deputy of Farrukh bey, the former *sancakbeyi*, acknowledged to Bayram bey, the *vakıf* administrator, that Farrukh bey owed the *vakıf* 310 *sultani*. Farrukh bey had collected this sum from the revenues of Bayt Jālā and Bayt Laḥm for the year 962, which were due in 963. Bayram bey then subtracted 50 *sultani* from the 310 due, because he had taken 5 *kintar* of olive oil, equal to 50 *sultani*, from the village of Jufnā which was actually part of Farrukh's income. So Farrukh owed the *vakıf* 260 *sultani*.[105]

Here, two months after the official date of its founding, the *vakıf* administrator was claiming revenues for the *vakıf* which had been collected a year earlier. However, Farrukh bey may not have been rightly entitled to those taxes at all, as he only became *sancakbeyi* some time in the summer of 1556/963. The man who was the *sancakbeyi* in the spring of that year, the season when accounts were usually made, was Kaytas bey. Coincidentally, it was Kaytas bey who was again the *sancakbeyi* in August 1557 when the administrator claimed the money for the *vakıf* from Farrukh bey. Finally, Farrukh had confirmed in April 1557 (Jumādā II 964) that three-fourths of the grain due from Bayt Laḥm for the year 963, 15 *ghirāra* of wheat and 10 *ghirāra* of barley, should be delivered to him in Jerusalem.[106] No further mention was made of this grain, whether it too was redirected to the *'imaret* storehouses or actually delivered to Farrukh bey. All of this accounting for the *'imaret* seemed to take place without reference to the people of the two villages. One might have expected them to be mistakenly overtaxed in the process of redirecting past and present revenues from the *sancakbeyi* to the *vakıf*, but no complaints were recorded to that effect.

It obviously took several years to organize the accounts of the new *vakıf*. In the village of Jīb, the change was already noted in 961. A month and a half after the note of the change was made in the survey register an order was sent to the kadi and *sancakbeyi* of Jerusalem at the request of the *vakıf* administrator, reminding them to make sure the designated taxes were being directed to the *vakıf*.[107]

Perhaps the interests of the *sancakbeyi* prevented the immediate transfer of the revenues from Bayt Jālā and Bayt Laḥm to the *vakıf*. A series of *sijill* entries from May–September 1555 (962) recorded the accounting of what the villagers owed to Kurd bey the *sancakbeyi*. These entries contained the usual reports of wheat, barley, and grapes owing, less the share allotted to the village leaders. In Bayt Laḥm, where the population was mixed, the obligations to the *sancakbeyi* were recorded as being divided along religious lines, presumably under the aegis of separate leaders. However, there was no difference between Muslims and Christians concerning the robes or the percentage which were the right of the leaders.[108] In May 1555 (Jumādā II 962) five leaders of Bayt Laḥm were said to owe 6⅔ *ghirāra* plus 12 *mudd* of barley and 13⅓ *ghirāra* plus 24 *mudd* of wheat from the revenues of 961 which were due in 962. The three Muslim leaders owed one-third of each grain and the two Christian leaders two-thirds.[109] As suggested earlier, this uneven split is curious, in view of the fact that the survey indicated the population of Bayt Laḥm to have been roughly half Christian and half Muslim in the mid-sixteenth century.[110] Perhaps the Christians of Bayt Laḥm were more prosperous than the Muslims, or were more involved in grain growing as opposed to other crops, such as grapes.

Christians and Muslims within the village were clearly organized into separate communities, and not solely for the collection of the *cizye*. Each had its own leaders. However, they could and did function as a unit before the administration. Five men, of whom two were Christians, all leaders of Bayt Laḥm, together and equally borrowed 20 gold *sultani* from Hasan *subaşı*.[111] In September 1555 (Dhū'l-Qa'dā 962), the elders of the Muslims and the elders of the Christians guaranteed each other before Gazanfer *subaşı* of Jerusalem, that they would be present in, cultivate, and maintain the village. If any one of them was absent, the others could be held responsible for his share of the cultivation, and by extension, the taxes from it.[112]

Bayt Jālā and Bayt Laḥm together demonstrate that the Christian peasants carried the normal burdens of both Christians and peasants in the Ottoman empire. For Christian peasants the *cizye* was another tax to pay, another payment to negotiate with the tax collector. For the man deputized to collect the *cizye*, the deputy of the deputy, accomplishing his task meant multiple encounters with the Christian villagers since the *cizye* was apportioned into multiple payments. *Cizye* collection tied another line of contact into the countryside from the authorities, one which immediately unravelled into subcontracted strands. In both villages, the transfer of revenues from the *sancakbeyi* to the *vakıf* was an occasion for confused remittances and assessments. There is no indication from the workings of tax payment, however, that the incorporation of the villages into the *vakıf* affected the peasants immediately, other than to alter the name of the man who collected their taxes.

ʿInab

The village of ʿInab, today called Abū Ghosh,[113] lies about 13 kilometers west-northwest of Jerusalem, where the hills begin to descend towards the coastal plain. Then, as now, it sat on the main road from the coast to Jerusalem. In the nineteenth century, the Abū Ghosh family in the village led one of the main rural factions around Jerusalem.[114] ʿInab in the mid-sixteenth century was a modest-sized village of twenty-four households, with a tax assessment of 3,600 *akçe* per year. A producer of grape syrup, the village was chiefly occupied with cultivating the usual grains and olive oil. Revenues were divided between the *vakıf* of the Ḥasaniyya *medrese* in Jerusalem (2/3)[115] and a *tımar* holder (1/3), who also received the tithe, goat tax, and *bad-i hava*.

One common feature of the villages discussed thus far has been the regular succession of officials who replaced each other every year or two as revenue recipients – either as *tımar* holders or leaseholders of revenues. All warrants (*berat*) to *sipahi*s, the *sancakbeyi*, and other officials were valid only for one year. The relatively rapid rotation of officials allowed the government to transfer individuals according to imperial needs and aimed to impede any tendency to build local power bases. In contrast, ʿAli Bali b. Sinan *sipahi* can be traced as the *tımar* holder of ʿInab for at least eight years. He also served as a *subaşı* and was the leaseholder of the *vakıf* share of ʿInab or the deputy of the *vakıf* administrator in some years. Thus, one *sipahi* here monopolized revenue-collection and policing functions in a single village over an extended period of time.

ʿAli Bali's relationship with the people of ʿInab, however, was difficult beyond the usual complications of tax assessment and collection. In November 1553 (Dhū'l-Ḥijja 960), he sued three villagers from ʿInab for olive oil which they owed from the crops of 959. When they acknowledged only a fraction of the sum which ʿAli Bali claimed they owed, the villagers were arrested for these debts.[116] One month later, ʿAli Bali was again before the kadi with four notables of ʿInab. No mention of debts was made. The notables, in this instance, gave a formal guarantee to cultivate and live in their village, keeping it free from wrongdoings or malicious acts, and fulfilling the rightful claims of their master, ʿAli Bali. They agreed to stand surety for each other's responsibilities.[117]

The following summer (1554/961), ʿAli acknowledged that he owed the *vakıf* 19 *sultani*, its share of revenues for the previous two years.[118] By winter, however, ʿAli and the *vakıf* administrator settled ʿAli's debt as lessee of the *vakıf* share for only 15 gold pieces, less 5 pieces of silver, explaining that the lands of ʿInab were said to be unworked and poor, though the village did seem capable of producing some revenues.[119] In September of the following year ʿAli Bali acknowledged his replacement in the *tımar* by Bayram *çavuş*, except that he maintained a claim to a share of the olive oil crop of the current year, to be collected in the future.

The conflict between ʿAli Bali and the villagers of ʿInab, not remarkable from the entries in the *sijill* presented above, was finally exposed before the kadi six months later in the spring of 1556. ʿAli Bali was not present in Jerusalem that day, but his actions were attested by three men of Jerusalem and two from the village of Bayt Fāsīn.[120] They asserted that he was the cause of the ruin of the village, and that its people had fled because of the magnitude of his oppression and abuses against them, for he took their possessions and jailed them contrary to *sharīʿa*. Because the village was ruined, the imperial road was cut. Five months after this, ʿAli Bali killed one of the villagers. Three further witnesses testified that they had confronted ʿAli Bali with these accusations, which he acknowledged, saying three times: "I ruined it."

Nonetheless, by the time this formal complaint was recorded, matters seemingly had already been worked out to the satisfaction of the peasants, for they had accepted Bayram bey, the administrator of the imperial *ʿimaret* in Jerusalem, as their master. He, it was asserted, was more suited to look after the village.[121] Under this arrangement, the people had returned to the village and were active at restoring and cultivating it, allowing the road to be reopened.[122]

Although one would think ʿAli Bali had been removed from the scene, at least where the village of ʿInab was concerned, this was not the case. In December 1557, he brought a suit against one ʿAlī b. Ismaʿīl al-Qiḥf for having taken olives which were part of his *tımar*.[123] ʿAli Bali might have only been tying up the loose ends of his former claims, were it not for evidence which firmly established him still to be in possession of the *tımar* share of ʿInab for the years 965 and 966.[124] He had succeeded in having himself reinstated, or else had never been thoroughly ousted. Moreover, the fourth survey records him as the *tımar* holder of the village.[125]

We have very few figures from the *sijill*s for tax payments in ʿInab in these years, but the ones available suggest a rather steady rate of production. Beneath the routine surface of these numbers, however, lay a hard struggle between the villagers and ʿAli Bali. The villagers were initially successful at pressing their claim against the *sipahi*, but over a period of several years he regained his position, probably due to some strong patron in the higher echelons of the military administration. Obviously there must have been a certain amount of tension for the *sancakbeyi* and the kadi, faced with the dual task of preserving the general well-being and the productivity of the peasants, as well as the loyalty, cooperation, and revenues of the *sipahi*. Also at stake here was the income of the *vakıf*. Finally, the situation threatened the imperial road, whose clear passage was certainly a chief concern of the Ottoman administrator.[126]

The case of ʿInab gives us another picture of how the villagers went about trying to safeguard their position: they could and did bring their complaints before the kadi, with the possibility of receiving a decision favorable to themselves. Unfortunately, we do not possess a written record of the means by which ʿAli Bali had the decision against him amended. He clearly had the power to restore his own position, even though he was manifestly destructive to the well-being of the peasants of ʿInab.

With ʿAli Bali's reinstatement, the regular assessment and delivery of taxes was resumed. Did he change his oppressive behavior? If so, only temporarily, for a few years later he was the subject of a petition filed before the sultan by the villagers. This time the quarrel was over the tax status of the village olive trees.[127]

Conclusion on the paying of taxes

Abū Dīs, ʿAyn Kārim, Bittīr, the villages of Banī Zayd, Bayt Jālā, Bayt Laḥm, and ʿInab establish by their examples some shared features of the villages in the district of Jerusalem. Few villages broke the basic wheat–barley–olive mold. ʿAyn Silwān, just beyond the southeast corner of Jerusalem's walls, served as the fruit and vegetable garden of the city. The Silwānīs were by custom privileged to hawk their produce around the town of Jerusalem, and paid their tithes calculated on the revenues of the gardens.[128] Far down in the Jordan valley, the village of Rīḥā (Jericho) was the eastern outpost of the district. Relatively large yields of grain there were varied by the cultivation and processing of indigo. A steady supply of water from the Jordan River, the presence of water buffalo, and the arid flats of the Jordan valley set this village apart from its counterparts in the mountains. In the higher valleys and mountain slopes, however, wheat, barley, grapevines, and olive trees normally defined the landscape.

This chapter has focused on matters of taxpaying. The mechanics of annual remittance punctuated the lives of the peasants and defined their relationship to authority. However, contacts between the peasants and Ottoman officials were not limited to the obedient delivery and collection of taxes; the process did not function so smoothly. A deceptively regular picture of rural taxpaying is drawn by the survey registers. In reality, the assessments, adjustments, deferrals, denials, remittances, and remonstrances which accompanied the annual transfer of revenue to its designated recipients described a more complicated and human situation.

Cases in which these exceptions and complications were adjudicated repeated themselves endlessly. They were a persistent preoccupation of the officials who attempted to collect their rightful revenues – whether granted or leased – from the revenues of the peasants. Patience was required. On the other hand, meticulous accounts were evidently kept in some fashion by both the villagers and the officials, not without confusion and disputes, but allowing for the continuance and eventual resolution of the debts. Payments were still legitimately due and demanded even after the tenure of an official was completed. In Bayt Jālā, Farrukh bey continued to settle his accounts after he had been transferred from his post as *sancakbeyi*. In Kafr Naʿma, northwest of Rāmallāh, the deputy of Mustafa bey claimed from the villagers the taxes for the year 960, olive oil due from 958, money from the vineyards from 956, 957, and 959; at the same time, the village owed olive oil to ʿAli *çelebi*, the former *sipahi* of the village from 956 and 957.[129]

Underlying the protracted process of annual tax payments was the more basic character of the taxes. These were recalculated annually. As the system was based primarily on the *kısm*, which taxed produce as a percentage of the total crop, variations were to be expected; the amount represented by the percentage could vary substantially. No correspondence with the imperial capital exists, nor any record in the kadi's proceedings, which indicates an annual interest on the part of the central imperial administration about how much the taxes actually amounted to for a particular year. A report was probably made, and certainly the amount collected from the sultan's *hass* holdings was reported. Rather, the mutual confirmation recorded in the *sijill* of a sum owing or a sum collected showed that the amount was fixed annually and accepted by both parties – the local official and the peasants – as a regular practice. The system had to be flexible in order to allow for natural variations in agricultural yields.[130] A *tımar* holder might come out ahead one year, when his one-third share represented twice the amount stated in his original warrant. Yet he could just as easily have barely enough to get by on if the year's crops were struck by drought or locusts. Despite the natural competition and antagonism between the taxed and the collectors in this system, they shared a common concern for and reliance upon the annual harvests.

CHAPTER 5

Between rebellion and oppression

Let no one cause any person to become fearful or oppressed contrary to the pristine *şer'iat* and the established *kanun*, so that the *re'aya*, forever protected, at ease and repose, may be occupied quietly with their own matters and common labors.[1]

Seasonal routines and the rhythms of agriculture formed the backdrop to the year's activities, providing a common calendar for both officials and peasants despite their different and even opposing agendas. Annual rhythms were predictably interrupted by unanticipated natural crises and disasters. Any common concerns over the vicissitudes of nature, however, were not enough to unite the peasants and Ottoman officials in a harmonious provincial polity. The two groups stood on opposite sides of the tax chest: the peasants filled it while the officials drained its contents. In the normal course of events, the officials spent considerable effort in calling the villagers to account for taxes owing and unpaid, and in bringing them before the kadi to acknowledge (and pay) their debts.

Contacts between officials and peasants were basically defined by fiscal matters. This did not, however, mean that they met only to discuss money. In order to ensure the financial base of the region, officials had to ensure general security, police their own ranks against abuses, contain the discontent of the peasants, oversee routine planting and harvesting, regulate the delivery of basic foodstuffs to Jerusalem and keep the water flowing into the city. They also had to prevent or discover more serious offenses committed by peasants such as leaving lands fallow, deserting villages, rebelling against authority and even physically attacking officials. The peasants, on the other hand, were preoccupied by this year's crops and taxes, next year's seed, with protecting themselves from greedy and obnoxious officials, and probably minimizing their association with officials generally. Moreover, there was no clear unity of purpose among the peasants or among the officials. As discussed above, officials might compete with each other for leases of revenues. Village leaders and other peasants may have found themselves at odds over payments made or outstanding. The Bedouin tribes in the region were another human factor, allied sometimes with the peasants, sometimes with the officials, as circumstances determined.

In the formulaic language of the documents, peasant behavior was often labelled "*tamarrud ve fesad*" (rebelliousness and disorder), while officials were accused of "*zulm ve ta'addi*" (oppression and enmity). The habitual attitudes and behavior of peasants and officials towards each other fell somewhere between the extremes of rebellion and oppression. The details of any case usually pointed to something less calamitous than these terms imply. Moreover, conflicts between taxpayers and revenue collectors around mid-sixteenth century Jerusalem normally erupted over issues less momentous than would require a direct appeal to Istanbul or draw the attention of imperial authorities in the capital to this outlying province.

Instead, peasants could and did turn to the kadi for redress against the various Ottoman officials in his jurisdiction. In even greater numbers, the officials themselves took their suits against local peasants before this same kadi. Surely there were some instances where officials abandoned a particular claim as too small or insignificant. But, more often, it was the peasants who lacked time or money to pursue complaints against officials; they may have been skeptical that their efforts would meet with some success. In spite of this caveat, the Jerusalem *sijill*s of the period are strewn with the complaints and petitions of local villagers seeking help in resolving their disputes with the local Ottoman officials. This fact alone suggests that they expected some assistance from the kadi.

The recorded grievances and suits of various officials reveal numerous strategies the peasants had for getting the better of local officials. And, complaints of the peasants provide some insight into what prompted them to these actions in the first place. Just as the kadi's records disproved the regularity of the fiscal system as reflected in the *tapu tahrir defterleri*, so too do they chronicle the give-and-take relationship between the peasants and officials, the range of acts each committed against the other. Officials certainly did the bulk of the taking, but the peasants were not hapless dolts, protected only by the benevolent concern of the sultan as expressed in his imperial decrees. This chapter examines the more irregular aspects of rural administration which elaborated the tax nexus.

"*Tamarrud ve fesad*" – "rebellious" peasants

Tahrir *making – surveying*

The Ottoman survey registers (*tapu tahrir defterleri*) themselves reflect the active role of the local peasantry in determining the terms of the Ottoman administration at the local level. These registers were compiled on the basis of information which was, at least in part, obtained directly from the peasants. Local residents were interviewed publicly about the status of lands and annual yields, and their replies were subject to confirmation by various indigenous authorities or notables.

However, any information-gathering scheme which depended on auto-reporting by the subjects of the investigation was also susceptible to errors purposely communicated by the subjects for their own benefit. Certainly, the peasants could not report completely ridiculous quantities for the extent of their cultivated fields and annual yields, since the lie would be too obvious. Further, villagers spread over a large region probably did not coordinate their efforts to deceive the survey-makers. The difficulties of communication alone would preclude such an effort. More likely is the case that in every instance of reporting or collecting, individuals tried to cheat to a small extent in their own favor.

In addition to the question of accurate reporting on the part of the villagers, there is also the matter of cooperation in general. One survey-maker named ʿAlī b. Muḥammad found that some villagers around Bayt Jālā, south of Jerusalem, were unwilling to give him any serious answers at all to his queries about the grape vines in their vineyards. He was treated with scorn and contempt: "write down what you want, 50,000 or more," they told him. When he continued to press these men for a substantive response, the survey-maker only elicited more mocking comments.[2] Ultimately, he turned to the kadi for assistance in completing the survey.

In any case, the numbers recorded in the survey registers were presented as estimates of average yields – not a very precise concept in the first place. As shown by the comparison of the survey figures and some actual records of payment (or in most cases non-payment) in Chapter Four, the variation between the expected revenues and actual payments could be enormous, changing according to the quantity and quality of a particular year's crop yield.

So, the Ottoman system of taxation, as efficient as it appears from the neat columns and rows of the *tapu tahrir defterleri*, could only collect recommended percentages and not actual sums when actually applied in a specific region. The survey registers laid down guidelines for the agrarian regime and enabled the central government to assign estimated revenues to its officials, but not precise sums.

Routines of planting and harvesting

Annual agricultural rhythms are fundamentally unchanging. Although the yields of a particular season may shrink or swell in the face of natural disaster or human intervention, the rhythm of activity remains more or less on a set cycle through the seasons. Around Jerusalem, the late autumn rains signalled the beginning of winter grain planting. Wheat and barley matured through the cold wet months and were harvested in spring, followed by summer vegetable and fruit crops, especially the olives and grapes which began to ripen in late summer. Each of the major junctures of this yearly routine was subject to the control of the Ottoman officials. They did not appear merely to collect taxes at the end of the harvest, but also had a say in determining what was planted where, and when. Thus the contact between officials and peasants was fundamentally regulated by the agrarian calendar.

The quality of any year's harvest was the principal determinant of the tax recipient's income. In southern Syria generally, and specifically in the *sancak* of Jerusalem, wheat and barley were the main cereal crops. Because revenues were levied as a percentage, the actual amount due from the peasants varied annually. Olives and grapes were taxed either according to a percentage or at a fixed rate per tree or vine, as determined by the customary practice. The villagers could not freely change the crop planted on a given area, say from wheat to olive trees or grape vines. If the crops were altered, the taxes would have to change as well, engendering confusion and loss of revenue, even temporarily an unacceptable occurrence. Nor could the government decide arbitrarily to change taxes from a percentage to a fixed rate.

The annual routine of supervision may be reconstructed from the complaints of officials regarding its contravention by the peasants. In general, no explicit permissions were issued to begin planting each year, as this basic task was obviously in everyone's interest. The villagers were supposed to work the lands within the villages and external parcels attached to them which had been recorded in the surveys. The crops planted remained unchanged from year to year, though fields were rotated in and out of use to allow the soil to recover. Peasants were bound to live in and cultivate the lands of their village year-round, not leaving anything fallow unnecessarily. If they planted unregistered lands outside the village before finishing that area, they were liable for a stiff fine.

In the case of the harvest, control was more rigorous. The ripe crop, ready to be reaped and threshed, now represented immediate subsistence and profit to both peasants and officials. However, grains or fruits were easily divided and disposed of once they came off the stalk or branch. Harvesting processes, therefore, required close supervision. Thus, the villagers formally announced the maturation of their crops before the kadi and the imperative to cut and thresh them.

The terms set out in the village of Naḥḥālīn show in detail how the responsibility for cultivation was assigned. Six peasants from Naḥḥālīn came before the kadi and pledged to work the land of their village piece by piece, to plow and cultivate it so that nothing lay fallow. Dibyān and Barīk were responsible for one-third, ʿAbd al-Muḥsin and his associate for one-third, and Muḥammad b. Ḥamīda and his associate for one-third. If any one of them cultivated the lands outside the village before he finished his own, then he agreed to be liable for a fine of 25 *sultani* in consideration for the land in the village which he had not cultivated. Any one who ruined (*ṭāḥa ʿalā*) his associate's land was liable for a fine of 25 *sultani* to the *tımar* holder and the same sum to the *sancakbeyi*.[3]

Control over planting extended well beyond a broad commitment to cultivate, and to do so within given boundaries. Farrukh bey, who held the village of Bayt Ṣafāfā as part of his *tımar*, obtained an imperial order in response to his complaint, dictating rather exceptionally that the villagers there were not to plant any part of the lands of their village without the permission of their master. The order was read before the kadi and witnessed by the leaders of the village. Any violations incurred a fine of 2,000 *akçe* (or about 50 *sultani*.)[4] Such threats, however, were not enough to dissuade Ḥamdān b. Aḥmad, who was brought before the kadi about two years later for having planted grapes, figs, and other things in the village lands without Farrukh's permission. No fine was recorded at the time.[5] It may be that the produce was taxed or confiscated, or that the fine was automatically applied upon confirmation of the offense, and therefore not explicitly noted.

Permission was also granted on an individual basis. Ibrāhīm b. Marwān of Bayt Fāsīn, who cultivated a piece of land in neighboring Bayt Ẓulmā, was allowed to plant whatever grain he wished there after the crops were sown in Bayt Fāsīn itself.[6] It seems that every incremental change in the cultivated area had to be approved officially, presumably to ensure that lands already under plow would not be ignored, and so that the correct tax assessment could be made. Thus, Ibrāhīm b. Khalīl of ʿAyn Silwān was allowed to plant barley in a new place called al-Birka.[7] Two peasants from Māliḥa were given permission to sow grains in what had been a vineyard,[8] but Yusuf b. ʿAbdallah, the *sipahi* of Sūbā, brought suit against two other peasants of Māliḥa for having planted grapevines without his permission – while he was away in Damascus – thereby obstructing the cultivation of other crops.[9] He forwarded a similar complaint to Istanbul and the reply came back strongly urging the kadi that no such irregularities be tolerated.[10]

From the number of complaints and suits brought by various *tımar* holders against villagers, it is clear that peasants did plant remote or unsurveyed land. These areas were probably not included, or not yet included, in the current *tahrir* and thus were mostly beyond the revenue collector's reach. So, one possibility open to peasants to circumvent or cheat the system on a small scale was to plant areas previously uncultivated or unknown, lands which were removed from the tax collector's path. Such fields probably did not cover extensive areas but were rather tucked away on remote hills or in less accessible wadis.

The key point of control over any crop came at harvest time. The villagers were required to report to the kadi that the crops had ripened and were ready to be cut before the harvest actually commenced. Every year at harvest time (March–April), the *ra'īs* and/or the elders and notables came to town with a sample of the new barley. This was presented to the kadi, evaluated by the chief measurer of the town market and witnessed by numerous officials.

Similarly, when new oil was pressed from the olive crop (August–September), it was brought before the kadi to be evaluated and priced.[11]

Representatives from a few villages came to make a general declaration for the entire *nahiye*. Typically, Muḥammad b. Kusba and Burjis b. Aḥmad of ʿAzariyya came before the kadi and testified that the grains of the region were ripe and ready to be harvested. In fact, they said, some of the crop had been cut ten days earlier and was already on the threshing floor.[12] The same procedure was observed for olives. From the olive-rich region of Banī Zayd, two peasants came to say that the ripe fruit had been knocked off the trees and pressed into oil.[13] Whether the crop was grains, grapes, or olives, a sample of the new harvest was brought before the kadi, to be witnessed and to have its ripeness and quality confirmed.[14]

Below is a table (Table 5.1) of the dates on which crops were reported as ripe. The announcement of the harvest was not necessarily the permanent duty of a particular village. The reports generally came from the villages closer to Jerusalem, especially from Abū Dīs, Ṭūr Zaytā, and ʿAyn Silwān. In most cases, the peasants reported that harvesting had begun some days earlier. This date is noted in square brackets.

Table 5.1 *Ripening of crops*

Date	*Crop*	*Village*
12 Jumādā I 960 – 26 April 1553 [mid-Rabīʿ II 960 – late March 1553]	grain	Ṭūr Zaytā, ʿAyn Silwān, Abū Dīs
8 Jumādā I 961 – 11 April 1554 [27 Rabiʿ II 961 – 1 April 1554]	grain	ʿAyzariyya
4 Dhū'l-Qaʿda 962 – 20 September 1555 [1 Ramaḍān 962 – 20 July 1555]	olives	Kūbar, Jufnā[15]
13 Jumādā II 963 – 24 April 1556	barley, legumes	Ṭūr Zaytā, Abū Dīs, Bayt Laḥm
15 Jumādā II 964 – 15 April 1557 [10 Jumādā II 964 – 10 April 1557]	barley	Ṭūr Zaytā
22 Ramaḍān 964 – 19 July 1557	grapes	Abū Dīs
7 Dhū'l-Ḥijja 967 – 29 August 1560 [27 Dhū'l-Qaʿda 967 – 19 August 1560]	olives, olive oil	Banī Zayd[16]
10 Shaʿbān 968 – 26 April 1561 [10 Rajab 968 – 27 March 1561]	barley	Rīḥā
21 Shaʿbān 969 – 26 April 1562 [c. 15 Shaʿbān 969–20 April 1562]	barley	Dayr Banī ʿUbayd, Abū Dīs, ʿAyn Silwān
9 Shaʿbān 970 – 3 April 1563 [4 Shaʿbān 970 – 29 March 1563]	barley	Rīḥā, Abū Dīs

Reporting of the harvest, in particular barley, was supposed to take place in two stages. The initial announcement was made to the kadi that the fields were ready to be cut. However, this alone did not allow the peasants to harvest. Though it seems that no penalty was incurred in cases when the harvest was begun before it was initially reported, usually the official who held the *tımar* or oversaw the *vakıf* supported by the village also had to be notified so that he could arrange for the supervision of the harvest. When he failed to do so, the peasants came to the kadi to complain. On May 21, 1557 (22 Rajab 964) villagers from Qubayba told the kadi that over one month had passed since the harvest had been reported as ready by the people of Ṭūr Zaytā,[17] and now the peasants complained that if the crops were left for one more day, they would be ruined. They therefore requested that the kadi give his permission for them to harvest, and that he appoint someone to oversee the procedure. (In this case, apparently the kadi was responsible for giving permission because the village was part of the imperial *hass*.) He named a man to supervise them, to protect their grain, to measure it correctly, and to allow no one the possibility of disposing of it improperly.[18]

Furthermore, if the village was shared between two tax-recipients, both had to supervise the harvesting. Thus, one finds Ferhad bey, the *sipahi* of Umm Ṭūba, and three villagers before the kadi complaining about Ḥusām al-Dīn, the *nazır* of the *vakıf*s which received half the village taxes.[19] Ḥusām al-Dīn had not given permission to harvest the grain and sell it, so they asked the kadi to come and apportion the shares. Ferhad was probably perturbed at the delay in realizing his own portion, and the villagers were genuinely worried over their own welfare. The kadi then ordered Ḥusām al-Dīn either to go himself and fix the shares, or to allow the villagers to harvest (presumably in his absence).[20]

In a system where taxes were generally calculated as a percentage of grains, the total harvest as it stood before cutting had to be assessed to prevent the tax collector being short-changed. Once the crop was harvested and bundled into sacks, baskets, jars or whatever, it was much more difficult to determine the total of the original harvest and so the correct percentage due from the peasants. However, it was equally critical to cut and thresh the grains as fast as possible once they were ripe, in order to prevent damage from sudden rains, winds, heat, or cold.

When the peasants reported to the kadi that harvesting had actually begun some days earlier, they generally pleaded that further delay would have harmed the crop and that there had been no time to come to Jerusalem beforehand. This may have been true, but it could very well have been an excuse allowing villagers to cache some of the harvested crop before the tax collector came to take his share. Other than planting hidden fields, concealment before assessment would have been the chief means by which the peasants could increase their share of an annual harvest.

Small wonder, then, that Mehmet *çavuş*, the tithe collector of Bayt Ḥanīna, brought suit against the notables there for having harvested the crop of beans, lentils, and vetch without his permission. Furthermore, he claimed, they proceeded to sell them without his permission, and only gave him his share afterwards. The villagers initially maintained that Mehmet had given them leave to harvest, but finally confessed that they had acted wrongly, for which they were arrested.[21] The threat of arrest, and perhaps other penalties, was enough of an inducement to keep the villagers of Qubayba and Umm Ṭūba, in the first example, from harvesting before they had been given proper permission, although they claimed to be in desperate straits. But it did not restrain the people from Bayt Ḥanīnā, as described in the last case.

After the grains were cut, they were brought to the threshing floor. It was from the threshed grain that the shares of the revenue collectors were divided off from the total yield. This was done in the presence of the collectors or their agents. The *tımar* holders and *vakıf* managers were supposed to attend to their villages in person in order to ensure a correct distribution of crop shares. But, if revenue holders failed to oversee this procedure, then they were not entitled to collect compensatory fees or claim any sort of "threshing duty." In the *kanunname* of the *sancak* of Safad, their responsibility was made clear:

> And in each province, let those *tımar* holders, who did not attend the sharing out of the harvest in the villages at the moment of the dividing, not demand anything, calling it some right like "tax on opening the threshing floors." And thus, when the threshing is completed, let them attend to the sharing out at the appointed time; let them not harm the peasants, and let them take the part assigned to them.[22]

Harvest time provided an opportunity for numerous abuses of the peasants by the *sipahis*. Although the officials were there to ensure the honest apportionment of shares by the peasants, the peasants likewise watched that the officials took only their due. If not, they protested to the kadi. The peasants who cultivated lands around Jerusalem sued Mehmet, the *wālī al-barr* (manager of the external lands) for his abuses against them during the threshing.[23] "And he took from every one of their threshing floors,[24] sometimes one *mudd*, or one-half or one-quarter of a *mudd* from the grains, and at times a quantity of straw or sometimes an [invented] straw tax." In reply to the charges, Mehmet maintained that he solicited these things from them as a donation.[25] This assertion was, however, contradicted by witnesses and the kadi ordered Mehmet to give up such collections in the future.

The organization of the harvest was fixed by practice and law. From a village in the *sancak* of Gaza, the peasants protested when the grain winnowers were chosen, not from among their own ranks as usual, but from outsiders. The outsiders did not conduct the winnowing properly, and thus the peasants requested that a man of their own choosing be put in charge of it again. The reply from Istanbul upheld the wish of the peasants.[26]

Whether it was the tax collector who succeeded in taking a bit more than his mathematically exact share, or the peasants who managed to put away some bit of the total before it was divided, such irregularities were probably a normal if minimal part of the threshing. A *sipahi* did not run to the kadi for every suspected kilo of missing wheat. For the villagers, not every loss incurred justified the bother of taking the case to Jerusalem. Certainly in the hectic days of harvesting and threshing, people would be unlikely to lose even a day of work unless the situation were intolerable. Even peasants cultivating in the immediate hinterland of Jerusalem, who did not have a long trip to town, waited until July, after the threshing season was ended, to lodge a complaint against the extra levies taken by the man who oversaw their work.[27]

Taxes were assessed and taken either in kind or in cash. When the harvest – grains in the spring, olive oil in the fall – was divided up, the peasants were obliged to deliver the share due to the *vakıf* or the *sipahi* in Jerusalem. Two hundred *mudd* of wheat were due from the *shaykh* of Banī Zayd, "transported by the peasants as was customary."[28] The repeated use of this and similar phrases leaves little doubt that such was the usual practice when taxes were calculated in kind.[29] Throughout the Ottoman empire, the villagers paying their taxes in kind were required to bring their crops to the nearest market-town, though they could not be forced farther than a day's journey, or beyond the closest market.[30]

When the taxes were due in cash, it was up to the peasants to sell their crops. However, this too required the permission of the village revenue collector. This permission was not always distinct from that given to harvest and thresh, but several complaints from *sipahi*s and others relate specifically to villagers who disposed of their produce before they were given leave to do so. In many cases, the peasants maintained that they had actually received permission to sell their produce, but then were unable to prove this. So, in the end, they were punished for the offense stated. In Bayt Kīsā, the olives were disposed of without the knowledge or permission of the *subaşı* in 963/1556.[31] Another year, a man from Kafr ʿAqab disposed of his wheat and barley without permission.[32] Saʿīd from the village of Māliḥa was accused of not having given over the *sipahi*'s share of gourds and eggplants before selling the rest. Saʿīd denied this, and offered his partner's testimony as proof, but it was not accepted.[33] Aḥmad b. Muḥammad of Ṭūr Zaytā actually acknowledged that he sold off almonds from a tree belonging to Ilyas *sipahi* of ʿAyn Silwān, but claimed before the kadi and Ilyas's agent that he had found a branch of the tree cut off and lying in his vineyard, so he simply stripped the almonds from it.[34]

The tension within the system is evident. Without an accurate account of each crop, each share, each sale, no tax collector was able to keep track precisely of what was his just due. It was impossible to be in every place at once, and so the business of the harvest and tax assessment was filled with these seemingly petty suits, which often involved the smallish revenues of individual peasants, not only the totals outstanding from whole villages. Peasants risked a fine by acting before receiving explicit permission, but presumably they acted in order to maximize their own share from the produce in question. If caught, they might lose the extra as well as a fine to the tax collector. If not caught, or not prosecuted, they could smirk quietly at having put one over on the officials in charge.

A repetitive stream of cases regarding quantities of grain or olives or grapes came before the kadi, occasionally interspersed with loads of vegetables or alkali (*qalī*) used to process soap.[35] However, from far down in the Jordan valley, two shaykhs of the village of Rīḥā (Jericho) made the steep trip up to Jerusalem in the spring of 964/1557, to notify the kadi that the time had come to process the indigo crop, a task requiring a cauldron. The kadi granted them the cauldron which the manager of the *vakıf* supported by the village revenues had purchased for that purpose, on the condition that they return it when finished.[36] By this action, the villagers notified the kadi and the *vakıf* manager that the indigo was ready for processing. The *vakıf* administrator, however, was obligated to assist the villagers whose revenues supported his foundation in their harvest activities. Here, the line between official control and assistance becomes ambiguous. Soon thereafter, Jericho was replaced in the endowments of this *vakıf* by a village which was closer to the city, whose revenues were presumably easier to collect; the request for the cauldron did not reappear in succeeding years.

A story of mudd

Correct assessment of the crop size and measurement of the quantities due were tasks integral to the functioning of the entire system. Standard weights and measures were used, but these varied, sometimes over a relatively short distance. On the other hand, this variation may indicate just how great these distances were in fact, and how localized life was for the bulk of the population. Often, weights and measures cited in the *sijill*s were identified as those of Jerusalem, Ramle, Gaza, or Nablus. Damascus, Aleppo, Cairo, and Istanbul, as well as smaller places in between, also had specific measures, though these are rarely found in the Jerusalem *sijill*s. In cases where measures were unspecified, however, or ambiguous, confusion and fraud might well result.

A few cases of measuring muddles from the Jerusalem *sijill*s will help convey a sense of the difficulty in assigning values to volumes and weights, and hence of converting quantities consistently to present-day measures. Moreover, these relatively simple and minor differences constituted part of the continual challenge faced by the officials in their day-to-day management of local affairs.

In 1553 (960), Mustafa *sipahi* came before the kadi and sued his own agents Yaḥyā and Ḥasan, claiming that they had collected the revenues of his *tımar* for him for the year 959, which were 438 *mudd* of wheat and barley, in large measures (*bi'l-kayl al-kabīr*). When asked about this, Ḥasan asserted that he had indeed taken the grain from the peasants in large measures; but when Yaḥyā was questioned, he claimed that he received the grain from Ḥasan in small measures (*bi'l-kayl al-saghīr*), although Ḥasan had taken it in large ones. The large measure was said to add 40 *mudd* to the total amount paid over, giving a total of 478 in small *mudd*. Mustafa assumed that his agents had embezzled the difference.[37]

There were (at least) two *mudd* volumes used locally to measure grains. Fortunately, the relative proportions are given: 438 large *mudd* equaled 478 small *mudd*, a ratio of roughly 9:10. Can one assume, however, that the substitutions were discovered every time small replaced large or large small?

Another case of large and small measures came before the kadi when one man sold to another 9 *mudd* of *hummus* (chickpeas) in Nablus measures. Upon delivery, the 9 *mudd* were measured out as 10 *mudd*, obviously a different *mudd*, as was indeed acknowledged.[38] The distance between the towns of Jerusalem and Nablus is roughly 55 kilometers. Although the two had separate measures, the villagers who peopled the hills between the two towns bought and sold among themselves, clearly using more than one set of measures, all familiar to them. But not necessarily so familiar to an outsider!

Small and large *mudd* were also the issue when Fakhr al-Din appeared on behalf of Farrukh bey, the *sancakbeyi* of Jerusalem, to claim the grain owed by the villagers of Jericho. The leaders of Jericho acknowledged a debt of 3,800 *mudd* of wheat and barley in Jerusalem measures, every 12 *mudd* being equal here to 13 *mudd*.[39] Again, the measuring was done in small *mudd*, the Jerusalem ones. Why were the large measures mentioned here as if standard, when no one from Nablus was involved? Were the larger measures perhaps more commonly used as well in the village of Jericho down in the Jordan River valley?

One bit of information clearly emerges from these three cases: the Jerusalem *mudd* was equal to about 9/10 of the Nablus *mudd*.

Non-cultivation and migration

Officials lodged complaints against peasants for leaving lands fallow because unnecessarily fallow land meant a reduced income to whoever claimed a share of the village revenues. Three villagers of ʿIsāwiyya got off lightly, required only to promise to restore to cultivation the piece of land left fallow which formed part of a *tımar*.[40] Others paid a more serious penalty. Rashīd b. Khiyāl of Rām was found to have left his lands untilled for five years. Rashīd protested to the agent of Mustafa bey, the *zaʿim* whose *tımar* included the village, that his brother was to have collected and delivered his share. This was not confirmed, and Rashīd was arrested until he could secure the wheat and barley, or its cash equivalent.[41] In a similar case some years later, another man from Rām was arrested. According to an agreement between the villagers of Rām and the *sipahi*, anyone who failed to cultivate their lands was liable for a fine of 5 *sultani*. When the man acknowledged his guilt, he was arrested against payment of that sum.[42]

In light of the attention paid to individual villagers who left plots fallow, it is not difficult to understand the concern aroused when people left their villages altogether. As described in Chapter Four, the *vakıf* administrator of Abū Dīs petitioned the sultan for an order that would return his absent peasants.[43] A fallow field meant a year's lost income, perhaps two. When one or more persons abandoned the village completely, the tax base was eroded, agricultural labor was lost, and land might be left uncultivated. One or two people leaving might herald the beginning of a larger exodus, and even greater loss. On the one hand, the officials' concern to enforce cultivation in its most minute aspects reflected the extent of control to which they aspired. On the other, the preoccupation with regulating cultivation and labor may testify to a chronic shortage of labor in this region.

Mehmet *sipahi* of Bayt Sāḥūr al-Wādī complained to the kadi about three men who had left for the nearby village of Abū Maqīra where they intended to remain. When confronted, the three confirmed Mehmet's claim and were required to return to Bayt Sāḥūr al-Wādī or face a fine of 200 *sultani* (16,000 *akçe*!).[44] So large a penalty was probably effective persuasion to return home. The size of fines varied, and was sometimes merely said to be "according to the *sharī'a*," without being specified. The threat of a fine was not always explicit. In the case of Ḥasan b. Abū Ḥāmil of 'Azariyya, who was accused of leaving his village, a guarantor was required to ensure his return. Ḥasan was meanwhile arrested until one could be arranged.[45]

It was not always so easy to prove who belonged where. When tax farmers of the imperial share (*hass*) of the revenues in Jerusalem tried to force several people from Ṣanāṣīn to return to that village, they ran into difficulties. Some of the sons and brothers of the villagers did not have their names recorded in the survey register, and on this basis they refused to return to the village. On what proper grounds could local officials then compel them to do so? The imperial reply to the petition they submitted for advisement instructed the *sancakbeyi* and kadi to resettle everyone – registered or not – who had left the village within ten years.[46] Thus the normal statute of limitations was in force, and the implication was that local knowledge would reveal who belonged in the village, enabling the officials to do their job. The villagers understood the system which the Ottomans had instituted, and tried to use it to their own advantage. However, the officials, with explicit imperial encouragement and authorization, ignored the strictly legalistic position taken here by the villagers.

Unregistered villagers were probably a fact of life for the Ottoman administration. Sons or brothers may have been too young to be registered at the time of the last survey, or they may have successfully avoided the clerk's notice. Strangers probably appeared from time to time, refugees from uncomfortable or unpleasant circumstances elsewhere. Yet concern to maintain the settled population in their villages overrode the niceties of formal registers and superior government force decided the issue.

An absent peasant, however, was not automatically returned to his village. There might be a legitimate reason for his desertion. When ʿAṭāllāh b. Musʿad of Bayt Laḥm was brought before the kadi by the *subaşı*, accused of leaving the village and abandoning his lands unworked, the kadi asked if the *subaşı* had harmed him in any way. Upon ʿAṭāllāh's reply that nothing had happened, he was required to return to Bayt Laḥm. The question initially put to him suggests that had there been some wrongdoing on the part of the *subaşı*, the outcome might have been different. ʿAṭāllāh probably would have been returned to Bayt Laḥm, but the *subaşı* might have been disciplined and/or removed.[47]

The statute of limitations regarding the forcible return of an absent peasant to his village was not a mere formula. Ten years' absence secured a person against being compelled to resettle in the village he had abandoned. Khalīl b. ʿAbd al-Raḥmān b. Hānī was originally from Salfīt, a village in the district of Nablus. In the spring of 968/1561, an agent of the *tımar* holder there came before the kadi of Jerusalem and insisted that Khalīl be sent back to Salfīt, having left only three years earlier. Khalīl insisted that he had moved to Kafr ʿAyn, in the Banī Zayd region of Jerusalem, eighteen years before. He produced two witnesses who swore to his long-time residence there, testimony which the kadi accepted. Khalīl was thus allowed to remain in Kafr ʿAyn. However, he was still required to pay any extraordinary (*ʿörfi*) duties outstanding to his former master, according to the Ottoman *kanun* quoted by the manager of the Haremeyn-i Şerifeyn *vakıf*s to which Kafr ʿAyn belonged.[48]

Officials' concern with peasant movement was inseparably tied to their preoccupation to ensure regular cultivation in the villages, their chief source of revenues. To this end, they consulted the survey registers and paid attention to the individuals in villages comprising their *tımar*s. Did some peasants also inform on each other to the revenue holders, settling private disputes or trying to win official favor? Exposure to the authorities could be used as a threat to hold over someone newly resident in a village. Migration by peasants, however, was usually a sign of hardship, whether due to official abuse or natural conditions.[49]

Water

South of Jerusalem, the officials were engaged in an ongoing struggle against the villages located along the course of the aqueduct which brought water to the city. The competition for water was between the town, the villagers, and the Bedouin who migrated in and out of the region. In this arid desert climate, the crucial conduit supplied the drinking fountains and baths of the city, supplementing the wells within the walls. The aqueduct pipes were of ancient origin, but had been repaired by Süleyman as part of the general Ottoman restorations of the city; they also established an endowment to maintain the system. The new *'imaret vakıf* also contributed funds to help insure the flow of water to the city.[50]

Several villages were located along the course of the aqueduct: Ṣūr Bāhir, Bayt Laḥm, Bayt Jālā, Arṭās, and Fāghūr. The peasants were allowed to take fixed shares of the water, but they frequently interrupted the water flow at unallocated places and times in order to irrigate their fields or water livestock. It was impossible to patrol the entire length of the pipe, which stretched over some fifteen or more winding kilometers northwards from 'Ayn Wādī Biyār up to Jerusalem. When the water was diverted or cut, however, the flow into the city diminished. Reports of interference with the water supply reached the kadi periodically, and each case was then investigated by a group of officials. However, as with the petty theft of other goods, water was probably also removed in smaller quantities whose disappearance went either unremarked or unchallenged.

The villagers of Bayt Laḥm were bound by a standing obligation regarding the consumption of water. In the presence of the kadi and one of the janissaries known as Kara 'Ali, who was the guardian of the pipe (*mashadd qanāt al-sabīl bi-Quds-i Sharīf*), sixteen notables of Bayt Laḥm affirmed their liability to pay 25 *sultani* to the *sancakbeyi*, whoever he might be. The fine was due in the event that they took more than the share of water assigned to them and their associates (the other villagers), or broke the pipe or committed any other action which interrupted the water flow, and did not report this to the guardian.[51]

Six months after this statement was recorded, in January 1554, one of the kadis and a *subaşı* were sent to Bayt Laḥm to investigate a complaint against the villagers, namely, that they had pierced an opening in the pipe and consequently cut the flow of water to Jerusalem. An on-site inspection by the investigators in fact found a new hole in the conduit. They thereupon seized the villagers and took them before the kadi in Jerusalem, where three men acknowledged that the pipe had indeed been broken and the new opening made.[52]

Fermans from Istanbul regularly addressed the chronic shortages of water reported in Jerusalem. In 1568 (975–6), an elaborate scheme was drawn up to incorporate the waters of an additional spring in the village of Artās south of the city into the network of the aqueduct, but it did not get past the planning stages.[53]

A sense of the routine frustrations caused by the pirate water channels is clearly conveyed in the complaint by the administrator of the *vakıf* which maintained the pipe and the janissary who was guardian of the pipe. One day, in the middle of the long, dry Jerusalem summer, they told the kadi how on most days the people of Ṣūr Bāhir, Bayt Laḥm, and Fāghūr created trouble by opening the covered channels of water. Whenever the two officials blocked a break in one channel, the villagers broke open another one, interrupting the water flow to Jerusalem.[54] Another similar complaint listed eleven separate breaks along the course of the pipe.[55] Again, in the two cases just cited, no penalties or fines were recorded against the villagers. With no other explanation available, it might be that the fines were automatic and so not specifically recorded. Alternatively, it may be that in cases where it was impossible to prove the guilt of individuals – peasants or Bedouin – in disrupting the water supply, no punishment could be meted out.

Yet even when they identified the offenders, officials were plagued with difficulties in their endeavors to prosecute. Mustafa *çelebi*, administrator of the *vakıf* of the pipe, recounted how he seized two of six villagers from Fāghūr whom he caught watering their sheep from a place they had broken open in the pipe. Mustafa insisted that the villagers pay him the fine, which they refused, so he did not release them but started off towards Jerusalem with the two men and their sheep. Upon nearing their village, however, a shout went up from the people there, who gathered around and rescued the confiscated animals. The two men were brought before the kadi and sued.[56] Notably, the villagers did not go so far as to attack Mustafa *çelebi*, nor could they prevent him from bringing the two men before the kadi as there were witnesses to identify them. But, they did take back their sheep before Mustafa could remove them to Jerusalem, presumably so as to ensure that the beasts did not inadvertently provide an unexpected feast or profit for some official.

The struggle over water was unending. Entries in the kadi's records on this subject continued for decades and centuries. In times of drought, the water flow to Jerusalem ceased entirely, as the water level in the holding basins at Solomon's Pools[57] south of the city fell too low to allow water to reach the city at all. In Süleyman's time, with the pipes newly repaired, the situation we have observed may have been relatively trouble-free compared to earlier and later periods.

The precise and supervised distribution of water was not a practice introduced by the Ottomans. Within each village, custom dictated the exact apportioning and rotation of the daily flow among the peasants. The *kanunnames* for the region do not include details of the arrangements, suggesting that the Ottoman officials did not interfere with local practice at the village level, but rather concerned themselves primarily with the supply of water to the town. In this context, and at those times when peasants were unable to resolve disputes among themselves, water issues were brought before the kadi. The practice was not limited to this arid region. Water supply for agricultural uses, as well as the regular and sufficient supply to cities, were a fixed concern all over the empire.[58] The kadi registers of Kayseri, for example, record disputes among villagers and officials over the construction of new water channels, the division of daily water-use rights and the taxes due to the supervisor of water distribution.[59] And, in those areas where water distribution or control was of key importance and required government regulation, such as in Egypt, the *kanunnames* do contain relevant clauses.[60]

Violence

Peaceful adjudication did not always resolve the disagreements and difficulties which arose between the Ottoman officials and the peasants. For one thing, the peasants did not always come before the kadi when summoned. One man of Bayt Ṣafāfā, who was guarantor for the debt of someone from Bayt Laḥm, refused twice to appear. A *subaşı* was finally sent to arrest him. The man was sentenced to be beaten according to *sharīʿa* for his rebelliousness and refusal to obey orders, in addition to being required to pay the debt for which he was originally summoned.[61] In another example, the villagers of ʿAjjūl owed two years' taxes to Mami *sipahi*, the *tımar* holder of nearby ʿAṭṭārā, where they also cultivated some land. The villagers refused to pay Mami the outstanding sum. Two officials were then sent who read a letter to these villagers commanding that they come before the kadi. When they again refused, the kadi requested that ʿAli bey, *tımar* holder of ʿAjjūl, bring them in. ʿAli answered that "he was unable to produce them, for they were rebellious and persistently fractious" (*mutamarridīn wa-mustamirrīn ʿalā-'l-ʿisyān*). The matter was thus recorded, to be passed on to a higher authority, presumably the *beylerbeyi* of Damascus or the sultan.[62]

In the village of Kafr Ṣūm, more forceful measures finally compelled the peasants to obey the officials and pay their debts. Kafr Ṣūm was linked to several attacks on *subaşı*s. Moreover, the *sipahi*s assigned to a *tımar* there frequently complained about tax arrears. On August 5, 1555 (17 Ramaḍān 962), Yusuf *sipahi* presented to the kadi a litany of the abuses perpetrated by the peasants of Kafr Ṣūm. He himself had gone to collect what was due him and received not only a refusal, but a shower of stones and arrows. The *subaşı* who subsequently went to the village received the same response. A third official was then sent to bring in the villagers. They refused him as well, and drove him out of the village.[63]

Six months later, the scene was repeated. Mehmet bey *sipahi* complained to the kadi and the *kethüda* of the *sancakbeyi* that the people of Kafr Ṣūm, which was part of his *tımar*, persistently rebelled against his authority, refusing to pay what was rightfully due to him. Feeling his situation threatened and unable to assert himself over the villagers, Mehmet asked the *sancakbeyi* for permission "to ride out against the people of the village, to settle what was due him from them, and to take their possessions from them so that they be an example to other rebellious persons."[64] Permission was granted to Mehmet. Two days later permission was also given to Yusuf bey *sipahi*, who had four years' worth of back debts due from the peasants of Kafr Ṣūm, to ride out with the *sancakbeyi* against them.[65]

The disciplinary foray against Kafr Ṣūm was not wholly successful. Although there were no further reports of physical attacks against officials there, in the years immediately following the villagers remained unforthcoming with their taxes. They sent Süleyman *sipahi* away when he came for his share, advising him to get a certificate from the *sipahi* commander (*alaybeyi*) whose nearby fields they cultivated. The latter was collecting Süleyman's revenues along with his own. Süleyman thus petitioned the sultan for help, which arrived in the form of an order to the Jerusalem kadi to investigate the matter and take the proper action.[66] Three years later, Yusuf *sipahi* was again trying unsuccessfully to extract back taxes from the villagers.[67]

Kafr Ṣūm was a particularly difficult village to control in this period. But it was not the only scene of violent confrontation between officials and the local peasants. Attacks against *subaşı*s and *sipahi*s, while not frequent, did occur at regular intervals. ʿAşur *subaşı* and his men were attacked, wounded, and robbed near Rāmallāh by some people from Dayr Dibwān. In this attack, the villagers wounded him, chased his party to Rāmallāh, tied them up, and robbed them. One villager subsequently appeared before the kadi to return the stolen property – cloth, horse blankets, and an embroidered filigree belt worth 10 *sultani*. ʿAşur accepted them back and there was no mention of further proceedings.[68] Only a month earlier, ʿAli, the *subaşı* of Banī Zayd, had come before the kadi, wounded and leading his wounded horse, to report that he had been attacked by the people of Jufnā al-Naṣārā, a village seven kilometers to the north of Rāmallāh.

In the village of Kharabta, in the sub-district of Ramle, Cevher the *subaşı* of the some *vakıf* villages got into a fight with two villagers over the accounting of the revenues due. Cevher ended up being stoned.[69] In another incident, Hasan *subaşı* reported being knifed one evening while loading grain from the threshing floor in Jabʿa.[70] And, the villagers were not the only ones to attack Ottoman officials. Şehsuvar *subaşı* was set upon by Arabs (Bedouin) when he was on his way to Bayt Dhakariyya, 10-15 kilometers south of ʿAyn Kārim.[71]

Such attacks are not surprising. This province, and others, were not especially peaceful places. Reports from travellers in Palestine recount the perils of the roads, where armed guards were an absolute necessity. Both villagers and officials gave accounts before the kadi of Bedouin assaults. Imperial orders reflect the tension, repeatedly addressing the problems of pacifying the countryside and securing the rural roads.[72] This common worry, however, created no special affinity for the Ottoman officials among the peasants or vice versa. Because of the stubborn refusal of the peasants in the *vakıf* villages of the ʿ*imaret* to pay their dues, the governor of Damascus was ordered to dispatch a Janissary commander (*bölükbaşı*), six janissaries, and ten men from the Jerusalem citadel in order to enforce the collection of annual revenues from them.[73]

And yet, one aspect of the officials' behavior towards the villagers was remarkable. Once the *sipahi*s decided that the people of Kafr Ṣūm needed to be punished, they first had to get permission to do so from the kadi. And, it seems, they actually sought it. This demonstrates a high level of discipline among the *sipahi* ranks, at least in this period. In general, though, a persistent problem addressed in imperial orders was the officials' custom of making the rounds in an area to collect revenues, meanwhile making excessive demands on the hospitality of the local peasants.[74] The pre-eminent position of the kadi is also evident, since he had to authorize such actions. At the same time, even when the peasants complained to the kadi about the officials, as we shall discuss below, it was more over abuses in taxation than arbitrary violence at the hands of these men.

An imperial order from some years later defined the limits of actions allowed against the peasants. In the province of Nablus, the peasants were rebellious and had refused to pay any taxes, despite numerous invitations to do so by Ottoman officials. The governor and *defterdar* of Damascus and the kadi of Jerusalem requested permission to burn down and destroy some villages to set an example for the others. This request was firmly rejected by the sultan, on the grounds that, "it is not proper to sack entire villages, [since in such case] it is inevitable that many obedient and inoffensive Muslims with their families and households will also perish on account of a few rebels among them."[75] The sultan went on to recommend that persuasion, intimidation, finally arrest and punishment be used instead to force people to pay their taxes.[76] With some insight, the order ends by observing:

> ...the rebellion and insurrection of so many villagers is not without reason. In all probability they have become unable to endure [any longer] the oppressive and iniquitous acts of the sanjak-beg's men and of the intendants (*ümenā*) and tax-collectors (*ʿummāl*), and were compelled to follow the road of rebellion. [Therefore] you shall not be negligent and not allow anyone among the intendants, tax-collectors, and your men to commit oppressive and iniquitous acts... [77]

Official Ottoman policy allowed for strong measures to be taken against peasants who would not fulfill their obligations. However, collective punishment was not sanctioned, lest innocent persons be harmed along with the guilty. The well-being and productivity of the peasants were of primary concern, as it was the profits of their labors which constituted the main source of revenues to the empire. This attitude is most strongly illustrated by the closing admonition to the governor and kadi, that perhaps the peasants were not to be blamed for their actions, that their violence was prompted by injustices committed against them.

"*Zulm ve ta'addi*" – "oppressive" officials

Many fewer complaints were filed by the peasants against the officials than were recorded by officials against the villagers under their jurisdiction. This is understandable for many reasons. The officials were based in Jerusalem, with ready access to the kadi. Unlike the peasants, they did not have to make a special trip into the city in order to pursue a complaint. They were better off and could afford to pay the costs, however minimal, of bringing a matter before the kadi. There was not an automatic identification between the interests of officials and kadis; notwithstanding, the kadi was an Ottoman official, and was universally perceived as such. This is attested on the part of the peasants by the fact that they turned to him for support against the injustices of other officials, whom they saw him as having the power to discipline. In the eyes of the officials, however, it was the kadi's task to aid them in assuring their livelihood, that is, the steady collection of revenues due from the villagers. Imperial expectations, too, were that the kadi and the *sancakbeyi* would look to the maintenance of order and prosperity for the general welfare of the empire.

In the formulaic language of the kadi's records the action most frequently taken by the peasants against the Ottoman officials was "to lodge a complaint" – *taḍarrara.* The ledgers of outgoing orders from Istanbul repeated the phrase: *zulm ve ta'addi ederler diyü...bildirdiler* – "they [the peasants] reported that they [the officials; sometimes the Bedouin] were unjust and oppressive," as a summation following the details of the report. Complaints were filed against officials for more and less serious offenses. Confrontations often evolved from complications in tax collection, although we will not take up matters of simple debt here, having previously done so. The other claims are worth examining to elucidate the more difficult aspects of the official–peasant relationship.

Certain administrative abuses must have been common all over the empire, as illustrated by the general orders issued against them.[78] These included miscollection of tithes, the imposition of extra tasks or taxes, the unauthorized appointment of assistant kadis, physical violence, and other obnoxious actions.

One of the more explicit demonstrations of peasant dissatisfaction against their masters was executed with their feet.[79] Several instances have already been mentioned where officials filed suit against peasants for having left their villages. The administration clearly recognized that such actions, though objectionable, were not necessarily unprovoked, and an investigation into the circumstances of peasant flight was a required part of settling these cases. One specific solution showed a degree of flexibility in the system, as well as the potential advantages the peasants might eke from it. Here, two leaders of Ṣūbā came before the kadi and a representative of the *sancakbeyi*, to complain that Sinan *sipahi*, who had a *tımar* in the village, attacked them on behalf of the *subaşı* of the region, and in this way they (the *subaşı* and his men) ruined their village.[80] At this, the leaders left the village and abandoned the obligation to pay their master. The complaint was recorded, to be forwarded to the responsible authority. But meanwhile, Sinan and the two leaders reached an agreement that the villagers would pay taxes at a rate of one-fourth and undertake not to deceive him, nor plant outside the village before they finished sowing inside it.

The statutes against runaway villagers were firmly fixed; the two men would not be allowed to remain absent after having been apprehended. Moreover, the potential damage here was perhaps greater because the two men who left were leaders and their action might encourage others to abandon the village as well. Since the survey register notes that the village was normally taxed at a rate of one-third, the agreement to lower the rate to one-fourth nonetheless constituted a form of assistance to the villagers, to help them recover from the damage inflicted on them. However, the relief was temporary as the survey register compiled two years later showed the village taxed at the traditional rate of one-third.[81]

A complaint brought by the notables of ʿAyn Silwān demonstrated the force of custom that was on the side of the peasants. Since before the Ottoman conquest, they said, the villagers of ʿAyn Silwān used to come to Jerusalem and peddle vegetables from baskets as they walked around the city. One winter day, an official tried to stop this and force them to sell their produce only in the Bāshūra, the permanent vegetable market.[82] They brought the matter to the kadi, who, having heard corroborating testimony from a group of Muslim witnesses, upheld their right to hawk their goods on foot within the city walls.[83] Had they been forced to sell in the market, these peasants would have incurred the added expense of renting a shop. The villagers of ʿAyn Silwān were not necessarily representative of all peasants of the province, living so close to Jerusalem and being directly involved in its daily economic life. On the other hand, they were not the only people with vegetables or other produce to sell, nor was theirs the only village close to the town. The experience of the Silwānīs was probably more typical for peasants in the immediate region of Jerusalem. While in town, they naturally brought their case before the kadi for immediate settlement.

Tax code complexities

The local Ottoman tax code (*kanunname*), whose sections were set out in Chapter Three, contained precise, if complex details regarding taxation in the district. Predictably, disputes arose over the way in which taxes were to be collected in particular villages, as a result of the more complicated paragraphs of these statutes. Some people of Dayr al-Shanna and Bayt Sāḥūr al-Wādī came to challenge the local *sipahi*, who wanted to collect taxes on their olive trees by *kısm*, taking a fixed percentage as was specified for *rumani* olive trees in the *kanunname*. The peasants maintained that the trees had always been *haraç*, that is, taxed at a fixed rate per tree as for *islami* trees. Moreover, they had a copy of the new imperial survey register to prove their claim. Having examined the document, the kadi found in favor of the villagers, admonishing the *sipahi* to collect the taxes properly.[84]

The fixed rate tax on olive trees was preferred where it was traditional, and one assumes that, on average, the tax of one *akçe* per two trees was less than the fifty percent of the produce due as *kısm*. In the village of ʿInab, the unpopular *sipahi* ʿAli Bali also tried to change the way he collected the tax on olive trees from the fixed rate to a fixed percentage. The peasants of ʿInab sent a petition of protest to the sultan saying that until the time of the complaint, ʿAli Bali took one *akçe* for every two trees "and it was written thus as well in the imperial *defter*, and it was recorded in the *sijill* that things were thus in previous years... But this year, the *sipahi* said 'your trees are not *islami* [taxed at a fixed rate], but they are *küffari* [taxed at a percentage].'"[85]

Although the outcome of the latter case is unknown, and there is no information in the survey registers available to support the claim of the peasants, ʿAli Bali's honesty is suspect. His previous reputation among the villagers was bad. Moreover, as in the first case, where the peasants' claim was confirmed, it seems that the fixed rate of one *akçe* per two trees did not work to the advantage of the *sipahi*s. In a good year, they did not share in the profits of a bumper crop, and in a poor year they could not take advantage of the higher price of oil. Thus, the *sipahi*s attempted to change the status of the olive trees, a change which the villagers were quick and able to resist.

A more involved dispute broke out between the villagers of Qulūnya and the *sipahi* there over the tithe. Initially, Badr al-Dīn, in his own name and as representative of the peasants, complained to the sultan that the *sipahi*s were trying to take the tithe directly from the villagers, when it was supposed to be deducted from the *vakıf* share. At the same time the *sipahi*s were in fact also collecting the tithe from the *vakıf* administrator. The *sancakbeyi* and kadi of Jerusalem were ordered to investigate the matter.[86]

ʿAli *sipahi* then brought suit against the owners of olive trees and vineyards in Qulūnya, claiming that his warrant (*berat*) and copy of the latest survey showed that the tithe was to come "from all the revenues" and not "from the money of the *vakıf*," as the villagers had claimed was the customary practice there. They cited the imperial order in their favor. However, the order to the kadi said only that he should ascertain the truth in the matter according to the *berat* and the survey. On the basis of those documents, the kadi decided in favor of the *sipahi*.[87] In fact, the copies of the surveys (II and III) from almost thirty-five and twenty years earlier stated that the tithe was to be taken "from all the revenues," although no specification was made in the more recent one, drawn up only a few years before.[88] Were the villagers attempting to bluff not only the *sipahi*, but the sultan as well, when they claimed to have paid the tithe customarily "from the money of the *vakıf*?"[89] There is no doubt here that the peasants both understood and felt the difference between the two kinds of tithe levies. And, the difference was great enough to prompt a concerted, if underhanded and unsuccessful, effort to change the status of their village.[90]

The peasants of Ṭūr Zaytā tried much the same ploy, but with less elaborate justifications. When brought before the kadi, they claimed that their tithe was "from the money of the *vakıf*." The *subaşı* representing the claim of the *sancakbeyi*, however, produced a copy of the imperial survey register, which was examined by the kadi and found to state that the tithe was indeed "from all the revenues," and not "from the money of the *vakıf*."[91] The copies of the survey registers examined in the present study confirm the kadi's findings.

However, a year or so later, the case was reopened in the midst of some confusion. Owners of some vineyards in Ṭūr Zaytā brought the *vakıf* administrator before the kadi, accusing him of taking the tithe "from all the revenues," contrary to *sharīʿa*, *kanun*, a copy of the *kanunname* from the imperial survey, and an imperial order which they showed to the kadi. The administrator, for his part, claimed the tithe was "from all the revenues," and he also produced a copy of the survey register and the *kanunname*. Examining all of these documents, the kadi concluded that the tithe "from all the revenues" was to be taken from the grain crops, and that the tithe "from the money of the *vakıf*" was paid from the taxes on the trees and vineyards of the village. Moreover, the kadi also found that the surveys neglected to list the percentage of the grape syrup due in taxes from the village vineyards.[92]

So, just as the *sipahi*s tried to force a change in the status of olive trees to their advantage, the peasants maneuvered to alter the tithes in their favor. In many instances, the parties were eventually brought before the kadi in order to settle the matter. The kadi then untangled the correct practice from the opposing claims, finding now for the peasants, now for the officials, as the law dictated. Settlements might be only temporary, as the repeated suits showed. In fact, not long after the kadi deftly separated the grains from the trees and vines in Ṭūr Zaytā, an order arrived from the sultan in response to a petition on the part of the *sipahi*s. Now, it seemed, the matter was further complicated because lands once sown with grains had been planted with vineyards.[93]

Exactions after taxes

Other complaints by the peasants against officials were less ambiguous or involved than the intricacies of taxation. Mehmet *subaşı* was accused of stealing livestock from the villagers of Jabʿa. The charge was made by

Muhalhal b. Ṣāliḥ, who was joined a few days later by his brother Ḥasan and another man. These three men claimed Mehmet had attacked them while they were in the village of Ṭarafīn earlier that month, taking twenty-one head of cattle and six donkeys. Mehmet replied that he had taken twenty-three animals – twelve cows, six calves and five donkeys – but justified himself, saying that he had taken them while the villagers were being rebellious.[94] When asked to give proof of the misconduct of the peasants, the *subaşı* was unable to bring proper evidence, whereas the villagers brought two more of their community who gave sworn testimony that Mehmet had taken the cows and donkeys as they had first claimed. He was thus required to return them. Here, as in the case of Mustafa *çelebi*, who tried to confiscate sheep in Fāghūr when he found them being illegally watered, an official seems to assume the right to confiscate animals in response to alleged peasant insubordination.

Significant injuries, such as the theft here of many animals, brought the peasants to the kadi. Small claims against the officials, however, appeared infrequently in the *sijill*s, especially by comparison with the familiar entries recording petty debts claimed by the officials from the peasants. The time and expense involved in pursuing a case in town may have dissuaded the villagers from bringing forward smaller claims more frequently. However, when their treatment by the officials exceeded the bounds of petty annoyance and threatened their livelihood and status in a serious manner, the peasants knew not only how to go to the kadi in Jerusalem, but how to file a petition to the sultan in Istanbul as well.

Abuses on a large scale were reported directly to the sultan by the villagers of Ludd, in the *nahiye* of Ramle. Their complaints may have been speeded to Istanbul because the village belonged to the *vakıf* of the imperial *ʿimaret* in Jerusalem.[95] At all events, the existence of two similar petitions to the sultan, filed ten years apart, suggests that imperial attention was no guarantee against abuse either.

The first petition was filed in early October 1556 (end of Dhū'l–Qaʿda 963.) A long list of complaints stated that the manager of the *vakıf* did not come to collect revenues himself, but instead sent men from the Jerusalem garrison, who quartered themselves and their mounts with the villagers, overcharged the Christian peasants in calculating the *cizye*, took extra grain, honey, oil, and rice for themselves and excessive fees wherever possible. As usual, the reply from Istanbul was an order to investigate the claims of the petitioners and prevent any future abuses.[96] Ten years later, a similar petition was received from the peasants of Ludd. It contained a catalogue of offenses committed against the villagers and described the numerous ways in which officials harmed them. The tithe, which was to be taken in kind, was instead collected in cash, with the price of the crops calculated above the fixed price; fines for petty offenses were raised arbitrarily; taxes were levied on unproductive fields or orchards; and sheep were taxed more than was customary.[97] As with the theft of livestock above, it seems likely that the combination of abuses made this case outstanding and not their existence *per se*, which on a smaller scale may have been common everywhere.

The story, it turns out, was even more complicated, not simply a straightforward case of greedy officials. Some two weeks before the last petition discussed above was answered, an imperial order went out to the governor of Damascus and the kadis of Jerusalem and Ramle. In it, the sultan reiterated that complaints had been received against the *vakıf* administrator from several of the villages endowed to the *vakıf* of the imperial *ʿimaret*, accusing him of bringing about the ruin of the villages and their mosques. At the same time, however, the order quoted a letter from the governor and the kadis which described how certain iniquitous villagers had themselves been perpetrating misdeeds against their fellow villagers, while the administrator acted with great integrity. Once again, the sultan ordered a complete investigation and the punishment which accorded with its findings.[98]

This case did not end here one suspects. The evidence from just these ten years, however, offers much detail regarding official–peasant relations and the conduct of rural administration. First, the peasants were not particularly shy about sending off their complaints to Istanbul. Though they may have ridiculed the survey-makers whom a new and remote sultan sent out to count their persons and property, the villagers were quite ready to appeal to that same ruler for relief against the wrongdoings of his own officials. He was, after all, the sultan. Second, the inventory of abuses contained in the two petitions illustrates the range of possibilities available to officials for stealing from the villagers, on whatever scale. Third, the original complaint, which stated that it was the garrison troops sent by the *vakıf* administrator who committed the offenses, adds another group to the list of officials active in the countryside. The administrator, busy with the many duties of running the *vakıf*, sent soldiers out to collect taxes in his place, with seemingly disastrous results. Finally, as in the false claim regarding their tithe from the villagers of Qulūnya, the petition from Ludd may not tell a true story. If such was the case, then the peasants, accused by the kadis of mischief against their own villages, tried to take advantage of the distance between Istanbul and the Palestinian countryside to gain the sultan's backing against his own officials. Was it the past history of abuse which the peasants counted on to lend credibility to their new complaints? Or their seemingly natural defenseless state vis-à-vis the imperial officials?

No continuous stream of grumbling villagers choked the roads and boats to the sultan's capital. The peasants who travelled to Istanbul in order to press a petition into the sultan's hand were the exception, not the rule. Yet the opportunity to make such a complaint was available and was a realistic, if difficult and costly option for the person(s) who felt oppressed. If the cases of deception described above really were premeditated acts, then some among the peasants clearly understood how to manipulate the authorities and the system to their own advantage.

Other disruptive factors

The Bedouin

Bedouin tribes who lived in and moved through the area of southern Syria, and Jerusalem in particular, were a permanent presence in the rural areas. In some of the survey registers, they were listed after the name of a village, and certain tribes can be located regionally.[99] Bedouin appeared frequently in the kadi's registers and imperial orders: in reports of attacks on the roads, raids against villages, in league with peasants against the Ottoman officials, and, in a slightly later period, as allies of the *sancakbeyi* against the peasants. Because of the proximity of many Jerusalem villages to the surrounding desert, there was probably continual contact between peasants and Bedouin, so much so as to make their exchanges an integral part of the local economy.[100] The variety of these reports suggests that it would be difficult to fix fast the place of the Bedouin in the network of relations between officials and villagers.

One chief preoccupation of the Ottoman administration in this area was to keep control of the Bedouin. The pacification of the Bedouin in southern Syria was one of the initial achievements of the Ottomans after they conquered the area from the Mamluks.[101] At least until the end of Süleyman's reign (1566), the Bedouin were kept relatively quiescent by the Ottoman governors. Hostage-taking from among the Bedouin leaders themselves was used with some success as a means to guarantee the conduct of the tribesmen. Another tactic of the government was to employ the Bedouin, coopting them into the *tımar* system in some places, elsewhere as guardians of the roads, or escorts for the pilgrimage caravan to Mecca and Medina.[102] Thus, three families from the tribe of Hutaym were recorded in the fourth and fifth survey registers as part of the *vakıf* of the *ʿimaret*, later as part of the *sancakbeyi*'s revenues. They were responsible for collecting and delivering the ripe grain from Jericho, and perhaps other places in the Jordan River valley, which belonged to the Jerusalem *ʿimaret* and the *sancakbeyi*. Each tribal group itself had to pay an annual tax of twenty-seven sheep and/or goats.[103]

Destructive raids against the villages occurred despite the Ottoman efforts to restrain the Bedouin. ʿUlyān b. Ismāʿīl of Bayt Liqyā came to the kadi in February 1553 (Rabīʿ I 960) to report that the Zāyida Arabs[104] had wrought havoc in his village. The fields had been trampled and the bean crop eaten, while the people were terrorized and powerless to stop the Bedouin. Two men were wounded and ʿUlyān's own sister killed.[105]

Incorporating the Bedouin into the system was not necessarily a guarantee of security to the villagers. Shaykh Ibrāhīm, who had in the past held the lease of the *hass* share of the village of Ṭurmus ʿAyyā, made a request to the sultan that the lease be returned to him. He already managed the interests of the *vakıf* supported by the remaining portion of the village revenues. When he had held the *hass* lease as well, Shaykh Ibrāhīm explained, then no outsiders interfered in the village, and "both the *vakıf* and the *hass* benefitted."[106] But now, "the *hass* agents have leased that share to some powerful people and rebellious Arab shaykhs who come and abuse the villagers so that most of them have left. As a result, both the *vakıf* and the *hass* have suffered."[107] The shaykh had touched a responsive chord; the sultan's reply was unequivocal: do not allow such people to hold leases. The peasants should not be dispersed.

The villagers were not always the target of the Bedouin. When the situation dictated, peasants sought Bedouin protection or came to their assistance. Thus, some years after the murder in Bayt Liqyā, a leader of that same village named Badr was the cause of great trouble. He put together a band of men, attacked another village where he killed several people, and then fled, taking refuge with the Bedouin in the province of Gaza.[108] Another incident found Şehsuvar, the *subaşı* of Bayt Natīf in 1554, under attack by a combined force of Bedouin and peasants. He had been on his way to a village called Bayt Dhakariyya, southwest of Jerusalem near Fāghūr and Naḥḥālīn. On the way, Şehsuvar came upon some Bedouin whom he tried to arrest, chasing them towards Naḥḥālīn. There, however, the people of Naḥḥālīn and others joined the Bedouin against the *subaşı*, shooting his horse and one of his men with arrows, and then preventing them from escaping towards Jerusalem. In the report made before the kadi of Hebron, where they fled instead, the entire incident was verified by all of the people. Either they did not try, or they were unable to act in collusion to lie about what happened so as to protect themselves.[109]

The Bedouin cannot be categorized absolutely either as the allies of the villagers or in their more traditionally perceived role as the permanent antagonists of settled cultivators. One further example emphasizes the range of Bedouin activities and settlement arrangements. Two shaykhs came before the kadi from the village of Fāghūr, south of Jerusalem: Shaykh Ibrāhīm b. Hamza of the tribe of al-Da'ājina and Shaykh Sa'fān b. Ṣa'b of the Banū 'Addā. They gave the kadi a guarantee for the cultivation of the village, each one for one half of it, identical to the guarantees made by villagers and their leaders, including a promise to finish sowing the lands inside the village first, and recognition of a monetary fine to be imposed if they failed.[110] Here, the Bedouin were not the supporters of the settled cultivators; they themselves were the cultivators, having undertaken to plant summer and winter crops so that the land not be fallow.[111]

Thus it is difficult to state which of the various roles was most "typical" of the Bedouin during this period: raider, ally, brigand, or farmer? Most were probably nomadic or semi-settled, with the great confederations still based in the Syrian and Arabian deserts. Certainly their most well-known face has been that of the troublesome nomads, who made the region treacherous during the end of the Mamluk regime, as well as in later periods. During the tenure of Ibn Farrūkh, the commander of the pilgrimage caravan in the early seventeenth century, the peasants found themselves the target of attacks by this local chieftain – who also held rank as an Ottoman official – and his Bedouin troops.[112]

Our notion of the size of the Bedouin population in the province is even more vague than that of the number of peasants. And probably to a greater extent than with the peasants, Bedouin matters were not regularly brought before the kadi, certainly not the small-scale tax claims and reports of petty abuses cited above. Yet during the years of the mid-sixteenth century, the Bedouin seem to have been less of a threat than in either the preceding or following century.

Nature

Interruptions to the normal course of rural work and administration were not all caused by human agents. Nature was the source of much hardship, troubles which the officials and peasants had to face together. The careful allocation of water was a constant source of tension between all groups, as seen above, yet its overall scarcity threatened soldiers, judges, and peasants alike. Drought, locusts, and other misfortunes periodically disrupted the agricultural routine, forcing expectations to be reduced as the land and the people recovered.

Illness could harm cultivation if it decimated the rural population sufficiently, thereby removing the crucial source of labor. However, the major plague epidemics in this area seem to have been concentrated more in the latter part of the sixteenth century.[113] Too, the peasants may have been somewhat protected from the devastating effects of the illness if they remained isolated in the countryside while it was rampant in towns.

In the relatively short span of years under consideration here, locusts were reported several times. In the late fall of 1559, an imperial order was sent to the *beylerbeyi* of Egypt, authorizing him to sell grain to Turgud the manager of the *ʿimaret* in Jerusalem. This was in response to Turgud's report of shortages in the spring of 1559 due to locusts (*çekirge*) which attacked the crop. Furthermore, bugs (*bit*) had eaten the grain stockpiled earlier. In the spring of 1560, a petition of the *sancakbeyi* and kadis of Gaza and Ramle spoke of the previous three to four years, during which locusts and drought had destroyed the grain harvest.[114]

Locusts struck the villages around Jerusalem in the spring of 1561. Villagers from ʿĪsāwiyya, Naḥḥālīn, and ʿAyn Silwān declared themselves unable to pay their taxes. In the case of Bayram bey, who had leased the revenue shares of Bayt Ḥanīnā and Qusūr belonging to the *vakıf* of the Dome of the Rock, the locust attack was a valid reason to cancel his lease, because no profit could possibly be derived from the villages in such a year.[115]

Little help was available to the peasants under such circumstances.

Importing wheat was expensive and extremely difficult, although it was possible to ship some from Egypt. People had to rely on the stored reserves, and adapt their diet. Seed grain, saved for planting in the coming season, could be eaten as a last resort. When this was gone, the peasants turned to the officials for aid. The notables of Qulūnya approached the kadi and the manager of the *vakıf* supported by their village in January 1556 (Ṣafar 963) asking for a loan from the *vakıf*, because they had too little grain to be able to cultivate their fields.[116]

Similar requests came in the winter of 1562–3 from two villages in the *sancak* of Gaza which were part of the endowment for the water pipes running into Jerusalem. The rationale for using *vakıf* funds to provide interim assistance to the peasants was clearly spelled out in the kadi's decision. "Permission was granted to give them [the villagers who came to the kadi] and the rest of their community the means[117] from the funds of the *vakıf*, for the benefit of the *vakıf* [itself], fearing that the land would [otherwise] be unworked and without cultivation."[118] Clearly, the *vakıf* was better served by spending some cash to keep the mainstay of the endowment from collapsing. For, continued hardship in the village would ultimately force the peasants to find sustenance elsewhere, and though they might be brought back home, recovery would then be even more protracted than if they had stayed.

One of the more cataclysmic natural events of the sixteenth century occurred in January 1546, when a violent earthquake struck a large area of southern Syria, as far north as Damascus. The Jordan river dried up for three days and a tidal wave was reported on the coast at Jaffa. Many buildings in Jerusalem, Hebron, Nablus, and Ramle were badly shaken and partly collapsed. The death toll amounted to some tens in Jerusalem, and 560 in Nablus.[119] Information on the effects of the earthquake in the rural areas, however, is scanty. One statement declared that "there is no place in these lands which did not endure some harm."[120] Coming in the middle of the winter growing season, the earthquake may have damaged or even ruined the year's grain harvest. Within the villages, as in the towns, numerous houses probably collapsed or sustained damage.[121] But, although the short-term effects may have been devastating to the peasants, the higher average yields recorded in the fourth survey register and the absence of any continued hardships mentioned there suggest that the area had largely recovered in the intervening fifteen years.

The formulae of "rebellion" and "oppression" which appear over and over again in the *sijill*s reinforce a mythology of peasants revolting against evil exploitative officials. Reading beyond the standard phrases, however, the details of individual incidents show that peasants acted against officials or contrary to the laws in ways which could not be construed as collectively rebellious. They punched holes in water lines, stole grain from the threshing floor, beat up officials, and tried to cheat the tax collectors by various artifices. Had all these acts been coordinated and contrived to achieve a single goal, then one could label them the manifestations of a revolt. Yet they were individual actions, mounted by single persons, one village, or a village plus Bedouin help. There was no wider organization or coordination of forces throughout the *sancak*, no fixed and recognized leadership, nor any defined common purpose. The "rebellious" deeds of the peasants were meant to achieve some local, immediate benefit; they were not aiming to overthrow the Ottoman governor or bring down the empire.

Local peasants shared a common attitude towards the officials. These agents of government, with military and judicial power to support them, regularly extracted a fixed amount of revenue from the villagers. The amount, and its components, were codified. The peasants acknowledged and fulfilled this obligation to higher authority. However, they felt no obligation to make the collection of these revenues an especially easy endeavor for the officials, nor were they willing to volunteer one more grain of wheat or barley, one additional grape or olive, than officially obliged to render. Furthermore, the records show that the villagers were not hesitant to exploit the weaknesses of the system to their advantage. Thus, they stole from the threshing floor before the grains were apportioned, cultivated hidden fields, switched measures, and diverted water. When inspired or provoked, they attacked officials, testing the physical limits of authority and the length of the tax collector's arm. Frustrated officials might take the law in their own hands and become abusive. Often, they turned to the kadis to prosecute claims against the peasants.

Although they may appear to have been united in some fundamental dislike of officialdom, the peasants were not necessarily united among themselves. They were physically dispersed throughout the countryside. Some were quite willing to take advantage of their own strong position within the village to abuse weaker persons there. Familial or other ties between settled villagers and the Bedouin made common cause between them against other villagers. Moreover, a basic distaste for authority did not prompt the peasants to boycott all things official and Ottoman. Kadis, the religious-judicial officials, were the embodiment of the law and provided an address for redress against the military-administrator *sipahi*s and *sancakbeyi*s. Distance, cost, and suspicion did not deter peasants entirely from turning to these judges.

From the perspective of the officials, there was no systematic effort to bleed the peasants dry in this period. As with the peasants, individual interest probably motivated officials to try to abuse the system. And, like the officials, the peasants appealed to the kadis to correct such abuses. At some level, too, a sense of shared economic interest may have operated to prevent officials from overtaxing the rural population. The officials had an obligation to protect the villagers against Bedouin raids, an obligation which overlapped with their motivation to protect their income.

One must assume, I think, that the system did not work perfectly, and that just as we suspect officials of forever trying to take more than their due, we must suspect the peasants of forever trying to pay less than they owed – not simply out of spite, but because they continually looked out for their own interests in a tenuous agrarian economy. The losses incurred by the revenue collectors from the petty thefts of the peasants did not individually represent huge sums, but each time a peasant managed to plant a hidden patch, conceal a bit of the harvest, add a rock or two to the containers of threshed grain, sell the crop for a fraction above the official price – the incremental gain he achieved eased his existence marginally.

The peasants were certainly not getting rich from any of this petty pilfering, but rather padding against hard times, taking out a bit of insurance against disaster, and basically ensuring their own subsistence. Living close to the margin of subsistence – far closer than the officials – every small addition was meaningful. An element of defiance may also have goaded the peasants to steal from or cheat officials; these acts were minor tokens of the control they retained over their own lives.

Peasants probably kept as much as they could without bringing down the ire of the local officials and incurring harsh measures and coerced extraction of whatever surpluses they had held back. Officials certainly knew that their revenue collection efforts were not one hundred percent efficient, but the cost of achieving such efficiency would have been very high. For, administrative functions occupied these officials only part of the year, and, in theory, they spent a long summer season away on military campaigns. In any particular place, for any given month or year or decade, some equilibrium was reached temporarily between the forces and needs of the administration and the forces and needs of the local agrarian, taxpaying population.

CHAPTER 6

Realities and routines

Peasants in Ottoman history have most often stepped from the flat dimensions of the imperial survey registers into the three-dimensional world when they were either the victims of abuse or the villains of insurrection.[1] In the past, the key to understanding Ottoman provincial administration was in the prescriptive descriptions of the survey registers with their codifications of local taxes. The ideological underpinnings of administration were construed from the paradigm of the "circle of equity" and the formulae of imperial *fermans*. Peasants, according to this schema, would enjoy a reasonably secure and regulated existence. Where abuse existed, the system provided a mechanism of redress against greedy or harsh officials. Insistent orders to kadis and governors admonished them: investigate the problem, find the offending parties, punish them appropriately, and do not allow the offense to recur.

Another version of provincial administration cast the Ottomans in the permanent role of corrupt and callous occupation forces. The closing chapters of Ottoman rule in the various provinces have tended to color popular and, sometimes, scholarly perceptions of earlier periods. Social and economic dislocations accompanying the dismemberment and ultimate demise of the empire left a bitter memory in people's minds. Moreover, the legacy of the break-up was a constellation of states whose early independent histories in no way encouraged a sense of gratitude to the former empire. These predominant influences on memory, coupled with a hazy picture of the practical execution of rural administration for the earliest periods of Ottoman rule in the Arab provinces, have contributed to a dull and depressing image of ever over-taxed peasants struggling bravely but in vain against a continually oppressive progression of officials.

For this reason, I have concentrated on contemporary local records of administration and compared them only with the records of imperial expectation which shaped the attitude of low- and high-ranking officials. I have ignored the accounts of contemporary foreign travelers, whose observations and judgments unavoidably contained a comparison with their country of origin and its own ideology of rural administration. Except for points of nomenclature, I have also shunned the later records and observations made by foreign travelers, consuls, ministers, archaeologists, and anthropologists, which accumulated rapidly during the nineteenth and early twentieth centuries. Local sources were hostile to the Ottomans, while foreigners were often so imbued with their sense of mission – be it religious, philanthropic or historical – that their accounts were not very useful.

Peasant studies in the early Ottoman period, however, are not only possible, but may be carried out with great depth and variety. The combined use of the *tapu tahrir defterleri* and the *qāḍī sijillāt* allow comparative insights from both the imperial and the local perspective. The imperial *ferman*s recorded in the *mühimme defterleri* and sometimes in the pages of the *sijill*s, reveal the concerns communicated by the central government to the local authorities.

Any of these documents or series of documents taken in isolation would give a warped sense of the overall functioning of rural administration. The *tapu tahrir defterleri* are far too standardized, infrequent and distant to convey an idea of the variation and complexity of local administration. Entries from the *mühimme defterleri*, on the other hand, distort the picture in favor of the extraordinary, the wrongdoings of officials and indigenous persons, concentrating on the problems of running an empire. Finally, the perspective of the *sijill*s is too local, shutting out not only the context of the larger empire, but for the most part even the nearer reaches of the other Palestinian provinces. Together, however, the different sources complement each other.

None of these documents, however, constitutes a first-hand, first-person account of a sixteenth-century Palestinian peasant. The peasant "voices" that we seem to hear in the complaints and petitions were recorded by court clerks or official scribes. At best, they were recorded from the testimony of peasants themselves; if not, from the reports of officials who quoted them. Yet no citation should be assumed to be verbatim, for the repeated phrases suggest the formulae of bureaucratic convention.[2] Like Plato's forms, they are shadows of the real thing, or worse, reflections of mere models. Alongside the suspect voices, however officials recorded what peasants did, mostly when it varied from the norm or displeased them. These actions speak more directly, certainly more frequently, than any words.

The realities of everyday, every-month, every-year rural administration depended on interconnecting routines. Natural seasonal routines were largely predictable, but completely uncontrollable. Human routines, on the other hand, could be managed, influenced, and contained – by the power of other humans and by nature's forces. Peasant routines were primarily shaped by the rhythms of seasonal agriculture. The regular demands of the sultan through his officials were superimposed on the natural rhythms, but necessarily mitigated by them. In practice, the case of Palestine at mid-century demonstrates that administrative routines were adjusted through a continual process of negotiation and compromise between peasants and Ottoman officials.[3] From the initial survey registers, to the annual payments to revenue collectors, each stage represented another occasion on which peasants could moderate, postpone, or even try to cancel payments due. They put forward various reasons, some legitimate and substantiated, others manufactured.

However, the Ottoman sultan possessed enormous and effective resources for imposing the imperially determined routines on both his officials and the subject populations in the mid-sixteenth century. Imperial ideology recognized the restraints on authority and the use of force required to govern a flourishing domain. A highly developed rhetoric reiterated to the sultan's officials – the *sancakbeyi*s, kadis, and *sipahi*s – that they should act according to the laws of God and the sultan. In practice, however, physical force and the threat of violence were also used in provincial administration as a means to obtain revenues and control the local population.

The sultan could not control his officials perfectly. They were key military men as well as administrators, and he needed to ensure their willingness to fight the enemy, even at the expense of his need to discipline them for petty acts of abuse. Officials, on the other hand, could employ another coercive instrument to persuade the sultan and counteract the complaints of local taxpayers: the influence and patronage of powerful and high-ranking officials.

In part, the tensions between the sultan and his officials derived from the tug-of-war between them for control over revenues produced by the peasants. What we have seen, via the evidence of the *sijill*, is that the peasants were not passive victims or mere spectators in this contest. They participated actively in the struggle, defending the routines established by the sultan and their own custom. Therefore in mid-sixteenth-century Palestine a tacit alliance of purpose against the officials existed between the sultan and the peasants. More importantly, Süleyman possessed the power and will to enforce his side of this alliance, through the mechanism of the central Ottoman government.

Similar conditions may have prevailed around the empire at this time. However, little work has thus far been done on questions of peasant activity via records such as the *sijill*s. And, there are very few *mühimme* registers from Süleyman's time.[4] Palestine, and Jerusalem in particular, seem to have commanded significant imperial attention. The Syrian provinces had not been Ottoman for more than a generation and had already suffered one serious, if early, revolt. More importantly, Jerusalem's holy status prompted considerable imperial investment in restoration and new construction projects. Not only did Süleyman rebuild the walls and watercourses, but he added fountains throughout the city. Hurrem Sultan's *ʿimaret* took over the revenues from numerous villages around Jerusalem. The *vakıf* was added to by Süleyman after her death, and its villagers were not infrequent petitioners against official wrongdoings. Possibly, the extent of imperial expenditures here elicited a greater measure of attention to proper administrative practice than in other places. Jerusalem's well-being also directly reflected on the sultan in his capacity of leader of Islam.

Images of authority

From the peasants' perspective, the Ottoman government existed in a variety of incarnations. Local officials presented the most familiar, and obnoxious, face of authority. Among them, as noted in Chapter Two, were military-administrative and religious-judicial personnel. The *sancakbeyi*, *sipahi*s, *subaşı*s, janissaries, etc. dominated tax collection and the use of force. Kadis investigated and adjudicated the legality of actions according to the dictates of *sharīʿa*, *kanun*, and custom. It was to them that peasants brought their complaints of abusive behavior suffered at the hands of the *sipahi*s and others. These judges and other members of the *ʿulema*, on the other hand, were sometimes implicated in harmful actions against the peasants, whether as *vakıf* administrators in charge of revenue collection or as corrupt judges who took bribes or misused their offices. Complaints against judges, however, are rare in this period in Palestine, and those recorded concern the illegal appointment of deputy-judges (*naib*s), rather than abusive behavior against Ottoman subjects.[5] By the end of the century, more substantive complaints were forwarded to Istanbul.[6]

Peasant attitudes toward all these officials could range from overt and active hostility through a kind of considered deference. Despite their differentiation from the military-administrative officials, the kadis, as agents of the state, probably at best won grudging respect. Faroqhi points out that most complaint petitions were transmitted through the kadis on their way to Istanbul, and so their language could be tempered. Moreover, the kadis might make sure to cast themselves in the best possible light in drawing up the document, stressing – where appropriate – their own efforts to protect the peasantry.[7] As for the *sijill*s, they could hardly reflect accurately peasant feelings towards the kadi, since they recorded what transpired in his presence. Naturally, peasants seeking assistance would be reticent to express unfavorable feelings toward the kadi in the same breath as their request. And, any peasant outburst might not be considered germane to the recorded protocol of the case being judged. Perhaps the indignation of ʿAbd al-Laṭīf of Bittīr, described in Chapter Four, was recorded because of its exceptional fury.

"Utilitarian" is perhaps a general descriptor of the peasants' relationship to local authority. Kadis kept military officials in line. The military men might usefully control the Bedouin, but ultimately, they had the advantage of force and were self-interested revenue collectors. While it is hard to imagine that peasants objected to any increase in local security, they sometimes joined forces with the Bedouin against the sultan's men. Peasants sought Bedouin protection, however, and not vice versa. Although no friends of the state, the Bedouin might act as military agents for local rulers, or were even appointed to local office. In both cases, they mistreated the agrarian populace.[8] The antagonism between pastoral and sown, between nomadic and settled populations may be cliché, but the dichotomy retains some legitimacy. The two groups, meanwhile, shared a basic suspicion of the state and its purposes.

The sultan represented the more benevolent countenance of officialdom to the local peasantry. Several factors account for the disparity in peasant perceptions of sultanic authority as compared with its local manifestations. Distance certainly played a role; local officials were the immediate and intrusive agents of the remote and magnificent Ottoman sultan. And, the sultan cultivated an image as protector of all his subjects, accessible by petition to even the most humble. Numerous responses to peasant petitions in the *mühimme* registers confirm that the villagers believed in the efficacy of this process. Examples of peasant petitions also suggest they were sometimes used in a more sophisticated and calculating manner than that of a simple and desperate plea for justice. Peasants clearly identified the sultan with the ideology of the state, which reiterated the importance of the peasantry as a productive force and the obligation of good government to safeguard it from abuse.

Brown suggests another reason for peasant willingness to petition, and for peasant ability to hold such opposite images of what was essentially a single, though hugely graduated official apparatus. He ascribes this attitude to "the personalism of the peasant political outlook."[9] The maliciousness of the state was not to be seen as inherent in the state structure, but rather particular to the persons who acted on its behalf. Thus the sultan, an individual as well, could be exonerated. Nor was this assessment a simple misperception on the part of the peasants. For as we have seen from the *mühimme*, and as Brown reminds us, the sultans (and their agents) responded to these petitions. Imperial orders not only emphasize the ideology, but they enjoin the kadis to see to the removal of injurious persons and practices. In this way, the kadis, as the local arbiters of justice, are clearly a separate arm of officialdom from the military-administrative officials. Therefore, we find peasants appealing to them against the iniquities or offenses of the *sipahi*s, janissaries, and others.

This image of the sultan was further cultivated and reinforced in Süleyman's time and afterward. The language of the *mühimme*s evokes a sultan personally attending each and every matter sent to him with extreme diligence and concern.[10] At the same time, the formulae of the *ferman*s also emphasized the oppressive character of local officials. By the end of the sixteenth century, this literary device may have been especially amplified to establish as great a distance as possible between the well-intentioned sultan and his increasingly disobedient officials.[11] As we have seen in the cases presented here, the peasants endorsed this view and invoked its intent in their claims for justice.

Süleyman's own standing was substantially enhanced during the years of his reign, partly by virtue of his military successes, and partly through its careful cultivation by his grand viziers and *şeyhülislam*. For the peasants around Jerusalem, Süleyman was paradoxically very immediate in the physical presence of his constructions, but remote and moving farther away in his grandeur and magnitude.

Hierarchies of authority did not end with the officials. Local residents could be found integrated into the lower ranks of the military and judicial staffs, either as deputized revenue collectors, holders of sub-leases on tax collection rights, clerks or subordinate judges. The hierarchies also extended into the peasant population. Each village was represented by one or more leaders, the *ra'īs al-fallāḥīn*, who also represented the officials to the peasants. But there were other influential people in every village: the *akābir*, *a'yān* and *mashā'ikh*. Some must have had economic or moral power over people in each village. Others, including village women, perhaps had a mystical or medical talent. The *ra'īs al-fallāḥīn* and village notables acted very often on behalf of an entire village. But they also protected their own interests, and it is difficult to discern when they did so to the exclusion, or at the expense, of weaker people in the village.

The details of stratification within the village community remain unelaborated, though the peasants were obviously greatly differentiated among themselves. Again, further research is required. There was no incidental evidence of familial ties between villagers and townsmen, although some Christian villagers from Bayt Laḥm and Bayt Jālā were registered as resident in Jerusalem. In a slightly later period, one particular characteristic of Jerusalem was the emphatic separation between the rural and urban populations because of the unique religious importance of the city and hence the prevalence of prominent families of scholars there. In Nablus, by comparison, the urban notables originated from the surrounding countryside and maintained direct political and economic ties there.[12] Wherever these ties did exist, they wove the peasants into other hierarchies of power, wealth, and influence.

Illusions of power

In the preceding chapters, we have discovered a spectrum of measures used by the peasants against local officials: complaints to the kadi, petitions to the sultan, cheating, theft, and outright violence. Having discussed the range of peasant attitudes towards the officials, we must still ask more insistently what it was peasants thought they would achieve by their actions. They sought relief or redress of any specific grievance brought before the kadi. But they also engaged in a range of criminal activities against Ottoman officials, from petty theft from crops at harvest time to outright assault. Were acts of theft and attempts at fraud meant to harm the officials or only to further private peasant interests? What could they hope to accomplish when they shot arrows at government officers?

Most of these peasant actions may be understood as part of the arsenal of everyday forms of peasant resistance, "the *ordinary* weapons of relatively powerless groups: footdragging, dissimulation, false-compliance, pilfering, feigned ignorance, slander, arson, sabotage, and so forth..."[13] They were part of the local routine: repeated, modified, but regular. While such "weapons" were assuredly a nuisance for officials, they were also a means to reduce the inherent tension and competition between peasants and officials. Perhaps these petty actions were tolerated along with ongoing abuses by officials for the same reasons: the cost in manpower and political support to the central government of eliminating them was too high.

It seems, too, that peasant actions were not normally intended to provoke a crisis in local rural administration. When they intensified in number or effect, peasants were sending an unwritten message to the central government. In his written responses, the sultan at least paid lip service to the notion that disobedient and destructive peasant behavior probably had its roots in abuses by his own officials. Whether he could stop them or not was another matter.

Such forms of resistance are also called "avoidance protest, by which dissatisfied groups seek to attenuate their hardships and express their discontent through flight, sectarian withdrawal, or other activities that minimize challenges to or clashes with those whom they view as their oppressors..."[14] While flight may have been used as a means to avoid immediate confrontation, it was viewed with particular concern by the Ottoman administration in the mid-sixteenth century. The careful inquiries into reported cases and heavy fines reflect the active implementation of the laws on absentee peasants, and imperial care to eliminate the source of the problem. Damaging consequences might result from abuse, as was the case, for example, in sixteenth- and seventeenth-century Greece: "Then, whole villages emptied as peasants refused to tolerate the burden of additional heavy taxes. Spahis found themselves cut off from a prime source of income, and sometimes peasants would even successfully demand the immediate remedy of grievances as a condition of their return."[15]

No mass movement was apparent in Palestine, though individual instances were carefully investigated. Abuse was neither widespread nor continuous enough to induce peasants to leave their villages *en masse*. Population pressure does not appear to have been a severe problem either; despite the growth of the sixteenth century it was not enough to prompt large-scale migration. According to various estimates, the population in Palestine probably declined in the seventeenth and eighteenth centuries so that the totals in the mid-sixteenth and early nineteenth were roughly comparable.[16]

The Ottoman empire could not afford to have peasants mistreated overmuch, since all signs point to a chronic labor shortage; peasants were hard to replace, and they could not be abused to the point where they fled, or expired. This reality and imperial ideology reinforced each other, conspiring to promote a government policy which kept peasants in their villages and made it possible for them to return if they left. Even as later, peasant flight was interpreted as a sign of distress to be rectified.[17]

Pilfering, concealment, dissimulation, and fraud all conspired to attain the rather pedestrian goal of regular and secure subsistence. The reports of more blatant aggression might also be understood in this context, for we do not always have the full story of what prompted such attacks. Most often the incidents were reported by the officials who were their victims; it was not in their interest to disclose any personal wrongdoing which might have provoked the assault.

It is conceivable, too, that *sipahi*s, kadis or other provincial officials may have used these peasant complaints in order to harm their rivals. A petition to the kadi or to Istanbul might bring disciplinary action against someone, or even his removal and transfer. Alternatively, powerful patrons working behind the scenes may have been able in some cases to counter the effects of even the most true and damning petitions. ʿAli Bali, the *sipahi* in ʿInab, managed to retain his office despite the numerous protests against his behavior. In the eighteenth century, to cite another example, the Bedouin ruler of the Galilee, Ḍāhir al-ʿUmar, had well-placed friends in Istanbul who for a long time protected him in the face of repeated protests from the governors of Damascus.

Most of the cases brought before the kadi by local peasants were purely indigenous and self-interested appeals for help and relief from specific abuses committed against them by officials. No intent besides the obvious one was contained in their pleas. Yet on occasion the peasants tried to trick the kadis, or the sultan and his ministers, into declaring some false assertion to be true. The false petitions were filed to try to change tax status, but also to cover up abuse by other peasants and they emphasize the complex texture of relations in the countryside. The petitions to the kadi and sultan generally highlight the peasants' acceptance of procedural channels of protest to rectify oppressive conditions.

Although the Palestinian peasants were not great fans of the local Ottoman officials, there is no evidence in the mid-sixteenth century that they tried to expel them entirely. Above, we described the peasants' attitude of grudging acceptance towards the officials. The beatings and shootings inflicted by peasants were also part of a process of testing and establishing the limits of the authority of Ottoman officials. The severity of official reaction to such violent acts and the success of officials in punishing the perpetrators revealed the local capacities of the Ottoman administration. Examples of more virulent, widespread, and coordinated violence in later periods underscore just how moderate were the peasant actions of the mid-sixteenth century.[18] Yet even a wide-scale revolt such as that led by the *naqīb al-ashrāf* in 1703–5 was able to unify peasants and Bedouin with urban factors only in order to oust the *sancakbeyi.* This done, the coalition of forces rapidly dissolved and united peasant activism diminished.

There were no doubts about the overall strength of the Ottoman empire and no realistic aspiration to throw off Ottoman rule. In the time of Süleyman, would these peasants have questioned, not to mention challenged, the legitimacy of "His Eminence, the highest king, venerable emperor, guardian of the people, Sultan of the Greeks, the Arabs and the Persians, Sultan Suleyman son of Sultan Selim"?[19] Perhaps not; but they readily derided his local representatives. In April 1531, one Abu Bakr and his fellows in Bayt Jālā taunted the man compiling the survey register, saying: "if your sultan finds himself involved in a war with seven Franji rulers, and if he manages to win the war, then come to us; and your record is like the wind from the donkey."[20]

Peasants and the Empire

The Ottoman empire comprised a vast territory which stretched around the south shore of the Mediterranean, to Upper Egypt and Arabia, east to Iraq and Iran, north around the Black Sea, across Anatolia, into the Balkans and Greece. Only the fact of being subject to Ottoman rule gave the peasants living in all these lands a common tie; there was no such thing as an "Ottoman peasant." In the Balkans and Greece the peasants were mostly Orthodox Christians, who had been ruled by Byzantine, Hungarian, Frankish, German, or Slavic kings prior to the Ottomans. In Anatolia, the legacy was Muslim, Turkish, and Byzantine. The peasants of Syria and Egypt were Muslim and Christian, and had been ruled by Muslim Turks based in Egypt. Variations in climate, soil quality, rainfall, and crops added to these differences of political, cultural, and religious heritage.

Were there any commonalities among these many peasant populations? The kadi constituted one persistent shared feature among the subject populations over time and space. He was a key official in every town and province of the empire and his position as an arbiter between the peasants and the *sipahi*s should have been similar from one place to the next. Identical imperial orders were issued to kadis in all parts of the empire to prevent abuses and protect the taxpayers.[21] As around Jerusalem, peasants went or were brought to the local kadis in Anatolia, particularly when the villages were found in proximity to the kadi's seat.[22]

*Sipahi*s were certainly common figures where the *tımar* system was in effect, so that the basic relationship between this official and his subordinates, and the local peasantry may have characterized provincial administration generally. But by the end of the sixteenth century, the importance of the *sipahi*s was waning.

The *tımar* system itself typified provincial administration in many parts of the empire. Everywhere, customary practice helped fix the details of this administration. Rates of taxation depended at least partly on tradition and types of crops differed from place to place and with them the rhythm of the agricultural year and the nature of administrative control. The Ottomans did not initially impose any internal reorganization on the villages they conquered. As far as we know, for example, the *ra'īs al-fallāḥīn* was not a familiar institution in Anatolia or the Balkans in this early period, but a local Syrian phenomenon.

The *tımar* system did, however, impose certain common relationships on peasants and officials throughout the empire. It presupposed a close association and cooperation between the *sipahi* and the peasants of his *tımar*. A *sipahi* needed extensive knowledge of local agricultural practices and prospects to understand how to calculate his annual revenues. Yet the *sipahi*s were warriors, not farmers. And they certainly were not native to Palestine, or most other places to which they were posted. For such familiarity with local conditions, therefore, they relied on local people or other Ottoman officials who had been stationed for long periods in the region. These latter sometimes sub-leased the rights to collect revenues for the *sipahi*s, *sancakbeyi*s and even from the kadi, as *ex officio nazır* of some local pious foundations.

By the seventeenth century, local sub-leasing was a widespread phenomenon around Jerusalem, although perhaps more common in *vakıf* properties. The objective difficulties of revenue collection may have created similar situations around the empire. These local leases were different, however, from the tax-farming arrangements of imperial *iltizam*s which were gradually replacing the *tımar*s and which were so often cited as a cause of peasant oppression in later centuries.[23]

By the seventeenth century, however, the *sancak* of Jerusalem could be described as "a battlefield between several layers of ownership": the state; the military-governing elite; the local elite; and the cultivators.[24] The same was true in the sixteenth century, but the relative strengths of the contestants were different. The local elite played a minor role in the conflict. And the state and the cultivators, with the help of the kadi, seemed to be able to hold their own for the time being against the military-governing elite.

Palestinian peasants, therefore, shared many structural features of life common to peasants throughout the Ottoman empire: not only similar taxes, but even the *same* officials, same official language and decrees. At the same time, the *sancak* of Jerusalem was a unique focus of Muslim, Christian, and Jewish religious sentiment. Pilgrims arriving via Jaffa and Acco created or reinforced the links between religious communities around the Mediterranean. They also made Jerusalem an international city, a congeries of peoples, languages, and sects. The inland desert sea brought others to Jerusalem and acted as a counterweight to the pull of the Mediterranean. Locally at least, economic, familial, and military ties to the Bedouin and the *ḥajj* route to Mecca and Medina were as important as the maritime connections. These elements of the Jerusalem environment gave the region its specificity in the empire.

Local *fallāḥīn* presumably had far more contact with foreigners than peasants in most other places. This did not mean that a cosmopolitan atmosphere dominated the Jerusalem countryside – their observations on these foreigners would surely have been just as outlandish as the travelers' notes on the *fallāḥīn* they met – but only that these people may have been somewhat more worldly than their more isolated fellows. Peasants who came to Jerusalem crossed paths with many strangers. In villages like Bayt Laḥm or Bayt Jālā, Christian pilgrims must have been a regular curiosity; travelling Muslims also stopped at the many prophets' tombs found in local villages. The *fallāḥīn* belonged to several worlds, and yet local custom, climate, geography, agriculture, vernacular, and the uniqueness of Jerusalem as their urban centre gave their universe its own particular stamp.

Our traditional notion of the strong Ottoman central government has developed, at least in part, from examining so much of its history from the perspective of that center and sources originating from it.[25] Yet they distort our perception of state power. In order to assess that power realistically, we need to check the state's ability to enforce the norms and ideological aspirations it defined for itself. Unfortunately, we cannot accomplish this feat entirely, as even local reports in the *sijill*s do not recount the final resolution of conflicts, but only the adjudication. Nor are they an exhaustive chronicle of the encounters between peasants and local officials or a completely faithful rendering of the peasants' side.

However, the peasantry undoubtedly represented a limit to state power. The state possessed the means to coerce and control the peasants more thoroughly if it chose to devote all its resources to that goal. However, the Ottoman government had diverse objectives and priorities, making war abroad and keeping peace within the empire, disciplining officials, running the imperial bureaucracy, managing its cities, etc. Each of these constituted a limit on the energies available for the others. When we turn to the countryside, the gap between official expectations and actual agricultural revenues describes one limitation the peasants imposed on official power. Another is elucidated by the disparity between the intentions of ideology and the realities of rural administration. We have succeeded in identifying these gaps and some kinds of limitations they imposed on the state's ability to realize its goals. Yet we have not understood fully how extensive these limitations could be and therefore to what extent peasant behavior and attitudes regularly affected official actions. If expectations and realities ran on separate but parallel tracks, at what cost were they brought closer together and how did a widening gap contribute to the changing fortunes of the empire?

Palestinian peasants, like peasants in other times and places, were not a passive and abject undifferentiated agrarian mass. Variations in location, crops, taxation and religion affected their welfare and position within the villages. From year to year they might be struck by locusts, drought, Bedouins or abusive officials. For this reason, even prosperity was relative and temporary. While the general situation around Jerusalem in the mid-sixteenth century appears to have been reasonably stable and perhaps prosperous, peasant fortunes were always precarious. Peasants remained wary of anything which might compromise their subsistence and they disliked authority. They disliked officials and struck out at them when possible. But their actions were more often individual and selfish, not organized or coordinated.

Neither the suffering nor the actions of the peasants were heroic; they were routine. And they melded with the seasonally determined routines of plowing, planting, and harvesting, and with the officially imposed routines of tax collection. Together these routines shaped the rhythm of rural administration around mid-sixteenth-century Jerusalem.

Whether they filed petitions and complained or took matters into their own hands, the peasants seem to have been intent on enforcing the Ottoman taxation codes when officials violated them. Ideology may have been on their side, but reality generally conspired against them. On the other hand, they were not actually avid collaborators in the wider Ottoman imperial ambitions. Peasant interests were determined by an entirely separate schedule of concerns from those of the state. The two might intersect, but they were not congruent.

It is for this reason that the role of peasants in the history of large agrarian empires is being and should continue to be re-evaluated. Scott uses the metaphor of the submerged coral reef to describe the effects of the myriad individual acts which, like polyps, fuse unseen to sabotage or sink the ship of state.[26]

> Their individual acts..., in the end, make an utter shambles of the policies dreamed up by their would-be superiors in the capital. The state may respond in a variety of ways... Whatever the response, we must not miss the fact that the action of the peasantry has thus changed or narrowed the policy options available. It is in this fashion, and not through revolts, let alone legal political pressure, that the peasantry has classically made its political presence felt.[27]

One must stress that these political actions were those of individuals, especially in the cases discussed here. Even in the compromise between the peasants and Ottoman government which Inalcik says was basic to the nature of the empire, peasant support was tacit. Neither support nor protest were organized among the peasantry. In practice, then, each negotiated relationship between a peasant and an official was part of the broader compromise.

Although individual peasants may be visible only briefly – in a single petition or claim – one cannot forget that they were all individuals. And their separate actions added up to shape the empire which seemingly controlled them.

Appendix 1: The Villages

Computers and the *tapu*

A computer was used in order to handle the large quantities of data available on villages from the survey registers. A sample of the computer records made for each of the villages in the *sancak* is presented here. The charts give the information for some of the villages which are discussed in the text.[1]

Referring to the charts below: in the left-hand column, the possible categories relating to population, production, taxation, and distribution of revenues are listed. Not every register contained information for every category for each village.[2] Across, the columns are labeled I, II, ..., from the earliest to the latest register. In this way, the original data are presented in one standard format for every village.[3] The charts are presented here to illustrate the nature of the data. Noting the systematic progression of figures and the consistency of many categories, we see how easy it is to ascribe a statistical value to the data which is basically lacking.

The data from the five surveys for all villages were also sorted by item. The sorted data, displayed by single item, highlight the distribution and quantity of individual categories of people or produce. The sort-charts for *imams* and olive oil are included after the village charts in Appendix 2.[4] They offer a graphic demonstration of the changes and trends discussed.

No statistical computations were attempted. The computer facilitates the handling of large amounts of data, and the results allow one to identify basic changes in recording practices, concentrations of populations and crops, and some general trends in the countryside. Some basic calculations, such as those done by Toledano and Makovsky on population and production figures can also be performed by the computer. However, the interpretation of these totals remains difficult, due to the problems regarding survey-making and the inconsistencies from register to register. To proceed from the computing of simple aggregates and percentages to any kind of complex statistical analysis produces quickly diminishing results due to the ever-multiplying margin of error. Therefore, I have exploited the capabilities of the computer only as described, and concentrated on surveys III and IV which appear most detailed and original.

Abū Dīs

Item	*I*	*II*	*III*	*IV*	*V*
households	28	45	112	102	80
bachelors	2	1	6	1	
imam	1	1			
total[5]	mak[6]	3500	6250	13750	14000
kısm		1/3	1/3	1/3	1/3
wheat[7]	2/600	2/960	10/4800	15/7200	15/7500
barley	7/1470	4/1040	5/1300	15/3900	15/4200
summer crops[8]		d 1500			
tax on trees[9]		(16/17/+)	2050 (17/+)	1700	
goats	50	150	160	n 453	n 500
bees			21		
tax on grapes[10]			a 150		
olive oil				m 100/600	100/600
bad-i hava			u 230	510	1/2 499
tithe	207	350	2084	4537	5000
sancakbeyi[11]		x	x	x	
tımar					x
vakıf	x	x	x	x	x

ʿAyn Kārim

Item	*I*	*II*	*III*	*IV*	*V*
households	10	28	39	38	39
bachelors		1		3	
imam		1			
total	mak 2500	mak 2500	3990	4950	5000
kısm			1/3	1/3	1/3
wheat			5/2400	5/2400	5/2500
barley			4/1040	4/1040	2/560
summer crops			46	a 500	a 940
tax on trees			+ 260		+ 450
goats		s 150	n 118	n 250	n 200
bees	83	200			
tax on grapes				460	
grape syrup			184	(20) 550	(20) 550
olive oil			m 10/60		
bad-i hava			1/2 90	1/2 100	100
zeʿamet					x
tımar		x	x	x	x
vakıf	x	x	x	x	x

Bittīr

Item	*I*	*II*	*III*	*IV*	*V*
households	9	13	53	38	22
bachelors		1		6	4
imam		1			
total	mak 3000	mak 2500	2331	4299	4900
kısm			1/3	1/3	1/3
wheat			1.5/720	3/1440	3/1500
barley			2/520	4/1040	5/1400
summer crops			824	d + 1000	d + 1100
goats		250	n 26	n 165	n 200
bees		100			
grape syrup			e 267	(17/20) 819	(17/20) 900
bad-i hava			1/2 100	225	103
tithe	300	500	774	1418	1500
ze'amet				x	
tımar		x	x		
vakıf	x	x	x	x	x

Bayt Jālā

Item	*I*	*II*	*III*	*IV*	*V*
households			? 36	2	6
Christians[12]	129	151/6	220/20	171/47	239
kısm	1/3	1/3	1/3	1/3	1/3
wheat	6/1800	8/3840	7.5/3200	15/7200	24/12000
barley	6/1250	8/2080	9/2340	8/2080	30/7400
tax on trees		(20) 500			
goats		500	n 200	n 400	n 2000
bees		200			
tax on grapes	500	250	(17/20)3074	(17/20)13400	(17/20/+)5600
tax on olives	500[13]	1000			
presses				1/80	1/80
bad-i hava		550	120	1100	920
cizye[14]	129@70	157@80	240@80	218@80	239@90
total	=7740	=12560	=19200	=17440	=21510
hass-i şahi[15]		x			
sancakbeyi			x		
tımar	x	x			
vakıf	x	x	x	x	x

Bayt Laḥm

Item	*I*	*II*	*III*	*IV*	*V*
households	39	46	152	106	
bachelors			10	1	
imam		1			
Christians	60	81/2	152/10	143/5	287
total		10190			
kısm	1/3	1/3	1/3	1/3	1/3
wheat	5/1500	12/5760	20/9600	25/12000	30/15000
barley	5/1050	12/3120	20/5200	20/5200	11/3080
goats		s 400	n 437	n 1300	n 1500
bees		360			
tax on grapes	1200	150	+ 3000	+ 11200	+ 15000
tax on olives	1200[16]				
bad-i hava		400	u 230	1280	420
cizye	61@70	83@80	164@80	149@80	287@80
sancakbeyi			x		x
tımar	x	x			
vakıf	x	x	x	x	x

'Inab

Item	*I*	*II*	*III*	*IV*	*V*
households	5	10	24	28	37
bachelors	2	1		6	
imam		1			
total		3240	3600	4880	5070
kısm	1/3	1/3	1/3	1/3	1/3
wheat	1/300	4/1920	4/1920	4/1930	4/2000
barley	1/210	2/520	1.5/390	2.5/650	5/1400
tax on trees			370	800	320
goats		10	n 30	n 52	n 272
bees		10			
grape syrup			m 10/20	m 150/300	75/150
olive oil	1/100[17]				
bad-i hava		1/2 20	1/2 85	1/2 100	
tithe	407	80	115	325	338
tımar	x	x	x	x	x
vakıf	x	x	x	x	x

		Rīḥā			
Item	*I*	*II*	*III*	*IV*	*V*
households	50	59	57	50	51
bachelors		7	6		
imam		1			
blind			1		
crippled			1		
total	mak 8000	12000			
kısm[18]					
wheat		15/7200	25/12000	25/12000	24/12000
barley		15/3900	25/6500	25/7500	36/10080
summer crops			e! 70	d + 13000	d + 13000
water buffalo		10	204	750	500
goats		s 10	n 30	n 50	n 920
durra (sorghum)		3/780			
olive oil				3000	3000
bad-i hava	300	100	196	250	500
sancakbeyi			x		x
ze'amet		x			
vakıf	x	x	x	x	x

Appendix 2: The Sort-charts

These charts include the sort-charts of *imams* and *zeyt* (olive oil). These were derived for all villages in the *sancak* of Jerusalem from the five survey registers. The table is divided into columns (I–V) representing the five survey registers, with the villages of the entire *sancak* of Jerusalem labelled 1–221 down each page on the left side.

Chart numbers for some villages discussed in the book

Abū Dīs (1)
ʿAyn Kārim (15)
Bittīr (58)
Bayt Laḥm (35)
Bayt Jālā (32)
ʿInab (88)

Item = Imam

Village	I	II	III	IV	V
1	1	1			
2					
3	1				
4		1			
5		1			
6		1			
7					
8					
9					
10		1			
11					
12		1			
13					
14					
15		1			
16					
17		1			
18					
19					
20		1			
21		1			
22					
23		1			
24		1			
25					
26					
27					

28		
29	1	
30	1	
31		
32		
33	1	
34		
35	1	
36		
37	1	
38	1	
39	1	
40		
41		
42		
43		
44	1	
45	1	1
46	1	
47		
48	1	
49		
50		
51		
52		
53	1	
54		
55		
56	1	
57	1	

Item = Imam

Village	I	II	III	IV	V
58		1			
59		1			
60		1			
61		1			
62					
63					
64					
65					
66		1			
67					
68		1			
69					
70					
71		1	1		
72					
73					
74					
75			1		
76					
77		1			
78					
79					
80		1			
81		1			
82					
83		1			
84		1			

85		
86		
87		1
88		1
89		1
90		1
91		
92		1
93		
94		1
95	1	1
96		
97		
98		1
99		
100		1
101		
102		
103		
104		
105		
106		
107		
108		
109		1
110		
111		
112	1	1
113		
114	1	1

Item = Imam

Village	I	II	III	IV	V
115		1			
116					
117					
118	1	1			
119		1			
120					
121		1			
122					
123					
124		1			
125					
126		1			
127		1			
128					
129					
130					
131					
132		1			
133		1			
134		1			
135		1			
136					
137		1			
138		1			
139					
140					
141		1			

142		
143		
144		
145		
146		
147		
148		
149		
150		1
151		
152		
153		
154		
155		
156		1
157		
158		
159		
160		
161		1
162	1	1
163		1
164		1
165		
166		
167		1
168		
169		1
170		1
171		1

Item = Imam

Village	I	II	III	IV	V
172					
173					
174					
175		1			
176					
177					
178					
179		1			
180					
181		1			
182					
183					
184					
185					
186		1			
187					
188					
189					
190		1			
191					
192		1			
193					
194		1			
195		1			
196		1			
197		1			

198	
199	
200	1
201	
202	1
203	1
204	
205	
206	
207	2
208	
209	1
210	
211	1
212	1
213	
214	1
215	1
216	1
217	
218	1
219	1
220	1
221	

Item = Zeyt

Village	I	II	III	IV	V
1				m 100/ 600	m 100/ 600
2					
3					
4	2400		m 950/ 5700	m 1200/ 7200	m 1200/ 7200
5			m 500/ 3000	m 500/ 3000	m 500/ 3000
6			m 370/ 2420	m 100/ 3600	m 100/ 3600
7			m 240/ 1440	m 200/ 1440	m 200/ 1440
8			m 5/ 30	m 20/ 120	m 20/ 120
9					
10	qt 20/ 4000		m 1250/ 7500	m 1500/ 9000	m 1500/ 9000
11			m 50/ 300	m 60/ 360	m 60/ 360
12					
13			m 250/ 1740	m 300/ 1800	m 300/ 1800
14					
15			m 10/ 60		
16	qt 5/ 528			m 300/ 1800	m 300/ 1800
17					
18			m 180/ 1080	m 200/ 1200	m 200/ 1200
19	45				
20	qt 3/ 900		m 300/ 1800	m 400/ 2400	m 400/ 2400
21					
22					
23					
24					
25					
26			m 8.5/ 50	m 40/ 240	m 40/ 240
27					

28	qt 3/ 600		m 51/ 126	m 220/ 1420	m 110/ 660
29					
30	qt 6/ 600		m 30/ 180	m 1500/ 9000	m 1500/ 9000
31			74	m 100/ 600	m 100/ 600
32					
33	110		m 20/ 120	m 600/ 3600	m 600/ 3600
34			m 30/ 180	m 50/ 300	m 50/ 300
35					
36			m 20/ 120	m 300/ 1800	m 300/ 1800
37			m 250/ 1500		
38			m 50/ 300		
39	qt 50/0000		m 3000/18000	m 3200/21000	m 3500/21000
40		qt 1/ 400	290	m 100/ 1200	m 100/ 1200
41					
42					
43					
44			m 5/ 30	m 50/ 300	m 50/ 300
45			900	m 200/ 1200	m 200/ 1200
46					
47			400		520
48	qt 2/ 400	1500	m 300/ 1800	m 400/ 2400	m 400/ 1200
49			95	100	100
50			m 130/ 780	m 150/ 900	m 150/ 900
51	qt 1/ 300				m 500/ 900
52					
53					
54					
55			262	200	200
56			m 300/ 1800	m 550/ 3300	m 550/ 3300
57			m 25/ 150	m 25/ 150	m 25/ 150

Item = Zeyt

Village	I	II	III	IV	V
58					
59					
60			m 5/ 300	m 50/ 300	m 50/ 300
61			m 2000/12000	m 3500/21000	m 3500/21000
62				m 100/ 1200	m 100/ 1200
63			610	m 200/ 1200	m 200/ 1200
64			m 100/ 600	m 150/ 900	m 150/ 900
65					
66	qt 5/ 1000		m 475/ 2850	m 500/ 3000	m 500/ 5000
67					
68					
69			m 5/ 30	m 250/ 1500	m 250/ 1500
70					
71			4713	m 1000/ 6000	m 1000/ 6000
72	qt 50/ 1000		m 1008/ 6048	m 3000/18000	m 3000/18000
73				m 120/ 720	m 60/ 360
74					
75			m 175/ 1050	m 300/ 1800	m 150/ 900
76					
77					
78			m 150/ 600	m 100/ 600	600
79					
80			m 283/ 1698	m 283/ 1698	m 283/ 1698
81			174	300	600
82					
83			m 167/ 1002	m 167/ 1002	m 167/ 1202

84					
85				m 60/ 360	m 100/ 200
86					
87			m 24/ 144	m 50/ 300	m 50/ 300
88	q.0.5 qt 1/100	qt 2/ 800	m 150/ 900	m 200/ 1200	m 200/ 1200
89			m 50/ 300	m 100/ 600	m 100/ 600
90	r 395		m 200/ 100	m 300/ 1800	m 300/ 1800
91					
92			m 15/ 128	m 50/ 300	m 50/ 300
93			m 10/ 60	m 110/ 660	m 110/ 660
94	qt 10/ 2000		m 550/ 3300	m 1000/ 6000	m 500/ 3000
95			m 130/ 660	m 500/ 3000	m 500/ 7000
96			m 100/ 600	m 340/ 2040	m 40/ 2040
97			m 50/ 300	m 150/ 900	m 150/ 900
98				m 50/ 300	m 50/ 300
99			m 3.5/ 60		
100	qt 28/8400		m 2000/12000	m 2600/18600	m 2600/18600
101					
102			m 181/ 1090	m 100/ 600	m 100/ 600
103			m 250/ 1500	m 400/ 2400	m 400/ 2400
104			m 30/ 180	m 200/ 1200	m 200/ 1200
105			m 250/ 1500	1200	1200
106					
107				m 50/ 300	m 50/ 300
108			m 200/ 1200	m 100/ 600	m 100/ 600
109			m 50/ 300	m 150/ 900	m 150/ 900
110			19 d 60	19 d 60	m 20/ 120
111			m 25/ 150	m 20/ 120	m 2/ 520
112			m 200/ 1200	m 150/ 900	
113			m 55/ 330	m 100/ 600	m 100/ 600

Item = Zeyt

Village	I	II	III	IV	V
114			m 50/ 300	m 25/ 1500	m 250/ 1500
115	qt 20/ 4000		m 1900/10800	m 3000/18000	m 3000/18000
116					
117			m 25/ 120	m 200/ 1200	m 200/ 1200
118					
119			m 10/ 60	m 50/ 300	m 50/ 300
120					
121			m 25/ 1500	m 250/ 1500	m 250/ 1500
122					
123					
124	qt 1/ 200		m 50/ 300	m 100/ 600	m 100/ 600
125				m 250/ 150	m 250/ 110
126	qt 1.5 / 300		m 20/ 120	m 50/ 300	m 50/ 300
127	qt 10.5/ 3000		m 1700/ 8400	m 3100/18600	m 3100/18600
128					
129					
130				m 100/ 600	m 100/ 600
131			m 20/ 120	200	200
132			m 22/ 132	m 200/ 1200	m 200/ 1200
133					
134					
135			m 15/ 90	m 50/ 300	m 50/ 300
136				m 50/ 300	m 50/ 500
137					
138				3000	3000
139			m 20/ 120	m 20/ 120	m 20/ 120
140				m 100/ 600	600
141			m 250/ 1500	m 200/ 1800	m 200/ 1800

142				
143		m 145/ 870	m 300/ 1800	m 300/ 1800
144				
145				
146	r 25/ 50			
147		m 6/ 48	m 50/ 300	m 50/ 300
148	3000	m 15/ 90	m 20/ 120	m 20/ 120
149				
150				
151				
152	r 3/ 60			
153		m 50/ 300	m 100/ 500	m 100/ 500
154				
155		m 5/ 30	m 80/ 480	m 80/ 480
156		m 400/ 2400	m 500/ 3000	m 500/ 3000
157		m 62.5/ 375	m 150/ 900	m 150/ 900
158				
159				
160		m 50/ 300	m 100/ 600	m 100/ 600
161		m 50/ 300	m 50/ 300	m 50/ 300
162				
163		m 12/ 72	m 20/ 120	m 20/ 120
164				
165		m 90/ 540	m 150/ 900	m 150/ 900
166		m 20/ 120	m 20/ 120	m 20/ 120
167				
168				
169				
170		m 15/ 94		
171				

Item = Zeyt

Village	I	II	III	IV	V
172					
173					
174					
175					
176					
177					
178			m 50/ 300	m 50/ 300	m 50/ 300
179					
180					
181					
182					
183					
184					
185					
186					
187					
188					
189					
190					
191					
192			m 80/ 480	m 100/ 600	m 100/ 600
193					
194					
195					
196			M 270	M 45/ 470	M 45/ 470
197			m 1200/ 7200	m 1200/ 7200	m 1200/ 7200

198			m 927/ 1060	1060	1500
199					
200	1580				
201					
202					
203	qt 5/ 1500				
204					
205					
206					
207	qt 6/ 1279		m 100/ 600	m 100/ 600	m 100/ 600
208					
209					
210					
211					
212					
213					
214	200				
215					
216	5/ 1500	qt 10/1000	m 350/ 2100	m 350/ 2100	m 350/ 2100
217			m 100/ 600	m 300/ 1800	m 300/ 1800
218					
219			250	1080	1000
220			m 100/ 600	m 180/ 1080	m 180/ 1080
221					

Appendix 3: Village leaders, notables, and elders

Abū Dīs

al-Asad b. Shu'ayb	*ra'īs*	960, 961, 963 964
Mūsā b. Mus'ad	*ra'īs*	960, 963, 964
	shaykh	962
	a'yān	963
'Abd al-'Azīz b. Ibrāhīm Basīṭa	*ra'īs*	960, 961, 963, 964
	a'yān	963
Khalīl b. 'Ulyān	*ra'īs*	960
	shaykh	960
Jibrān b. 'Alī al-Ba'jī	*ra'īs*	960, 963, 964
	shaykh	960, 962, 970
	a'yān	963
Khalīl b. Ḥaḍāra	*ra'īs*	960, 961
	shaykh	960
Sālim b. 'Uthmān	*ra'īs*	960
	shaykh	960
Majd b. Zayn	*ra'īs*	960
'Isā b. Mus'ad (brother of Mūsā)	*ra'īs*	960
Ghādir b. Sa'd Abū Hawsh	*ra'īs*	960
Ramaḍān b. Sa'd Abū Hawsh	*ra'īs*	961
	shaykh	969, 970
Kisya b. 'Abd al-Dā'im	*ra'īs*	961
Mūsā b. Abū 'Ulyān	*ra'īs*	961
	shaykh	962
Salim b. Jarrad	*shaykh*	962?
al-Asad Muḥammad b. Na'īb	*shaykh*	962
Salim b. al-Ba'ji	*shaykh*	962?
Muḥammad b. 'Alī b. al-Basīṭa	*ra'īs*	963
Ibrāhīm b. Khalīl b. 'Ulyān	*ra'īs*	963
Nimr b. Muḥammad b. Abū Dahīm	*ra'īs*	963, 964
	a'yān	963
	shaykh	970
Masīf b. Abū Dahīm Nāmir	*ra'īs*	964
	shaykh	970
Maḥārib b. al-Asad	*shaykh*	970

ʿAyn Kārim

Aḥmad al-Fahl		*ra'īs*	960, 963
Za'n b. Dibyān		*ra'īs*	960, 963
Muḥammad b. Khalīl al-Aʿma		*ra'īs*	960, 961, 963
Dibyān b. ʿAlī		*ra'īs*	961, 963, 969
Khaṭṭāb b. Ghānim		*ra'īs*	961
Aḥmad b. Dīb		*ra'īs*	963

Bayt Jālā

Ibrāhīm b. Budayr	C[1]	*ra'īs*	960, 968
		aʿyān	968
Khalīl b. Abū Zaʿīda	C	*ra'īs*	960, 968
		aʿyān	968
		akābir	968
Muhannā b. Ghanīm	C	*ra'īs*	960
Khalīl b. Rabīʿ al-Mukarbil	C	*ra'īs*	960, 962
Salāma b. Khamīs Sulaymān	C	*ra'īs*	960, 962, 963?, 968
		aʿyān	968
		akābir	968
Rabīʿ b. Ghanīm	C	*ra'īs*	962, 968
		aʿyān	968
		akābir	968
Ilyās al-Dabb b. Musallam	C	*ra'īs*	962
-Khalīl b. Ibrāhīm al-Qissis	C	*ra'īs*	962
Yūsuf b. Akhīṣar	C	*ra'īs*	962
Nāsif b. Mūsā	C	*ra'īs*	963
Zaytūn b. Buqʿatā	C	*ra'īs*	963
Naṣār b. Ibrāhīm	C	*ra'īs*	963
Jirjis b. ʿAṣfūr		*ra'īs*	968
		aʿyān	968
		akābir	968
Mūsā b. al-Fawwāl		*ra'īs*	968
		aʿyān	968
		akābir	968
-Yūsuf b. Mūsā Abū Maʿīṭa		*ra'īs*	968
		aʿyān	968
Yūsuf al-Mukarbil		*ra'īs*	968
		aʿyān	968
Niqūlā b. al-Qissis Sulaymān		*ra'īs*	968
		aʿyān	968
		akābir	968
al-Qissis Sulaymān b. Niqūlā		*ra'īs*	968
		aʿyān	968
-al-Qissis Khalīl b. Ibrahīm		*ra'īs*	968
		aʿyān	968
		akābir	968

Mubārak al-Rāshid		*ra'īs*	968
		a'yān	968
-Yūsuf b. Mu'īla		*akābir*	968
al-Khūrī Sulaymān		*akābir*	968
Mubārak		*akābir*	968
Khalīl b. Za'īm [Za'īda?]		*ra'īs*	962

Bayt Laḥm

Ḥasan b. Jāziya		*akābir*	960
'Ulyān b. Bardawīl		*akābir*	960
'Alī b. Ḥasan b. al-Ajrūd		*ra'īs*	960
		akābir	960
'Īsā b. Zurayq		*akābir*	960
Khalīl b. Ibrāhīm Baṣbūṣī		*akābir*	960
al-Naṣrānī		*ra'īs*	961, 962
		shaykh	962
Sālim b. 'Aṭāllah (and 2 brothers)		*akābir*	960
Mansur? b. 'Aṭallah?		*akābir*	960
Ḥusayn b. Aḥmad		*akābir*	960
		ra'īs	961
Sarūr b. al-Ḥawāsī		*akābir*	960
'Abd al-Qādir b. al-Ḥawāsī		*akābir*	960
Mūsā b. al-Faqīh		*akābir*	960
Ḥamdūn b. al-Faqīh		*akābir*	960
Hilāl b. al-Najjār		*akābir*	960
'Abd b. Ḥarīz		*ra'īs*	960
		akābir	960
Ni'ma b. Ḥarīz		*akābir*	960
		ra'īs	960
Khalīl al-Naṣrānī		*akābir*	960
Dū'aṣ b. Sam'ān		*ra'īs*	960
Manṣūr b. Abū 'Aṭāllah		*ra'īs*	960
'Īsā b. Sam'ān	C	*ra'īs*	960, 962, 963, 964
		shaykh	962
Tūba b. Aḥmad		*ra'īs*	960, 961
		akābir	965
Akaya b. Bardawil?		*shaykh*	961
Ḥusayn b. Khalīl b. al-Ahmark?		*shaykh*	961
		ra'īs	961
Aḥmad b. 'Alī b. al-Afra'	M	*shaykh*	961, 962
		ra'īs	962, 963, 964
		akābir	963
Muḥammad b. 'Ulyān	M	*shaykh*	961, 962
		ra'īs	962
Ma'ālī 'Ulyān b. Abū Ḥusayn	M	*ra'īs*	960, 962, 963, 964
		akābir	965
Diyāb b. Ḥasan b. Ḥāziya	M	*ra'īs*	962, 963
		shaykh	962

ʿAṭāllah b. Lābiq al-Naṣrānī	*ra'īs*	962
Yāsif b. Sulaymān C	*ra'īs*	963
Zaytūn b. Yaʿqūb C	*ra'īs*	963
Naṣār b. Ibrāhīm C	*ra'īs*	963
?ʿAṭāllah b. Adir? al-Naṣrānī	*ra'īs*	963
?Ibrahim b. Faraj al-Naṣrani	*ra'īs*	963
Naṣr b. Faza C	*ra'īs*	963
Taʿīr b. Baṣbūṣ al-Naṣrānī	*ra'īs*	964
ʿAlī b. Muḥammad	*akābir*	965
Mūsā b. Muḥmmad	*akābir*	965
Bittīr		
ʿAbd al-Laṭīf b. Muḥammad	*ra'īs*	961, 962, 964, 970
Aḥmad b. Yaʿqūbī al-Hatīmī	*ra'īs*	961, 962, 964, 970
	aʿyān	970
ʿĪsā b. Daqqa	*ra'īs*	961
ʿĪsā b. ʿAlī	*ra'īs*	962, 964, 970
	aʿyān	970
ʿAlī b. ʿAbd al-Qādir	*ra'īs*	969
	aʿyān	970
ʿAlī b. ʿĪsā Daqqa	*ra'īs*	969
	aʿyān	970
ʿAlī b. ʿĪsā	*ra'īs*	970
ʿInab		
Sālim b. Rashīd	*akābir*	961
Ḥammād b. Qaṭāmish	*akābir*	961
ʿUbayd b. Ibrāhīm	*akābir*	961
Muḥammad b. Qanjar/Qanbar	*akābir*	961
	ra'īs	965
ʿAṭa b. Muḥammad b. Bayār	*ra'īs*	965

Notes

Money, weights and measures

1 See A. Cohen and B. Lewis, *Population and Revenue in the Towns of Palestine in the Sixteenth Century* (Princeton, 1978), 43; A. Cohen, *Economic Life in Jerusalem* (Cambridge, U.K., 1989), 129–30; and the *sijill* entries: JS 27:1589/p. 311; JS 28:151/p. 50, 726/p. 211, and 967/p. 256.

2 For further discussions of money see: H. Sahillioğlu, "The role of international monetary and metal movements in Ottoman monetary history 1300–1750," in *Precious metals in the later medieval and early modern worlds*, ed. J.F. Richards (Durham, 1983), 269–304, which includes a description of different coins, how they changed and their relative worth; and by the same author writing in Arabic specifically on the Arab lands, H. Sahilī, "Al-nuqūd fī'l-bilād al-ʿarabiyya fī'l-ʿahd al-ʿuthmānī," *Majallat Kulliyyat al-Adāb* (Jordan) 2(1971):105–15. Also see B. Lewis, "Notes and Documents from the Turkish Archives," *Oriental Notes and Studies* (Jerusalem) 3(1953):22.
On money-of-account see: Cohen and Lewis, *Population and Revenue*, 43–4; and I. Beldiceanu-Steinherr and N. Beldiceanu, "Règlement ottoman concernant le recensement (première moitié du XVIe siècle)," *Südost-Forschungen* 37(1978):7.

3 See Lewis, "Notes and Documents," 17. For a comparative perspective: 1 Jerusalem *qinṭār* = 5.5 Cairo *qinṭār*, cited in Cohen, *Economic Life in Jerusalem*, 162, n. 59.

4 This equivalence is for Jerusalem and the immediate area. Stated in: JS 31:2134/p. 431, and numerous other documents. In the coastal town of Ramle 1 local *mudd* = 2 Jerusalem *mudd*, according to a document from a slightly later period, JS 107:531, dated 1033/1623.

5 B. Lewis, "Studies in the Ottoman Archives – I," *BSOAS*, 16(1954):489.

6 For extensive estimates of the present-day values of these weights and measures, see H. Inalcik, "Introduction to Ottoman Metrology," *Turcica* 15(1983):311–48, which has tremendous detail on Anatolia and the Balkans, but leaves the Arab lands largely untouched. Lewis' "Notes and Documents," 16–17 and the notes, and "Studies in the Ottoman Archives," 489–91 contain discussions of relative and absolute values for measures used in Syria in the Ottoman period. Older works, based on pre-Ottoman data include W. Hinz, *Islamische Masse und Gewichte* (Leiden, 1955), and Sauvaire's articles on metrology in the *Journal asiatique*, 7e et 8e séries.

1. Peasants, Palestine, and the Ottoman Empire

1 JS 30:1060/p. 294, dated 21 Ramaḍān 962/9 August 1555.
2 JS 30:7/p. 2, dated Muḥarram 962/24 November–25 December 1554.
3 JS 27:26/p. 6, dated 29 Rajab 960/11 July 1553.
4 H. Inalcik, *The Ottoman Empire: The Classical Age 1300–1600*, (1973, reprinted with new preface: New Rochelle, NY, 1989), xiv.
5 David Ayalon, "Discharges from service, banishments and imprisonments in Mamluk society," *Israel Oriental Studies* 2(1972):33–4.
6 Background on the area around Jerusalem under the Mamluks is taken from Y. Friedman, "Eretz-Yisrael ve-Yerushalayim erev ha-Kibush ha-Othmani," in *Perakim be-Toldot Yerushalayim: BeReshit ha-Tekufa ha-Othmanit*, ed. A. Cohen (Jerusalem, 1979), 7–38. Friedman reviews the sources for this period: Arabic chronicles, and the accounts of Christian and Jewish travelers.
7 M. Sharon, "The Political Role of the Bedouins in Palestine in the Sixteenth and Seventeenth Centuries," in *Studies on Palestine during the Ottoman Period*, ed. M. Maoz (Jerusalem, 1975), 13–16.
8 S. D. Goitein, "al-Ḳuds," *EI*[2], 5:333.
9 Friedman, "Eretz-Yisrael," *passim.*
10 For a more detailed history of the early Ottoman empire and the conquests, see H. Inalcik, *The Ottoman Empire*, and R. Mantran, ed., *Histoire de l'empire ottoman* (Paris, 1989). Pitcher's historical atlas provides a clear cartographic description of the rise and expansion of the Ottoman empire, see D. E. Pitcher, *An Historical Geography of the Ottoman Empire from earliest times to the end of the sixteenth century* (Leiden, 1972).
11 See H. Inalcik, "Ottoman Methods of Conquest," *Studia Islamica* 2(1954):103–29.
12 Adnan Bakhit, *The Ottoman Province of Damascus in the Sixteenth Century* (Beirut, 1982), 12–14.
13 I. Metin Kunt, *The Sultan's Servants: the Transformation of Ottoman Provincial Government, 1550–1650* (New York, 1983), 107 and Figure 5. The list published by Kunt couples Jerusalem and Gaza as one *sancak*, possibly because they were granted together to one man, Üveys Bey. Other documents from the same period, i.e. the *tapu tahrir defterleri* discussed below, clearly distinguish the two as separate *sancak*s.
14 On the Ottoman policy towards the *ḥajj*, see S. Faroqhi, *Herrscher über Mekka* (Munich, 1990).
15 Manna' says that although the Bedouin threat was not completely eliminated, in the first half of the sixteenth century he found no indication of large-scale Bedouin actions in the records of the Jerusalem kadi, which exist from the year 936/1529–30. In the latter part of the century, reports of Bedouin activities became more frequent. See A. Manna', "Moshlei Yerushalayim mi-Bayt Farrukh ve-Yakhaseihem im ha-Bedouim," in *Perakim be-Toldot Yerushalayim: BeReshit ha-Tekufa ha-Othmanit*, ed. A. Cohen (Jerusalem, 1979), 201.
16 Discussed in Antoine Abdel-Nour, *Introduction à l'histoire urbaine de la Syrie ottomane (XVIe–XVIIIe siècle)* (Beirut, 1982), 339.
17 Michael Winter, "Military connections between Egypt and Syria (including Palestine) in the Early Ottoman Period," in *Egypt and Palestine: A Millennium of*

Association (868–1948), eds. A. Cohen and G. Baer (Jerusalem, 1984), 142–3. Winter maintains that the superior Egyptian troops could acceptably substitute for the Syrian forces when they were away, but the Syrians were never sent to Egypt in a reciprocal capacity. The Syrian desert frontier was primarily a border between the settled zone and the lands traveled by the Bedouin.

18 Amnon Cohen gives an account of the wall restoration project in his comprehensive work on the fortification of Jerusalem under the Ottomans: "Mifalo shel Suleyman ha-Mefuar be-Yerushalayim," *Cathedra* 57(1990):31–51.

19 For a thorough discussion of this project, see O. Salama and I. Zilberman, "Aspakat ha-mayim li-Yerushalayim ba-meot ha-16 ve-ha-17," *Cathedra* 41(1986):91–106.

20 On the making of the Süleymanic image, see C. Fleischer, "The Lawgiver as Messiah," in *Soliman le Magnifique et son temps* ed. G. Veinstein (Paris, 1992), 159–77, and C. Imber, "Süleyman as Caliph of the Muslims," in *ibid.*, 179–84.

21 Imber, "Süleyman as Caliph," 183.

22 See the list of surveys at the beginning of Chapter Three, and Appendix Two, which shows the startling appearance and disappearance of persons in this category in the surveys.

23 See the discussion of Mamluk rule in Palestine by Y. Drori, "Rishum Shilton ha-Mamlukim be-Toldot ha-Aretz," in *Eretz-Israel ba-Tekufa ha-Mamlukit* ed. Y. Drori (Jerusalem, 1992), 3.

24 On the development of the Arab towns under Ottoman rule, see, A. Raymond, "The Ottoman conquest and the development of the great Arab towns," *International Journal of Turkish Studies 1(1979–80):84–101.*

25 On the local developments, see U. Heyd, *Ottoman Documents on Palestine 1552–1615* (Oxford, 1960), 117–18; A. Cohen and B. Lewis, *Population and Revenue in the Towns of Palestine in the Sixteenth Century* (Princeton, 1978), 26–7; Bakhit, *Ottoman Province of Damascus*, 105–7; Abdel-Nour, *Introduction à l'histoire urbaine*, xv; and Nawfān Al-Ḥumūd, *Al-Askar fī Bilād al-Shām fī al-Qarnayn al-sādis 'ashr wa'l-sābi' 'ashr al-mīlādīayn* (Beirut, 1981), 133. For an overview of the trends which disrupted and altered the Ottoman state in the later sixteenth century, see H. Inalcik, *The Ottoman Empire*, 41–52 and Mantran, *Histoire de l'empire ottoman*, 224–6.

26 Mustafa Naima, *Tarih-i Naima*, 3rd edn. (Constantinople, 1281–3/1864–6), 1:40–4, as translated in Lewis V. Thomas, *A Study of Naima*, ed. N. Itzkowitz (New York, 1972), 78. Thomas has used a narrow translation of *re'aya* as "peasantry" here. On the origins and development of this family of sayings concerning practical justice and utilitarian ethics, see J. Sadan, "A 'Closed-Circuit' Saying on Practical Justice," *JSAI* 10(1987):325–41.

27 Fernand Braudel, *The Mediterranean and the Mediterranean World in the Age of Philip II*, trans. Siân Reynolds (New York, 1976), 2:1241.

28 For example, the Rīmāwiyīn found in Gaza and Ramle who came from Bayt Rīmā, or the people of Bayt Jālā listed as residing in Jerusalem. All of these people were Christians. See Cohen and Lewis, *Population and Revenue*, 32. Faroqhi also says that "only migrants to towns and cities remained legally attached to their villages of origin regardless of the time that had elapsed." See S. Faroqhi, "The Peasants of Saideli in the Late Sixteenth Century," *Archivum Ottomanicum* 8(1983):223.

29 For one special case, see, H. Inalcik, "Rice cultivation and the Çeltükci-Re'âyâ system in the Ottoman Empire," *Turcica* 14(1982):83–5, 88–103.
30 For a longer discussion of *fallāḥ* vs. serf, see C. Cahen, "La communauté rurale dans le monde Musulman médiéval," *Recueils de la société Jean Bodin XLII: les communautés rurales*, IIIe partie "Asie et Islam," (Paris, 1982), 22–3.
31 The spectrum of positions on both sides of the debate has been thoroughly reviewed by Halil Berktay; his own point of view places the empire among the world's feudal systems. See H. Berktay, "The Feudalism Debate: The Turkish End – Is 'Tax-vs.-Rent' Necessarily the Product and Sign of a Modal Difference?" *Journal of Peasant Studies* 14(1987):292–301 and nn.1–14. A special issue of the *Journal of Peasant Studies* (18:3–4, 1991) edited by H. Berktay and S. Faroqhi, entitled "New Approaches to State and Peasant in Ottoman History," is largely devoted to discussions of feudalism and the Ottoman empire, from both historical and historiographical perspectives.
32 R. S. Humphreys says: "To comprehend the peasant's world, we need to comprehend the whole set of mutual relations...within which he acted on a regular predicatable basis. Here, an almost endless series of questions arises..." *Islamic History: A Framework for Inquiry*, 2nd ed. (Princeton, 1991), 289.
33 Wickham provides the most lucid discussion of the current debate about feudalism in his "The Uniqueness of the East," *Journal of Peasant Studies* 12(1985):168, and in his earlier "The Other Transition: From the Ancient World to Feudalism," *Past and Present* 103(1984):3–36.
34 Wickham takes the former position, while Berktay holds to the latter. Both specifically address the nature of rent and tax in the Ottoman empire. See C. Wickham, "The Uniqueness of the East," 170–1; H. Berktay, "The Feudalism Debate," 301 ff., and *idem* "The Search for the Peasant in Western and Turkish History/Historiography," *Journal of Peasant Studies* 18(1991):167, n.42. Others who see rent and tax as different aspects of the feudal mode are V. Mutafchieva, *Agrarian Relations in the Ottoman Empire in the 15th and 16th centuries* (New York, 1988), 25, 168–9, and J. Haldon, "The Ottoman State and the Question of State Autonomy: Comparative Perspectives," *Journal of Peasant Studies, 18(1991):50–1.*
35 Ze'evi (on seventeenth-century Palestine) and Cuno (on late eighteenth-century Egypt) both stress the complexities of landholding arrangements. Ze'evi refers to "layers of ownership", while Cuno finds "a hierarchy of shared rights or claims." See D. Ze'evi, "An Ottoman Century – The District of Jerusalem in the 1600s," (PhD. diss., Hebrew University of Jerusalem, 1991), Chapter Five, and K. Cuno, "The Origins of Private Ownership of Land in Egypt: A Reappraisal," *IJMES 12(1980):246.*
36 For a more thorough discussion of the history of peasant studies, see T. Shanin, "Short Historical Outline of Peasant Studies," in *Peasants and Peasant Societies*, ed. T. Shanin, 2nd edn. (New York, 1987), 467–75.
37 C. Cahen, "La communauté rurale," 9.
38 Humphreys, *Islamic History*, 284.
39 I refer here to peasant studies which treat subjects prior to the mid-nineteenth-century Tanzimat reforms instituted by the Ottomans. From roughly that time to the end of the Ottoman empire, the quantity and quality of documentation changes significantly. As a result of this, and for the reasons governing interest

suggested above, the amount and variety of published research on that period is far greater than for the earlier eras.

40 S. Faroqhi, "Agriculture and rural life in the Ottoman Empire (ca. 1500–1878): a report on scholarly literature published 1970–1985," *New Perspectives on Turkey* 1(1987):24. Notable exceptions, in addition to the extensive work of Halil Inalcik and the research of Faroqhi herself, are studies on Tunisian peasants, including the work of Valensi on the eighteenth and nineteenth century which uses literary sources and anthropological field work, and Cherif, who uses a literary source from the sixteenth century. See L. Valensi, *Fellahs tunisiens* (Paris, 1977) and M. Cherif, "Témoignage du 'Mufti' Qasim 'Azzum sur les rapports entre Turcs et autochtones dans la Tunisie de la fin du XVIe s.," *Les Cahiers de Tunisie* 20(1972):39–50. Further, Cuno's most recent study and the forthcoming work by Barkey are examples of the new and profitable researches on peasants in the Ottoman period. See Kenneth M. Cuno, *The Pasha's peasants: Land, society, and economy in Lower Egypt, 1740–1858* (Cambridge, U.K., 1992) and Karen Barkey, *Bandits and Bureaucrats: The Ottoman Route of State Centralization* (Ithaca, forthcoming, 1994).

41 Humphreys, *Islamic History*, 298. *Sharīʿa*-court records, or *sijill*, were the records of proceedings before the kadi. *Awqāf* registers contained the administrative records of pious foundations (s. *waqf*; Turkish *evkaf-vakıf*). Faroqhi, too, points to the kadi registers as an underutilized source for regional studies, see "Agricultural and Rural Life," 25.

42 For a description of *defter*s see Ö. L. Barkan, "daftar-i khâqânî," EI^2, II:81–3, *idem*, "Research on the Ottoman Fiscal Surveys," *Studies in the Economic History of the Middle East*, ed. M. A. Cook (Oxford, 1970), 163–71, and B. Lewis, "The Ottoman Archives as a Source for the History of the Arab Lands," *Journal of the Royal Asiatic Society* (1951):144–8.

43 Compare, for instance, the lists of taxes and fees in Cohen and Lewis' work on the towns with the village information transcribed in the articles by Lewis: "Nazareth in the Sixteenth Century," *Arabic and Islamic Studies in Honor of Hamilton A.R. Gibb* (Cambridge, MA, 1965), 416–23; "Jaffa in the 16th century, according to the Ottoman Tahrir registers," *Necati Lugal Armagani* (Ankara, 1968), 436–46; and "Acre in the Sixteenth Century," *Memorial O.L. Barkan* (Paris, 1980), 135–9. E. Toledano, "The *Sanjaq* of Jerusalem in the sixteenth century," *Archivum Ottomanicum* 9(1984):279–319 and A. Makovsky, "Sixteenth-Century agricultural production in the Liwâ of Jerusalem," *Archivum Ottomanicum* 9(1984):91–127 both focus on the countryside but are almost entirely based on the survey registers. See also R. Jennings, "The Population, Society and Economy of the Region of Erciyeş Dağı in the 16th Century," *Contributions à l'histoire économique et sociale de l'Empire ottoman* (Louvain, 1983), 149–250 and M. Svanidzé, "L'Economie rurale dans le vilâyet d'Akhaltzikhé (Çıldır) d'après le 'registre détailé' de 1595," *Contributions à l'histoire économique et sociale de l'Empire ottoman* (Louvain, 1983), 251–66.

44 S. Faroqhi, "Rural society in Anatolia and the Balkans during the 16th century, I," *Turcica* 9(1977):166.

45 For a more extensive critique of the combined use of *tapu tahrir defterleri* and *qāḍī sijillāt*, see A. Singer, "*Tapu Tahrir Defterleri* and *Kadı Sicilleri*: A happy marriage of sources," *Tārīḫ* 1(1990):113–25.

46 See H. Inalcik, "kânûn" and "kânûnnâme," *EI*[2], 4:558–66.

47 The continuity between Mamluk and Ottoman regimes in the Arab provinces has not been studied as explicitly as that between Byzantium and the Ottoman empire. However, some treatment of the subject may be found in B. Lewis, "Notes and Documents from the Turkish Archives," *Oriental Notes and Studies* 3(Jerusalem, 1953), 1–52; Cohen and Lewis, *Population and Revenue*; and Bakhit, *The Ottoman Province of Damascus*.

48 See B. Lewis, "The Ottoman Archives as a Source," "Notes and Documents from the Turkish Archives," and "Studies in the Ottoman Archives – I," *BSOAS* 16(1954):469–501, and the more synthetic "Ottoman land tenure and taxation in Syria," *Studia Islamica* 50(1979):109–34; M.A. Bakhit continued specific work on the province of Damascus, based in part on the survey registers, in his *Ottoman Province of Damascus*; W. D. Hütteroth and K. Abdulfattah, *Historical Geography of Palestine, Transjordan and Southern Syria* (Erlangen, 1977); M. İpşirli and M. al-Tamīmī concentrated solely on the *vakıf* registers in *The Muslim Pious Foundations and Real Estates in Palestine* (Istanbul, 1982).

49 See Cohen and Lewis, *Population and Revenue*; Toledano, "The *Sanjaq* of Jerusalem"; Makovsky, "Sixteenth-Century Agricultural Production"; and D.S. Powers, "Revenues of Public *waqf*s," *Archivum Ottomanicum* 9(1984):163–202.

50 When this project began, the authoritative guide to these archives was A. Çetin, *Başbakanlık Arşivi Kılavuzu* (Istanbul, 1979). Most recently, an expanded and updated volume has been published, incorporating the new catalogues which are being prepared in the ongoing project supported by the Turkish government, *Başbakanlık Osmanlı Arşivi Rehberi*, T.C. Başbakanlık Devlet Arşivi Genel Müdürlüğü. Osmanlı Arşivi Daire Başkanlığı Yayın Nu:5 (Ankara, 1992).

51 I would like to thank Bernard Lewis for also making available to me his collection of photocopies of these registers.

52 On the dating of these registers see Singer, "*Tapu Tahrir Defterleri* and *Kadı Sicilleri*, 115–19.

53 For a full description of the volumes of the Jerusalem *sijill*s see J. Mandaville, "The Jerusalem Sharīʿa court Records," in *Studies on Palestine during the Ottoman Period*, ed. M. Ma'oz (Jerusalem, 1975):517–24 and "The Ottoman Court Records of Syria and Jordan," *JAOS* 86(1966):311–19; A. Cohen, *Yehude Yerushalayim ba-me'ah ha-16 [Ottoman Documents on the Jewish community of Jerusalem]* (Jerusalem, 1976), 9–13; B. Doumani, "Palestinian Islamic Court Records: a source for socioeconomic history," *MESA Bulletin* 19(1985):161–4; and A. Mannaʿ, "The *Sijill* as a Source for the Study of Palestine," *Palestine in the Late Ottoman Period*, ed. D. Kushner (Jerusalem, 1986), 351–62.

54 Inalcik, *The Ottoman Empire*, 104.

55 J. A. Reilly discusses this point in his analysis of the problems of using the registers as sources. See "Sharīʿa Court Registers and Land Tenure around nineteenth-century Damascus," *MESA Bulletin* 21(1987):164–5.

56 Galal El-Nahal, *The Judicial Administration of Ottoman Egypt in the 17th Century* (Minneapolis, 1979), 11.

57 Doumani's example of Bayt Jālā in the mid-eighteenth century is thus appropriate, but his more general conclusion implies that verification of payment is possible in most situations. This seems overly optimistic, as does the expectation that one can consistently verify the execution of imperial orders to the provinces.

If an order was sent only to the *sancakbeyi*, then it did not necessarily come before the kadi at all. See Doumani, "Palestinian Islamic Court Records," 171–2.

58 Surviving *sijill* volumes from Hebron date from 1283–4 A.H. (1867 C.E.) It is more likely that earlier volumes were lost, destroyed or are currently unknown, than that the Hebron court was established and began recording in this particular year. The catalogue of Hebron *sijills*, as well as other extant volumes for the *Bilād al-Shām* can be found in M. A. Bakhit, *Kashshāf iḥṣā'ī zamanī li-sijillāt al-maḥākim al-shar'iyya wa'l-awqāf al-islāmiyya fī Bilād al-Shām* (Amman, 1984), 89–101.

59 The *ahkâm defterleri* are found in the separate *Maliyeden Müdevver Defterleri* classification of the Başbakanlık Arşivi, and the rubric "*ahkâm*" serves as title to a wide variety of documents within the classification. Some of the registers however, are virtually identical in content though not in form to the *mühimme*. (They are long and narrow as opposed to the latter which are wider.) For the complete listing of *mühimme* volumes, see Çetin, *Başbakanlık Arşivi Kılavuzu*, 49–57. The cataloguing of the *Maliyeden Müdevver Defterleri* series is described on pp. 28–35.

60 For a detailed explication of the *mühimme defterleri* see Heyd, *Ottoman Documents on Palestine*, xv–xvii, 1–6. Heyd describes the diplomatics of the *fermans*, their compilation and dispatch, in the introductory chapters of his work. Translations and annotations of a selection of *fermans* are then presented. The first facsimiles and translations of *mühimme* were done by G. Elezovic, in *Turski Spomenici* (Beograd, 1952) and Lewis, in "Notes and Documents," V.

61 Berktay, "The Search for the Peasant," 133.

2. Aspects of authority

1 The opening page of TTD 289 summarizes this information; it shows two *za'ims*, six *tımarcı ba-tezkere*, and forty-eight *tımarcı bila-tezkere*. The *za'ims* were higher-ranking officers with holdings between 20,000–100,000 *akçe*; a *tımar* holder *ba-tezkere*, with an imperial certificate, had an income of over 6,000 *akçe* per year; a *tımar* holder *bila-tezkere*, without an imperial certificate, received under 6,000 *akçe*. See Lewis, "Studies in the Ottoman Archives," 480–1.

2 Cohen, *Economic life in Ottoman Jerusalem*, 37–8. A document from 974/1566 lists thirty-seven *müstahfizān* (garrison soldiers) and twenty-two *müteferrika* (soldiers from a separate corps) in the Jerusalem citadel, and thirty *müstahfizān* in Hebron, cited in Bakhit, *Ottoman Province of Damascus*, 98. Bakhit gives a detailed account of the fortresses and garrisons in Syria. On the *müteferrika* see Kunt, *The Sultan's Servants*, 39–40.

3 See Cohen and Lewis, *Population and Revenue*, for the list of revenues from the city of Jerusalem (95–104) and the town of Hebron (112–16), which shows large portions of urban-generated revenues reserved for these *vakıfs*. The *icmal* (summary) register which corresponds to the third survey, and shows gross changes in production divided according to revenue recipient, lists 50% of the grains and 77% of the olive oil collected from agricultural revenues as belonging to the *vakıfs*. It is unclear from the text, however, if this refers only to these large *vakıfs* or to all *vakıfs* in the province. See TKM 283/p. 4.

4 See Powers, "Revenues of Public *waqfs*," *passim*, for a list of public *vakıfs* in

Jerusalem. This does not include the *vakıfs* for Mecca and Medina, the Dome of the Rock, al-Aqṣā, the imperial *'imaret* or the foundations of Abraham in Hebron. On the water system, see Salama and Zilberman, "Aspakat ha-mayim."

5 This is a general picture of the *subaşıs*. The description of their tasks and authority varied somewhat over time, and from place to place. For more examples from around the Ottoman empire see: J. H. Kramers, "*Ṣu-bashi*," *EI*, 4:491-2; Inalcik, *The Ottoman Empire*, 108, 113, 117; Kunt, *The Sultan's Servants*, 13, 26; R. C. Jennings, "Kadi, Court and Legal Procedure in 17th-Century Ottoman Kayseri," *Studia Islamica* 48(1978):158, 165; G. Káldy-Nagy, "The First Centuries of the Ottoman Military Organization," *Acta Orientalia* 31(1977):160, n.47; H. Gerber, "*Sharia, Kanun*, and Custom in the Ottoman Law: the court records of 17th-century Bursa," *International Journal of Turkish Studies* 2(1981):142–3; and M. İlgürel, "Subaşılık Müessesesi," *Journal of Turkish Studies* 7(1983):*passim*.

6 No single list of these divisions was found in the *sijill*. Rather, they were identified from scattered references. The villages listed as dependencies of the town (*tawābi'ihā*) included: Abū Dīs, 'Azariyya, al-Ṭūr, Buqay'at al-Ḍān, Qulūnya, Qalandya, Jadīra, Rafāt, Bir Nabāla, Bayt Ḥanīna, 'Ayn Kārim, Bayt Fāsīn, Bayt Mizmīl, Bayt Ṣafāfā, Māliḥa, Umm Ṭūba, Ṣūr Bāhir, Bayt Sāḥūr, ['Ayn] Silwān, Dayr al-Shanna, and Dayr Abū Thawr (JS 26:18/p. 5). Banī Zayd referred to the group of villages in the northern area of the Jerusalem district. If Bayt Laḥm and Bayt Jālā were in fact wholly separate jurisdictions, it was perhaps due to their large size, and their Christian populations. Possibly the two were part of Bayt Natīf, on which see JS26:53/p. 12, and JS 28:1254/p. 483, which seems here to have included Bayt Zakariyya in this division. The *subaşı* for the *'imaret* villages was appointed sometime after the *'imaret* was set up, the final *vakfiye* having been dated 964/1557. The first reference to it is from that year, see JS 33:2800/p. 525.

7 JS 26:53/p. 12.

8 JS 28:364/p. 109 (961/1554) and JS 40:2401/p. 475 (968/1561).

9 JS 26:734/p. 154; JS 44:549/p. 916.

10 JS 35:933/p. 181. See the section on 'Ayn Kārim in Chapter Four for the details of this lease.

11 JS 26:442/p. 998.

12 JS 33:370/p. 79.

13 JS 43:2733/p. 485.

14 JS 40:2350/p. 465.

15 JS 30:140/p. 39.

16 D. Possot, *Le voyage de la Terre Sainte (1532)* (Paris, 1889), 161.

17 In Māliḥa: JS 40:1360/p. 283; in Bayt Ta'ammur: JS 28:807/p. 228.

18 On kadis and the Ottoman judicial system see: H. Inalcik and C. Findley, "Mahkama: The Ottoman Empire," EI^2, 6:3–5; Jennings, "Kadi, Court and Legal Procedure," *passim*; Gerber, "*Sharia, Kanun*, and Custom," 132–4; and Bakhit, *The Ottoman Province of Damascus*, 119–32.

19 For a description of the Ottoman religious hierarchy, and the ranks of kadis, see U. Heyd and E. Kuran, "'ilmiyye," EI^2, 3:1152–4; and R. Repp, *The Müfti of Istanbul* (London, 1986), 27–72.

20 Bakhit, *The Ottoman Province of Damascus*, 123.

21 JS 28:1003/p. 261: *...al-mawlā bi-qaḍā' al-Quds al-Sharīf wa-madīnat sayyidina Khalīl al-Raḥmān...wa-qal'at Bayt Jibrīn wa-tawābi'ihā...* Bayt Jibrīn was a

village located in the province of Gaza, along the route east to Hebron and Jerusalem. In the mid-sixteenth century, the Ottomans repaired the fortress there and manned it to increase security on the roads, which were subject to Bedouin attacks. On this, and the imperial orders relating to the rebuilding, see Heyd, *Ottoman Documents*, 115–16. On the special position of the Jerusalem kadi see Heyd, *Ottoman Documents*, 42.

22 See the list of fees in H. Inalcik, "Adâletnâmeler," *Belgeler* 2(1965):78 and in Bakhit's discussion, *The Ottoman Province of Damascus*, 125–7. A longer discussion of fees, in the context of the decline of the office of kadi, is found in U. Heyd, *Studies in Old Ottoman Criminal Law*, (Oxford, 1973), 212–15.

23 H. Inalcik, "Suleiman the Lawgiver and Ottoman Law," *Archivum Ottomanicum* 1(1969):135.

24 On this see the *ferman* in Heyd, *Ottoman Documents*, 55–6; H. Inalcik, "mahkama," 3; and Inalcik, "Adâletnâmeler," Document V.

25 Evliya Çelebi lists the officers (*ağalar*) he found under the kadi of Jerusalem when he visited in the mid-seventeenth century. These include a *muhzır başı*, police inspector, chief architect, engineer, steward, cashier, treasurer, *subaşı*, market inspector, *şehir kethüdası*, the head of the (cloth?) market, the guild *şeyh*s, and the *mütevelli*s of the 700 *vakıf*s in the city. (*Evliya Çelebi Seyahatnamesi* (Istanbul, 1935), 9:463. Jennings gives a detailed description of the court staff as it worked in Kayseri, also in the seventeenth century, in "Kadi, Court and Legal Procedure," 136–7.

26 On *vakıf* administration, and on the role of the *nazır* in particular, see J. R. Barnes, *An Introduction to Religious Foundations in the Ottoman Empire* (Leiden, 1987), s.v. "*nâzır*".

27 See Toledano, "The *Sanjaq* of Jerusalem," 281–6, and also Faroqhi, "Peasants of Saideli," 225–6 for more details on *mezra'a*s. The distinction between *mezra'a* and *kita-i arz* is one of size – the latter consistently were shown to yield smaller amounts of revenue, and one of settlement – *mezra'a*s might become villages and vice versa, but the smaller *kita*s never acquired a permanent population.

28 Toledano, "The *Sanjaq* of Jerusalem," 314. Forty-nine Christian households from the villages of Bayt Laḥm and Bayt Jālā were also registered as living in Jerusalem itself at this time. See Cohen and Lewis, *Population and Revenue*, 86.

29 Toledano, "The *Sanjaq* of Jerusalem," 307–8. As discussed above, only adult males were recorded in the population lists. The taxpayers among them included heads of households and men over fifteen who were still bachelors (*mücerred*). Other persons listed were those exempt from taxes: religious persons and the infirm. See Cohen and Lewis, *Population and Revenue*, 14–16.
The debate over the size of the pre-modern household, in the Ottoman empire and elsewhere, is not closed. Initially, Barkan set a coefficient of 5 to be used with household figures in order to estimate total population, with the addition of ten percent of that total for the population not counted at all. See O. L. Barkan, "Essai sur les données statistiques des registres de recensements dans l'Empire ottoman aux XVe et XVIe siècles," *JESHO* 1(1958):21–3. Erder's work on pre-industrial population changes suggests that this method has a large margin of error. She suggests using an age pyramid instead, which gives the proportional relation of adult males to total population in stable societies. However, she specifically includes a proviso against using this method to estimate small popu-

lations such as a village, because of the possibility of special conditions. See R. L. Erder, "The measurement of preindustrial population changes," *Middle East Studies* 11(1975):296–9. Throughout this work, I will refer to figures for adult males only.

30 Toledano, "The *Sanjaq* of Jerusalem," 311.

31 A complete list of these is found in Toledano, "The *Sanjaq* of Jerusalem," 284–5.

32 Figures for the towns are taken from Cohen and Lewis, *Population and Revenue*, 94, 111; figures for the rural area from Toledano, "The *Sanjaq* of Jerusalem," 308. Cohen says that figures for the Jewish community in Jerusalem may be as much as twenty percent higher in actuality than the numbers recorded here, based on his researches in the Jerusalem *sijills*. See his *Jewish Life Under Islam* (Cambridge, MA, 1984), 34.

33 Cohen and Lewis, *Population and Revenue*, 94. This final survey is problematic, though it may still offer a sense of the direction of change, as well as the disparity between town and countryside. See Singer, "*Tapu Tahrir Defterleri* and *Kadı Sicilleri*," 102, n. 23 and 118–19.

34 See the discussion of this in Cohen and Lewis, *Population and Revenue*, 20–2.

35 See A. Singer, "The Countryside of Ramle in the sixteenth century," *JESHO* 33(1990), Table 2. Also D. H. K. Amiran, "The Pattern of settlement in Palestine," *Israel Exploration Journal* 3(1953):182. Amiran contrasts the stability of settlement in mountain towns to the fluctuations in towns along coast. In the mountains, 80% of the towns were continuously settled through history, as opposed to 39% for the plain. Amiran also indicates (p. 195) that rural settlement followed these trends but more so. If this was the case, then Ramle's countryside may be a more accurate barometer for the general rural situation, which showed some contraction already just after mid-century, whereas in the mountains, rural settlement remained stable, although it was no longer expanding.

36 On Palestine and the power of local Bedouin chiefs see Chapter Four: "Desert, Village and Town: A Unified Social Structure," in Dror Ze'evi, "An Ottoman Century" (Ph.D. diss., Hebrew University of Jerusalem, 1991).

37 Literally: "head of the peasants," or "head of the people of the village of ... "

38 JS 26:282/p. 62 and JS 27:379/p. 73.

39 JS 31:1563/p. 319, JS 28:1389/p. 354, and JS 31:2362/p. 489.

40 JS 30:390/p. 119; JS 33:1821/p. 338.

41 Although one finds many people called *shaykh* (the singular of *mashā'ikh*), *akābir* and *a'yān* are found only in this, their plural form. See L. Valensi, *Tunisian Peasants in the 18th and 19th centuries* (Cambridge, U.K., 1985), 51–6, where *akābir*, *a'yān*, and *shaykh* are key terms designating the locus of authority within the tribe. She stresses that these plurals designate collectives, groups representing power, and not individuals.

42 Note that the *sipahi* was sometimes said to possess the *takallum*, the "spokesmanship" of his *tımar* village. This seems to refer to his responsibility for and claim on the tax revenues of the village.

43 JS 31:2640/p. 539.

44 JS 31:132/p. 29. In the text the dual *ra'īsan* is used, although the syntax would indicate that all three *akābir* were also leaders. " ... *akābir fallāḥīn qaryat al-Aṭrūn wa-hum Ḥamīda b. Aḥmad wa-'Amīra b. 'Umar wa-'Umar b. Maṭar al-ra'īsan al-ān* ... "

45 JS 26:565/p. 124.
46 JS 40:1700/p. 349 and JS 30:1686/p. 463.
47 JS 27:470/p. 89 and JS 27:609/p. 119.
48 Khalīl b. Ibrahīm (961/1554): JS 28:833/p. 232 and 1231/p. 313. Bashīr b. ʿAbd al-ʿAzīz (968/1561): JS 40:1785/p. 364 and 1845/p. 373.
49 JS 33:2069/p. 386: ... *wa-ʿalā al-nāẓir al-qiyām bi-muṭlaqihim wa-khilaʿihim ʿalā jārī ʿādatihim al-qadīm* ...
50 See N. Stillman, "Khilʿa," *EI*², 5:6–7; F. Köprülü, "Hil'at," *İslam Ansiklopedisi*, 5/1:483–6.
51 JS 43:3047/p. 534: ... *fī naẓīr thaman khilaʿihim* ...
52 JS 27:640/p. 124; JS 30:415/p. 125.
53 TTD 289/p. 141, p. 157.
54 TTD 289/p. 125 and TTD 516/p. 43.
55 See Appendix 3 for the lists of *ru'asā*. These are probably incomplete, as they were collected from separate *sijill* entries; no comprehensive listing has been discovered.
56 Details concerning the *shaykh al-yahūd* and the organization of the Jewish community of Jerusalem in the sixteenth century come from the Jerusalem *sijill* as well, as analyzed and presented by Cohen, *Jewish Life under Islam*, 37–9, and *passim*.
57 One exception to this will be discussed below, an extraordinary case which involved the abusive behavior of a *ra'īs*, who was replaced by those who lodged the complaint against him. See below, at note 96.
58 Cohen, *Jewish Life under Islam*, 53.
59 See the sample list of villagers and titles given in Appendix 3.
60 See JS 31:573/p. 126, where the leaders of the Jews, the Christian monasteries, and the Syrian, Coptic, and Melkite Christians are listed, as well as the leader of the Christians of Bayt Laḥm. The Jews in Jerusalem are listed as one community. However, in Safad the survey registers show the community of Jews as being divided into numerous quarters, according to their origins: Portugal, Cordova, Castile, Italy, Germany, etc. (See Cohen and Lewis, *Population and Revenue*, 156–60.) It would be interesting to discover if each had a separate *shaykh*, but thus far there is no evidence for such a conclusion.
61 JS 25:538/p. 114 and JS 30:468/p. 138: ... *shaykh bilād Banī Zayd* ... ; JS 31: 2441/p. 505: ... *shaykh nāḥiyat Banī Zayd* ...
62 C. Cahen, "Notes sur l'histoire des croisades et de l'Orient Latin. II. Le régime rural syrien au temps de la domination franque," *Bulletin de la Faculté des Lettres de Strasbourg* 21(1951):304, 306–7. Cahen bases his information on Ibn Jubayr, in *Recueil des Historiens des Croisades, Historiens Orientaux*, III (Paris, 1884; Repr., 1967), 449.
63 Ibn Taymiyya, *Al-Siyāsa al-sharʿiyya fī islāḥ al-rāʿī wa'l-raʿīya* (Beirut, 1966), 3. My thanks to Michael Cook for this reference. For the definition of *dihqān* as possessor of land or other immovable property, see E.W. Lane, *Arabic–English Lexicon*, s.v.
64 Aḥmad b. ʿAbd al-Wahhāb Al-Nuwayrī, *Nihāyat al-arab fī funūn al-adab* (Cairo, 1923–42), 8:257–8. ... *wa-'lladhi yaʿtamiduhu mubāshir al-kharāj bi-bilād al-Shām annahu bi-ilzām ru'asā' al-bilād bi-taghlīq arāḍīhā bi'l-zirāʿat wa'l-kirāb* ...
65 For a listing of these see D. P. Little, *A Catalogue of the Islamic Documents from Al-haram aš-Sarīf in Jerusalem* (Beirut, 1984).

66 Cited in M. H. Burgoyne, *Mamluk Jerusalem: An Architectural Study* (London, 1987), 67. Burgoyne gives only the English "headman" which I assume is translated from *ra'īs*.
67 Little, *Catalogue*, 203.
68 Cohen and Lewis, *Population and Revenue*, 40.
69 JS 32/p. 195 (mid): *... ve her mahalle ve her karyenin papaslarin ve reislerin getürüb ...*
70 M 29/504, as cited by Heyd in *Ottoman Documents*, 92.
71 H. Gerber, *Social Origins of the Modern Middle East* (Boulder, 1987), 41.
72 JS 1:968/p. 240. My thanks to Jon Mandaville for this reference.
73 A. E. Vacalopoulos, *The Greek Nation, 1453–1669* (New Brunswick, 1976), 187–91.
74 My thanks to Dror Ze'evi of Tel Aviv University for sharing with me his findings regarding the seventeenth century.
75 A. K. Rafeq, "Economic Relations between Damascus and the Dependent Countryside, 1743–71," in *The Islamic Middle East, 700–1900*, ed. A. L. Udovitch (Princeton, 1981), 662–3.
76 On eighteenth-century Palestine, see A. Cohen, *Palestine in the 18th Century* (Jerusalem, 1973).
77 G. Baer, *Fellah and Townsman in the Middle East* (London, 1982), 109, 131–2.
78 JS 28:970/p. 257 and JS 28:1108/p. 287.
79 JS 31:1563/p. 319.
80 JS 33:2049/p. 381 and JS 33:2069/p. 386.
81 JS 27:1806/p. 355. "Master": Arabic *ustādh*, was used in the *sijill* documents to refer to the *tımar* holder, *vakıf* administrators, or other persons with a claim to the revenues of a village.
82 JS 28:1084/p. 281.
83 JS 31:1784/p. 362.
84 JS 28:1215/p. 309.
85 JS 27:860/p. 169.
86 JS 30:390/p. 119. (20 Jumādā II 962/12 May 1555)
87 TTD 289/p. 71 and TTD 516/p. 64.
88 JS 31:2177/p. 442: *... fī dhimmatihim wa-fī dhimmat jamā'atihim ahālī al-qarya al-mazbūra ...*
89 JS 33:872/p. 174 and 890/p. 183: ... *naẓīra mā khaṣṣahu min maḥṣūl zaytūnihi wa-zaytūn aqāribihi bi-'l-qarya* ... and ... *naẓīra mā khaṣṣahu 'an faṣl zaytūnihi wa-zaytūn ṭā'ifatihi* ... It is unclear whether the use of the word *ṭā'ifa* here means simply "group, community" or if it identifies a semi-settled or settled Bedouin tribal group.
90 JS 31:533/p. 118: *... mā 'alā ṭā'ifatihi min al-kharāj 'an 23 nafar tamaman ... Kharāj* is used interchangeably in the *sijill* with *cizye* to refer to the head-tax on non-Muslims. It had a wider meaning however, being used to mean the tax on trees which was not the *kısm*.
91 JS 31:537/p. 118.
92 TTD 516/p. 55, p. 65.
93 JS 31:537/p. 118: *... ba'da al-taftīsh ... fa-lam yahar 'alayhim wa-lā 'indahum azyad min dhālika ...*
94 JS 33:915/p. 188.
95 JS 31:132/p. 29. The village of al-Aṭrūn (Latrun) was in the *nahiye* of Ramle, to

the west of Jerusalem in the coastal plain. Al-Aṭrūn lay farther west along the same road from Jerusalem as ʿInab, at the point where it emerged from the hills into the plain.

96 JS 31:2362/p. 489.
97 JS 40:1657/p. 342.
98 See Cohen, *Jewish Life under Islam*, 37.
99 For a brief description of the Islamic law of *kafāla* see J. Schacht, *An Introduction to Islamic Law* (Oxford, 1964), 158–9.
100 JS 30:1179/p. 328.
101 JS 30:1203/p. 334.
102 JS 30:1333/p. 371.
103 JS 40:2276/p. 451.
104 JS 28:1656/p. 414.
105 JS 28:1239/p. 479.
106 ʿInab – JS 27:1324/p. 263: ... *wa-taḍāmanū wa-takāfalū fī al-ʿimāra wa'l-iqāma bi-qaryatihim wa-ʿadam al-fasād wa'l-shanāʿa biha wa-fī'stiḥqāq ustādhihim* ...
107 In this document they are called *mashāikh* (JS 30:1333/p. 371); elsewhere in the same year four of the five men named can be identified as leaders. The fifth was a leader in the preceding year.
108 JS 30:1333/p. 371: ... *innahum taḍāmanū wa-takāfalū kull minhum kafl al-ākhar fī al-iqāma wa'l-ʿimāra wa'l-ḥaḍāra bi'l-nāḥiya al-mazbūra aʿlāhu ʿalā annahu kull man ghāba minhum wa-ṭuliba min al-ākhar yaḥḍirahu lahu wa-matā ṭuliba minhum aḥḍarūhu jamīʿuhum aw wāḥid minhum* ...
109 JS 31:649/p. 145. Another such guarantee was provided for this village several years later, for which see JS 39:2487/p. 526; and for the village of Bīr Zayt, JS 40: 148/p. 27.
110 JS 39:2487/p. 526 and JS 40:148/p. 27.
111 JS 27:1565/p. 306.
112 JS 26:673/p. 143. For similar cases see: JS 27:2522/p. 504; JS 31:193/p. 42, 1129/p. 236.

3. The rules of local administration

1 JS 29/pp.148–149. Evasıt Şevval 962 (28 August–6 September 1555).
2 As discussed in Chapter One, the *defter*s referred to are:

I	TTD	427	924–5/518–19
II	TTD	1015	937/1531
III	TTD	289	952/1545
IV	TTD	516	967/1560
V	TTD	515	1004/1595–6.

3 A collection of *kanunname*s, mostly concerning rural organization and taxation, from all parts of the Ottoman empire was published from the *tapu tahrir defterleri* by Ö. L. Barkan, *XV ve XVI ıncı asırlarda Osmanlı imperatorluğunda zirai ekonominin hukuki ve mali esasları. Kanunlar* (Istanbul, 1943). R. Mantran and J. Sauvaget, *Règlements fiscaux ottomans: les provinces syriennes* (Beirut, 1951) is a translation of selected *kanunname*s from the Syrian provinces, some of which are not in Barkan's *Kanunlar*. H. Lowry has recently published a comprehensive listing of *kanunname*s from the *Başbakanlık Arşivi* in "The Ottoman Liva Kanun-

names," *Osmanlı Araştırmaları* 2(1981):43–74. In addition, see Inalcik, "Suleiman the Lawgiver," 112–14, for a detailed description of the process of compilation.

4 See JS 34:p.75 copied in 956/1549; JS 29:p.39(a) dated 960/1552–3; JS 29:p.148–9 dated 962/1554–5; and JS 29:p.181 dated 963/1555–6.

5 H. Inalcik, "Islamization of Ottoman Laws on Land and Land Tax," in *Festgabe an Josef Matuz. Osmanistik-Turkologie Diplomatik*, ed. C. Fragner and K. Schwarz (Berlin, 1992), 101.

6 Inalcik, "Islamization of Ottoman Laws," 103–4.

7 Barkan, *Kanunlar*, 220–7.

8 M. L. Venzke, "Special use of the tithe as a revenue-raising measure in the 16th-century sanjaq of Aleppo," *JESHO* 29(1986):239.

9 See S. Shaw, "The Land law of Ottoman Egypt (960–1553)," *Der Islam* 38(1962):114.

10 *Çift* was a technical term used for the amount of land which could be plowed by a pair of oxen in one day. It was used as a measure of land throughout Anatolia and the Balkans. It does not appear in the Jerusalem surveys at all, but I found one occurrence in the *sijill*. ʿAlī b. ʿAbd al-Nūr of Kharabtā in the sub-district of Ramle left his village and his lands uncultivated, having moved to another village for the years 967 and 968. He was asked for the *rasm al-çift* which was due at 5 *sikke* for each year (JS 40:2875/p. 555). The normal *çift resmi* found in Anatolia or the Balkans was 22 *akçe* (H. Inalcik, "Osmanlılarda Raiyyet Rüsûmu," *Belleten* 23(1954):581 and H. Bowen, "akce," *EI*[2], 1:317–18.). Five *sikke*, gold coins equal to *sultani*, was an enormous sum. Most likely, this was the fine called *çift bozan resmi* which was levied as a penalty on the peasant for having left his lands uncultivated.

11 *Kısm*: the percentage at which grains, and sometimes other crops, were taxed in a village. *Haraç*, in contrast, was a fixed money tax per unit. This should not be confused with the more general use of the term *haraç* (Ar. *kharāj*), which includes more than one form of land tax. On *haraç*, and its development during the Ottoman period, see B. Lewis, "Ottoman Land Tenure and Taxation in Syria," *Studia Islamica* 50(1979):116, 119; and B. Johansen, *The Islamic Law on Land Tax and Rent* (London, 1988), 98–103 and *passim*.

12 *Rumani* and *islami* designated different rates of taxation for olives. The former was set as a percentage of the crop; the latter as a fixed rate in cash. In hard times, the percentage was an easier burden to bear but when the harvest was plentiful, the set cash levy was to the advantage of the peasants. For more on *rumani*/*islami* see Lewis, "Notes and Documents," 41, n. 38; Cohen and Lewis, *Population and Revenue*, 151, n. 20; and Mantran and Sauvaget, *Règlements fiscaux*, 6, n.4.

13 The *sahib-i arz* was the possessor of the land i.e. the person with a legitimate claim to the revenues of a given area of land.

14 This is explained further by the text of the Damascus *kanunname* (TKM 521/195, p. 2, 1005 A.H., and Barkan, *Kanunlar*, p. 221 #6): "the tithe of some *mezraas* which are not *dimos* [*maktu*] is recorded as 'from all the produce' [and] is grains. But the tithe of the *haraç* is taken 'from the money of the vakıf,' because it means the tithe was from the *haraç*... For this reason, most of the Syrian lands are *haraç*." Mantran and Sauvaget discuss this clause and find it too elliptical to be thoroughly explicable (Mantran-Sauvaget, p.7, #6, n.1). I would suggest it implies

that a large portion of the Syrian lands were *vakıf*, as reflected by the prevalence of *haraç* taxation, if the two can be understood as directly and consistently linked.

15 That is: these places be counted with grains and other items on whose *total* the tithe was taken before the *kısm* was assessed. Produce which paid *haraç* tax, not *kısm*, then paid tithe on the *haraç*, and not "from all the produce."

16 Twice the rate recorded for *islami* olive trees.

17 The problem is that there is no indication in the registers distinguishing one sort of place from the other. When added to the fact that olive trees and/or olive oil were recorded in the surveys along with two or three other items in one of the collective categories, it becomes virtually impossible to sort out how much of anything is being recorded. Perhaps this is the reason for such variation in recording styles of these different crops. And, it was perhaps due to the growing importance of olive oil that it was recorded separately and distinctly from the third survey on.
The Damascus *kanunname* gives a further look at the subtleties of assessing land status (TKM 521/195, p. 2; Barkan, *Kanunlar*, 221 #7-8):
"Some lands were [planted with] trees, but were sown. From places with trees *haraç* is taken, and from sown places [among the trees] *haraç* is taken. And from sown places *kısm* is taken. And the *erbab-i tımar* take tithe from the grains which were entirely sown [i.e. not among the trees];
In some places they do not sow grains, but vegetables. In such places, from every *feddan* ten *akçe* are taken; in their terms called '*hukuk*.'
In this *vilayet*, in places which are '*sultani*' in some villages, there are vineyards and gardens from which a quantity of *haraç* was assigned; afterwards the young shoots of the vineyards and the trees of the gardens [orchards] died, and their places were sown; [now] if they intend to pay the *haraç* which was assigned first, saying 'this is our *mülk*,' they may not proceed thus; the *kısm* of the villages, no matter how it is (?), according to the *kanun* it is the custom that *kısm* be taken."

18 Mecca and Medina.

19 The full text of the *kanunnames* is found in TTD 516 and TTD 515.

20 Makovsky, "Agricultural Production," 101–3, gives the complete breakdown of *kısm* rates for villages in the province of Jerusalem.

21 This becomes more complicated when we look at the assessment of tithes below. The only detailed explanation of various *kısm* rates specifically for Bilād al-Shām is found in Nuwayrī (d.1332). He says *kısm* was assessed at one-half for rain-watered crops, one-third or one-fourth for most lands, one-fifth or one-sixth for *mezra'a*s which were cultivated by renters, and one-seventh or one-eighth for coastal or border lands. There were no villages taxed at one-half in this area. This fact is the most telling indication of how dependent the peasants here were on the capricious winter rains and irrigation to get through every agricultural cycle. See Al-Nuwayrī, *Niḥāyat al-arab*, 8:258–9. Lewis, "Notes and Documents," 16, and Makovsky "Agricultural Production," 102, also discuss this.

22 TTD 427 and 1015, no mention; TTD 289/p. 226; TTD 516/p. 83; TTD 515/p. 95; Makovsky, "Agricultural Production," 102.

23 Makovsky, "Agricultural Production," 114.

24 Cohen, *Economic Life in Ottoman Jerusalem*, 74–5.

25 Cohen, *Economic Life in Ottoman Jerusalem*, 35–7.

26 Rīḥā (Jericho), ʿAwja, and Nuwayʿima.
27 Jerusalem *kanunname*, TTD 516: ... *ve külliyen Haremeyn ül-Şerifeyn ve Kuds-i Şerif ve Halilürrahman...hazretlerinin evkafi avariz-i divaniye ve tekalif-i örfiyeden ve öşürden defter-i atikde muaf ve müsellem kayd olunmağin defter-i cedid'de dahi kemakan muaf ve müsellem kayd olundu.*
28 This *vakıf*, or part of it, is often referred to as *simāṭ al-Khalīl*, lit. "the food table of Abraham," because it included a large soup kitchen. See Mujīr al-Dīn al-Ḥanbalī, *Al-Uns al-jalīl bi-ta'rīkh al-Quds wa'l-Khalīl* (Amman, 1973), 2:98; H. Sauvaire, *Histoire de Jérusalem et Hébron* (Paris, 1876), 257, n. 1; and Cohen and Lewis, *Population and Revenue*, 73.
29 On the tombs of Moses, Jonah, and Lot, see U. Heyd, *Ottoman Documents*, 76, 155, 158 and T. Canaan, *Mohammedan Saints and Sanctuaries in Palestine* (London, 1927), 194, 292, 294.
30 That is, recorded as producing substantial revenues.
31 The village ʿAzariyya is sometimes written ʿAyzariyya. This is the village which was known as Bethany.
32 See Powers, "Revenues of Public *waqfs*," 163.
33 *Kırat* (Arabic: *qirāṭ*) is a share equal to 1/24 part of anything being counted. The revenue due (*hasıl*) from a village is divided into *kırat*, as were pieces of land or trees.
34 TTD 289/p. 55: "*el-ʿöşr ʿan cümlet-i mütehassıl gayri ez hisse-i Sahra ül-Şerife.*"
35 This systematic notation of tithe assessment appeared more frequently in the third survey register and afterwards.
36 The intention here is tithe-paying *vakıfs*.
37 TTD 289/p. 149; TTD 516/p. 50.
38 Abū Dīs: TTD 1015/p. 214; ʿAyn Kārim: TTD 1015/p. 242. And see Appendix 1.
39 TTD 289/p. 82. All figures appear in the *defter* except the "total value produced" which I have calculated in this and the two following examples by simply multiplying the *hasıl* by the *kısm*.
40 TTD 289/p. 135.
41 TTD 289/p. 55.
42 To calculate the percentage of total value of village production taken in *kısm* and tithe, where x = total revenues, *kısm* = 1/3, and the tithe = 1/10: (a) When the tithe was "from the money of the *vakıf*," the tithe was (1/10) × (x/3); since the tithe came from the *kısm* share, the total taken from the village was only x/3, or thirty-three percent. (b) When the tithe was "from all the revenues," it was figured as 1/10(x). The *kısm* was then (1/3)(x–x/10) and the total taken from the village (*kısm* plus tithe) 3x/30 + 9x/30 = 12x/30 or forty percent.
43 Examples of such instances are discussed more fully in Chapter Five: "Tax code complexities."
44 Venzke found similar changes in tithe assessments around Aleppo at the same time. She links these to an imperial attempt to extract more revenues from shrinking agricultural revenue receipts, caused by a decline in agricultural productivity. See Venzke, "Special Use of the Tithe," 239. Venzke's detailed work on tithes around Aleppo has only moderate bearing in this area due to (1) the difference in the agricultural situation noted above; and (2) the fact that in the *sancak* of Aleppo the tithe was being imposed where it had not previously existed (M. L. Venzke, "Aleppo's *Mâlikâne-Dîvânî* System," *JAOS* 106(1986):460), a fact

which she says gives the state a political presence where before it had been shut out (455). Such is not the case here.

45 For the details about the tithe regime and a discussion of the abuses against it, see Inalcik, "Adâletnâmeler," 72–5.

46 See below, Chapter Four, "Abū Dīs," for an example of this.

47 H. Gerber, "The Ottoman Administration of the Sanjaq of Jerusalem, 1890–1908," *Asian and African Studies* 12(1978):65.

48 See B. Lewis, "'arūs resmī," *EI*[2], 1:679.

49 See B. Lewis, "bād-i hawā,"*EI*[2], 1:850.

50 Cohen and Lewis, *Population and Revenue*, 102.

51 See Ö. L. Barkan, "avâriz," *İA*, 2:13 and H. Bowen, "'awāriḍ," *EI*[2], 1:760–1. Bowen notes there that the term *'avariz hane* was a "contribution unit" and not necessarily a single household. For a thorough discussion of the changing importance of the *'avariz* in Ottoman fiscal administration, see L. Darling, "The Ottoman Finance Department and the Assessment and Collection of the Cizye and Avariz Taxes, 1560–1660," (PhD. diss., University of Chicago, 1990), 156–77.

52 Heyd, *Ottoman Documents*, 71–2.

53 See, for example, the *cizye* records of Bayt Jālā and Bayt Laḥm in Appendix 1.

54 Barkan dates the sections of the Damascus *kanunname* referring to the increase to 977/1569–70, *Kanunlar*, 226. The *kanunnames* of Gaza and Nablus are from the survey of 1005/1596–7. On the *cizye* see C. Cahen and H. Inalcik, "djizya," *EI*[2], 2:559–66 and Cohen and Lewis, *Population and Revenue*, 70–2.

55 See "Agricultural Production," 115.

56 *Maktu'*, (Arabic: *maqtū'*), "cut" and *kısm* (Arabic: *qism*), "division" were the two means of taxing the total production of crops. In the first, a set sum was collected from the total yield; in the second a fixed proportion. For a detailed explanation of these terms, see Makovsky, "Agricultural Production," 98–100.
The above percentages were derived from Makovsky's figures, which were calculated in U.S. bushels "for the sake of intelligibility and convenience." In addition, Makovsky's figures were only estimates, because not all villages included both the tax assessed and the rate of assessment. Out of 173 villages for which information was recorded in the second survey, only forty-two listed separate figures for wheat and forty for barley. Beginning from the third survey, recording was far more uniform and complete; 167 villages out of 178 included these data (pp.109–11). Makovsky's calculations also omit the produce of the *mezra'as*. It would be virtually impossible to include the produce of these plots in the totals, because they almost never recorded a breakdown of crops, but only a single figure. Nor is there any basis on which to estimate what proportion of the total they represented. Therefore, one must be conscious of their absence in the computation.

57 TKM 283/p. 2–3.

58 In the *icmal defteri*, the following equivalents were given: 1 *kintar* = 100 *tuman*; 1 *tuman* = 800 *dirhem*.

59 According to the suggestion of A. Cohen, this probably means "leased out taxes" of varying composition.

60 The *icmal* gives figures in Istanbul *kile*, the detailed survey register in Jerusalem *ghirāra*, both being measures of capacity for grains.

61 On "money-of-account" see: Cohen and Lewis, *Population and Revenue*, 43–4.

Neither the price per unit of measure nor the units themselves changed during the short period under discussion. See Makovsky, "Agricultural Production," 120.

62 See M. Cook's tables in *Population Pressure in Rural Anatolia, 1450–1600* (London, 1972), 112–13, for an example of the information from Anatolian villages.

63 TKM 283/p.2.

64 Amiran, "Pattern of Settlement," 73.

65 See Table 3.1, above. According to the *icmal defteri*, revenue rose from 30.5 kintar to 276 kintar, TKM 283/p. 3. Makovsky has converted olive oil measures into pounds, and finds that income from this item rose from 15,200 to 653,300 pounds, or 4,300%, "Agricultural Production," 112.

66 According to al-Nuwayrī, writing about Bilād al-Shām under the Mamluks, *al-sayfī* included sorghum, millet, sesame, rice, *nigella*, coriander, cucumbers, *wasma*, safflower, cotton, and hemp. Al-Nuwayrī, *Nihāyat al-Arab*, 8:258.

67 The *kanunname* for the *sancak* of Jerusalem lists, in addition to olive trees: walnuts, dates, mulberries, and other fruit trees. TTD 516/p.1, lines 5–8 of the *kanunname*, which precedes the accounting section and is unnumbered.

68 See the chart for ʿInab in Appendix 1.

69 See, for example, the charts in Appendix 1 for Abū Dīs, where everything is listed under *harac-i aşcar*, and Bayt Jālā, where it is all under *harac-i kurum*; and Makovsky's table, "Agricultural Production," 115.

70 For a comprehensive discussion of soap production and olive oil supply to Jerusalem, see Cohen, *Economic Life in Ottoman Jerusalem*, 74–97.

71 Olive oil is only recorded in about twenty-five villages in the first survey, three in the second. In those years it was recorded in *kantar*s (Ar. *qinṭār*); from the third survey quantities are in *mann* (50 *mann* = 1 *kantar*). What the drop in "price" signifies here is unknown. There is too little evidence from the survey registers to discuss it, and when set in the realm of money-of-account discussions, one becomes submerged in supposition.

72 See Cohen and Lewis, *Population and Revenue*, 55, 62–3, 96, and 101; and A. Cohen, *Economic Life in Ottoman Jerusalem, passim*. For more on olives and olive oil see Chapter Four, "Nāḥiyat Banī Zayd."

73 Makovsky, "Agricultural Production," 112.

74 This northern region of the *sancak* will be discussed in Chapter Four.

75 Some villages presented here are listed in the charts in Appendix 1, the same villages which will serve as examples in the discussion in Chapter Four.

76 It is probably a bad assumption that in a given village everyone paid an equal share of the taxes. Some means of pro-rating payments must have existed based on people's relative share in the total production.

77 "*Hasıl*:" included wheat, barley, *harac-i aşcar*, olive oil, animals. It did not include *bad-i hava* as these taxes were levied individually.

78 See B. Lewis, "Ottoman land tenure and taxation," 123.

79 From *icmal defter* #283.

80 There is no indication about which *vakıf*s this category included.

81 Labelled as "part of the *vakıf* of Halilürrahman and Sahra-i Şerife.

82 Venzke, "Special Use of the Tithe," 321.

83 In the villages of Bayt Jālā, Bayt Laḥm, Bayt Kīsā, Bayt Liqyā, and Buqayʿat al-Ḍān. The *mir-i liva* was then assigned other revenues.

84 Powers, "Revenues of Public *waqfs*," 199.
85 See Heyd, *Ottoman Documents*, 128–33.
86 E. LeRoy Ladurie, *The Peasants of Languedoc*, trans. J. Day (Urbana, 1974).
87 Inalcik, *The Ottoman Empire*, 110.

4. Real accounts and accounting

1 Peasant proverb quoted by Mrs. Finn, "The Fellaheen of Palestine," *PEFQS* (1879):44.
2 Hütteroth and Abdulfattah, *Historical Geography*, 12–14, 60–1.
3 In the 97–100th percentile of villages classified for size by numbers of *hane*, according to Toledano's calculations, "The *Sanjaq* of Jerusalem," 311.
4 Compare the *hane* figures in the Abū Dīs chart in Appendix 1 with the rates shown in Toledano, "The *Sanjaq* of Jerusalem," 309, Table III. Although the notation is cumbersome, I have included both Christian and Muslim dates in this chapter because the taxes due were quoted as being from the Muslim, or *hicri*, year. All conversions of dates were made using F.R. Unat, *Hicrî Tarihleri Mîlâdî Tarihe Çevirme Kılavuzu*, 5th edn. (Ankara, 1984).
5 In TTD 516/p. 29 this *vakıf* is more precisely defined as being "for Shaykh Aḥmad and Shaykh ʿAlī al-Hakkārī." It does not appear in Powers' list of the public *vakıfs* of Jerusalem which shows three foundations bearing the name of Salāḥ al-Dīn: a *medrese*, a *hanekah* (dervish monastery), and a *bimaristan* (hospital). Powers, "Revenues of Public *waqfs*," 166–9.
6 See Chapter Three, Table 3.2.
7 TTD 289: Abū Dīs p. 82, ʿAyn Silwān p. 125, Dayr Dibwān p. 130.
8 Figures are given as "number of *ghirāra*"/value in *akçe*.
9 All grain measures are given in *ghirāra*.
10 The tithe was recorded in gold *sultani*, and presented here in *akçe* to make clear the comparison of survey and *sijill* figures. Gold *sultani* were converted to silver *akçe* at 1:80.
11 JS 28:970/p. 257; JS 28:1108/p. 287. The standard list of crops given when citing taxes due was, with variations: *al-ḥinṭa wa'l-shaʿīr wa-baqiyat al-ḥubūbāt wa'l-ṣayfī wa'l-shitawī wa'l-kurūm wa'l-maqāthī*... "*Maqāthī*" (vegetable gardens) is the only reading of this word which makes any sense in the context of agriculture. It is used by Nuwayrī in his list of "summer crops."
12 JS 31:1563/p. 319; JS 31:1579/p. 321. The second half of the taxes due does not equal the first precisely. Slightly more wheat and less barley were assessed here. 72 *mudd* = 1 *ghirāra* (JS 31:2134/p. 431.) The remaining 1/5 of the year's taxes was perhaps the share of the village leaders.
13 JS 33:2049/p. 381; JS 33:2069/p. 386.
14 JS 44:1697/p. 283.
15 JS 30:645/p. 191. 1 *sultani* = 80 *akçe*.
16 *Kethüda*: see C. Orhonlu and G. Baer, "ketkhudā," *EI*^{2}, 4:853–5. This title was used for specific offices, but could also refer to any "authorised deputy official."
17 JS 27:834/p. 164.
18 JS 30:425/p. 127.
19 JS 33:1830/p. 340.
20 See Makovsky, "Agricultural production," Table V, p. 120.

21 This price is calculated from a *sijill* entry wherein it is recorded that the *ru'asā* of Abū Dīs sold to the *sancakbeyi* 2,200 *mudd* of barley, for 140 gold *sultani*, each *mudd* = 5 *akçe*. At this price, 1 *ghirāra* = 360 *akçe*. See JS 31:2640/p. 539.

22 This was calculated using the figures we have for grain taxes due for the year 963 above, which were 9 *ghirāra* wheat and 13 *ghirāra* barley. Using the notional prices in the registers, 480 *akçe/ghirāra* wheat and 260 *akçe/ghirāra* barley, a money equivalent of 7,700 *akçe* was due. This was one-third of the total of grains, which was 23,100 *akçe*. If we assume that the price of wheat was also thirty-eight percent higher, then this total is corrected to 31,878 *akçe*. However, this represents only grains, and the tithe is calculated on all tithable yield in the village. In Abū Dīs, non-grain yields were twenty-five percent of the total for grains, based on TTD 516 figures. So a re-corrected total for the village is 39,847.5 *akçe*. Finally, if we remember that the tithe here is calculated "from all the revenue" (*'an cümlet el-mütehassil,*) then we need to add the tithe to this last figure in order to get the total yield of the village in money equivalent: 50,247.5 *akçe* of which 130 *sultani*, or 10,400 *akçe* represents a tithe of twenty percent. Note: throughout the calculation, an equivalent of 1 *sultani* to 80 *akçe* was used. This was originally assumed from the *cizye* payments, which were 1 gold coin per adult male, stated as 80 *akçe* in the register. The assumption is born out by the evidence of the *sijill* entry about the sale of barley to the *sancakbeyi*, where 2,200 *mudd* of barley were sold for 140 gold *sultani*, and every *mudd* is said to be worth 5 *akçe*. 5 × 2,200 = 11,000; 11,000 divided by 140 = 78.5 (JS 31:2640/p. 539).

23 JS 26:282/p. 62.

24 The *mustaḥaqqīn*, or those who had a rightful claim to the revenues.

25 *wa-yakhshā 'alā māl al-waqf al-ḍayā' wa'l-talaf*

26 JS 28:1572/p. 394 1 Sha'bān 961/2 July 1554.

27 Nūḥ: JS 28:160/p. 53; Muḥammad al-Fākhūrī: JS 44:1697/p. 283.

28 Arabic: *qaḍā*, the area of a kadi's jurisdiction.

29 This village was also called al-Ṭūr in the survey registers and in the *sijill*, and should be the present-day village of al-Ṭūr lying due east of Jerusalem on the Mount of Olives.

30 *Çift* here refers to the plots which the peasants were responsible for cultivating in the village.

31 The *raiyyet rüsūmu* refer to all the various taxes to which the *re'aya* were liable, the *çift resmi*, *'öşr*, and *bad-i hava*. (Inalcik, "Osmanlılar'da Raiyyet Rüsūmu," 594.) Here, it may refer to the *çift bozan resmi*, see Chapter Three, n.10, or simply to the latter two taxes which were normally collected in this region.

32 JS 32: p. 124.

33 See S. Faroqhi, "Political Activity among Ottoman Taxpayers and the Problem of Sultanic Legitimation (1570–1650)," *JESHO* 35(1992):28, for a similar conclusion.

34 *Kanunname* of Erzurum from 947/1540, Başbakanlık Arşivi [BBA] – Tapu Tahrir Defteri [TTD] #700: "*Ve reaya tâifesi ki elinde yeri olub müteferrik ola sipahi göçürüb yerine getürmek kanundur Ammâ on yıldan ziyade varub bir yerde mutavattın olan kimesneyi göçürüb getürmek memnu'dur.*" Cited from Barkan, *Kanunlar*, 65. Other examples of these statutes in Barkan are from Trabzon (p. 60), Sofya (p. 253), and Silistre (p. 283).

35 *Taṣarruf* has a specific connotation with regard to the rights of the peasants. It

denoted the right to use and possess a particular piece of land, a right which could be inherited and could not be taken away as long as the land was worked. (See Lewis, "Ottoman Land Tenure and Taxation," 116–18.) In this instance, "disposing freely" of the *fūl* constituted a violation of the limits on that use.

36 JS 30:140/p. 39.

37 C. R. Condor and H. H. Kitchener, *Survey of Western Palestine* (London, 1883; repr. Jerusalem, 1970), III:19–20, 60–1.

38 According to the survey registers, the *zaviye* was founded by Salāḥ al-Dīn, but Mujīr al-Dīn gives the founder as one Shaykh 'Umar b. 'Abdallāh b. 'Abd al-Nabī al-Maghribī al-Masmūdi al-Mujarrad who established the endowment in 703/1303. The *vakfiye* (endowment deed) described 'Ayn Kārim as "embracing land cultivated and uncultivated ... rocky and plain ... and derelict dwelling houses for its cultivators (*fallāḥīhā*), ... a small orchard, pomegranate and other [fruit] trees, watered from the village fountain, old [Rūmi i.e. Rumānī] olive trees, and caroub, fig and oak trees ..." (Cited in A. L. Tibawi, *The Islamic Pious Foundations in Jerusalem* (London, 1978), 11.) See also Mujīr al-Din, *Al-Uns al-Jalīl*, 2:45–6; and the first survey register: TTD 427/p. 277. All succeeding surveys copied this. On the Maghribīs, the commmunity of North African origin living in Jerusalem, see Cohen and Lewis, *Population and Revenue*, 34–5, 82–3; Goitein, "al-Kuds," *EI*[2], 329, 331; and Burgoyne, *Mamluk Jerusalem*, 261. On the *zaviye vakıf*, see Gideon Weigert, "A Maghribi Religious Endowment in Fourteenth-Century Jerusalem," *Cathedra* 58(1990):28–30.

39 Qulūnya was entirely endowed for the Madrasa al-Shaykhūniyya in Jerusalem, on which see Powers, "Revenues of Public *waqfs*," 179. The tithes of Qulūnya and 'Ayn Kārim together formed a *tımar*. They are found assigned together in TTD 289 (to Rayhān *sipahi*) and TTD 516 (to 'Abdallāh *sipahi*).

40 All figures here were recorded in *akçe* and converted to gold *sultani* at 80 *akçe*/*sultani*.

41 This figure is given in *akçe*, but was converted to *sultani* at 80 *akçe*/*sultani*.

42 JS 27:640 and 641/p. 124.

43 JS 28:1215/p. 309.

44 Both the third and fourth surveys estimate 5 *ghirāra*(=360 *mudd*) of wheat and 4 *ghirāra*(=288 *mudd*) of barley from 'Ayn Kārim. See TTD 289/p. 135 and TTD 516/p. 49.

45 TTD 516/p. 49.

46 JS 31:1784/p. 362.

47 JS 33:2027/p. 379.

48 JS 35:933/p. 181.

49 JS 39:2514/p. 532 and 2548/p. 540.

50 *ziyādatan 'alā Murād sūbāshī al-musta'jir al-sābiq bi-sulṭānī dhahab*," JS 39:2580/p. 545.

51 JS 39:2587/p. 547.

52 JS 40:2020 and 2021/p. 407, 24 Shawwāl 968/8 July 1561.

53 JS 43:1880/p. 341.

54 JS 43:2519/p. 446, 27 Dhū'l-Qa'da 969/29 July 1562.

55 See above, the first case presented in this section.

56 Mūsā al-Dabarī is also listed as being the *imām* of the Dome of the Rock. JS 31:2653/p. 542.

57 JS 28:1096/p. 284; JS 30:415/p. 125. In fact, the difference is remarked in the

second *sijill* entry which says "4,000 ʿosmānī, half of which is in compliance with its orginal sum [and half added later]." JS 30:415/p. 125: *nisfuha ḥifẓan li-aṣliha.*

58 Approximately one-third of the total revenues: 1/3(550 − 55) = 165.

59 JS 33:151/p. 36.

60 JS 31:2653/p. 542.

61 JS 33:1862/p. 349

62 They are also referred to as "*nahiye*" in the *sijill*, although this may reflect local Arabic usage, rather than the formal Ottoman divisions.

63 The most detailed and documented study of population divisions in the Jerusalem area is in U. O. Schmelz, "Population characteristics of Jerusalem and Hebron regions according to Ottoman census of 1905," in *Ottoman Palestine 1800–1914*, ed. G. Gilbar (Leiden, 1990), 29–31. Mrs. Finn lists five "fellah clans" in the Jerusalem mountain district ("The Fellaheen of Palestine," 34), and Macalister and Masterman give a catalogue of the eighteen sub-divisions of Judaea and Nablus, including the villages of each, which they say were valid until the mid-nineteenth century (R. A. S. Macalister and E. W. G. Masterman, "Occasional Papers on the modern Inhabitants of Palestine," *PEFQS* (1905):352–6).

64 Bedouins from the tribe of Banī Zayd reportedly attacked the city of Jerusalem in 884/1480 after the governor executed some members of the tribe as rebels: M. Sharon, "The Political Role of the Bedouins in Palestine in the Sixteenth and Seventeenth Centuries," in *Studies on Palestine during the Ottoman Period*, ed. M. Maoz (Jerusalem, 1975), 15.

65 JS 1:968/p. 240. Banī Zayd and Banī Ḥārith were also the names of two quarters in the town of Jerusalem in the first two Ottoman surveys. The names of the quarters came from those members of these tribes who settled in Jerusalem. See Cohen and Lewis, *Population and Revenue*, s.v. "Banī Ḥāri*th*," "Banī Zayd."

66 The sub-district of Banī ʿAmr lay on the western edge of the district of Jerusalem and included the villages of Artūf, Aṣlīn, ʿAlīn, Kafrūriya, Rafāt, Sārā, Shawā, and one other illegible name. They were located in the beginning of the coastal plain, already almost beyond the mountainous terrain of most of the district. Probably it was decided that they were more easily overseen from Gaza.

67 Cohen and Lewis, *Population and Revenue*, 81, 83.

68 See Burgoyne, *Mamluk Jerusalem*, 419.

69 It is possible that other villages in this area for which no specific reference was found linking them to Banī Zayd were in fact considered a part of that area. Macalister and Masterman's article discussing the "former divisions and local government of the Fellahīn of Judaea and the District of Nablus," listed eighteen districts, including Bani Zaid (Deir Ghassānah, ʿAttara, ʿAjul, ʿArāra, Mazraʿa, Kefr ʿAin, Beit Rīma, ʿAbūd, etc.) and Bani Hārith (northern: Beit Illu, Jemāla, Abu Kash, Surdah, Jifna, Bir ez-Zeit, Deir ʿAmmar, Mezraʿa, Dura, and Karāwa; southern: Saffa, ʿAin ʿArīk, Ain Kāniah, and others). See Macalister and Masterman, "Occasional Papers" (1905), 354–5.

70 See JS 39:2510/p. 531, 7 Dhūʾl-Ḥijja 967/29 August 1560, where the villages Batna, Batana, and Salfīt were among the villages mentioned as being part of the ʿ*amal* (district) of Jerusalem and whose villagers appeared before the kadi led by Muḥammad Abū Rabbān, shaykh of the villages of Banī Zayd.

71 *shaykh bilād Banī Zayd*: *bilād* either means "region" or is used as the plural of *balda, balad*, "village."

72 here: "region"

73 JS 31:2441/p. 565.

74 Many Christians from Bayt Rīmā migrated to Jerusalem, Gaza, and Ramle during the sixteenth century. More left than those remaining, although the number in the village grew a little. See Cohen and Lewis, *Population and Revenue*, s.v. "Bayt Rīmā." The population of Jufnā also declined, but its subsequent whereabouts were not immediately traceable.

75 JS 31:2441/p. 565, 22 Ramaān 963/30 July 1556: ... *al-waqfayn al-sharīfayn waqf al-masjid al-Aqṣā al-sharīf wa-waqf Khalīl al-Raḥmān*... The term "*waqfayn al-sharīfayn*" recalls the "*ḥaramayn al-sharīfayn*" which refers to the holy cities of Mecca and Medina. In the survey registers the references are either to *Khalīl al-Raḥmān*, the mosque of al-Aqsā, or the *Ṣakhra al-Sharīfa*, the Dome of the Rock in Jerusalem. Cohen says that the term "ḥaramayn" may also refer to "the mosques on the Temple Mount in Jerusalem and the Cave of the Ancestors in Hebron," see Cohen, *Jewish Life Under Islam*, 60. See also B. Lewis, "*ḥaramayn*," *EI*², 3:175–6.

76 ʿAbwīn, ʿArūrā, Bayt Rīmā, Dayr Dibwān, Dayr Ghassāna, Kafr ʿAyn, Mazāriʿ, and Qarāwā. Of the remaining four, three – Bayt Illū, Dajjāniyya, and Jammālā – lie just west of Banī Zayd. The last – Idhnā – is found directly west of Hebron.

77 See Cohen, *Economic Life in Ottoman Jerusalem*, 196.

78 Cohen, *Economic Life in Ottoman Jerusalem*, 176 ff. Soap-making had been an important manufacture in Jerusalem until the Mamluk period, during which time the government monopoly on olive oil brought about its decline. On this see S.D. Goitein, "al-Ḳuds," *EI*², 333. In the late nineteenth century and early twentieth century, soap comprised one of the chief exports from Palestine, along with oranges. Nablus and Jaffa were the main centers of production. For more on this see G. Gilbar, "The Growing Economic Involvement of Palestine with the West, 1865–1914," in *Palestine in the late Ottoman period*, ed. D. Kushner (Jerusalem, 1986), 196–7, 199. Soap from olive oil is still produced today in and around Nablus.

79 Figures from survey given in *mann*. (50 *mann* = 1 *kintar*).

80 For a discussion of this alternation, and some present-day statistics to illustrate the annual swings, see S. F. Nāṣir, *Zaytūn Filasṭīn wa-mushkilātuhu* (Bir Zeit, n.d.) 33–7.

81 Cohen, *Economic Life in Ottoman Jerusalem*, 197.

82 JS 30:1250/p. 346; JS 39:2510/p. 531. On the supply and purchase of olive oil in Jerusalem, see Cohen, *Economic life in Ottoman Jerusalem*, 74–81.

83 See JS 26:456/p. 101, 26 Jumādā II 967/23 March 1560, where 7 *kintar* olive oil equal 70 gold *sultani*; and JS 33:2834/p. 532, 22 Shawwāl 964/18 August 1557, where 50 *sikke* (= *sultani*) equal the value of 5 *kintar* olive oil. These, however, must be accounting prices, as the market price of oil changed during the year and was recorded in the *sijill*. See Cohen, *Economic life in Ottoman Jerusalem*, 140–5.

84 JS 33:879/p. 177.

85 Mujīr al-Dīn found that most of the people of Bayt Laḥm were Christians in his time, *Al-Uns Al-Jalīl*, II, 65. For a general discussion of the Christian population of villages in the province of Jerusalem, see Toledano, "The Sanjaq of Jerusalem," 311–14.

86 See TTD 515, p. 74 and p. 72.

87 TTD 289/p. 71 ff, dated to 952.
88 *Çavuş*: an imperial messenger. The *çavuş* in the sixteenth century was more than simply a messenger. He embodied imperial authority in whatever task he was delegated to perform, whether carrying orders, making arrests or supervising discipline. See M. F. Köprülü, "çavuş," *İA*, 2:362–9.
89 JS 27:282/p. 55.
90 See Cohen, *Jewish Life in Jerusalem*, 24–35. In fact, Cohen (p. 21) says that the *cizye* was set as a lump sum, while the names in the surveys were not checked, but simply recopied from one to the next. This is one of two principal forms of *cizye* payment under the Ottomans, known as *cizye ber vech-i maktu'*, or *cizye* calculated as a fixed sum. The other form was called *cizye 'ala 'l-ru'us*, or *cizye* calculated on the head (of each person). See C. Cahen and H. Inalcik, "djizya," *EI*², 2:559–66.
91 JS 31:537/p. 118.
92 Cohen and Lewis, *Population and Revenue*, 86 and 90. In TTD III, thirty households and three bachelors from Bayt Laḥm, nineteen households from Bayt Jālā; in TTD IV, twenty-six households, one bachelor and one blind man from Bayt Laḥm, twenty-one households and one bachelor from Bayt Jālā. These occur only in the third and fourth surveys.
93 See Cohen and Lewis, *Population and Revenue*, s.v. "Bayt Rīmā."
94 Islamic law traditionally did not levy the *cizye* on invalids, and this practice was upheld by the Ottomans. See "djizya," 561, 563. On the use of *fetva*s in Ottoman courts, see Jennings, "Kadi, Court, and Legal Procedure," 134–5.
95 JS 44:64/p. 11.
96 See Cohen, *Jewish Life in Jerusalem*, 21 ff.
97 JS 27:31/p. 7.
98 JS 40:1523/p. 316 and JS 44:311/p. 51.
99 Also sesame oil according to A. Cohen, "Local trade, international trade and government involvement in Jerusalem during the early Ottoman period," *Asian and African Studies* 12(1978):7.
100 When the British mandatory government of Palestine surveyed local industry in 1928, it found 452 simple olive oil presses in operation in villages. See S. Ilan, "Ha-Haklaut ha-aravit ha-mesortit," in *Nofei Eretz-Yisrael ba-meah ha-19* ed. E. Shiller (Jerusalem, 1984), 49.
101 See Cohen and Lewis, *Population and Revenue*, 63–4, on presses in the towns.
102 First page reference in each *defter* is to Bayt Laḥm, second to Bayt Jālā: TTD 427/pp. 273, 274; TTD 1015/pp. 199, 197; TTD 289/pp. 71, 76; TTD 516/pp. 64, 65; and TTD 515/pp. 72, 74. The *vakıf* supplied large quantities of grain to feed people in the holy cities of Mecca and Medina. See S. Shaw, *The Financial and Administrative Organization and Development of Ottoman Egypt 1517–1798* (Princeton, 1962), 269.
103 The draft deed, in Turkish, was published by S. H. Stephan, "An Endowment Deed of Khâsseki Sultân, Dated 24th May 1552," *Quarterly of the Department of Antiquities in Palestine* 10(1944):170–94; on Bayt Jālā and Bayt Laḥm, see 184, n.1. One copy of the final endowment deed in Arabic is located in the Türk ve İslam Eserleri Müzesi, #2192; it is dated mid-Sha'bān 964.
104 TTD 289/p. 107. These 2,500 *akçe* were the tithe on another *vakıf* supported by

the tax revenues of Jīb, plus the *bad-i hava* from the village. Sultan Selim was Süleyman's son and successor; he was entitled to the appelation "sultan" because of his princely rank.

105 JS 33:2934/p. 532. The document says Farrukh owed 270 *sultani*, but this is an error either in calculation or transcription.

106 JS 33:1821/p. 338.

107 JS 29/p. 25, Evahir Rebiülahir 961/26 March–5 April 1554.

108 JS 30:402/p. 122.

109 JS 30:390/p. 119.

110 See Chapter Two at n. 86.

111 JS 31:2752/p. 560.

112 JS 30:1333/p. 371.

113 See S.D. Goitein, "al-Kuds," *EI*[2], 5:334.

114 The Abū Ghosh family were the Yamanī leaders in the Judean Hills. See M. Hoexter, "The Role of Qays and Yaman Factions in Local Political Divisions," *Asian and African Studies* 9(1973):285 and *passim*.

115 For the references on this foundation, see n. 73, above, re: Dayr Dibwān.

116 JS 27:1075/p. 207.

117 JS 27:1324/p. 263.

118 JS 28:1336/p. 334; JS 26:380/p. 82.

119 JS 28:364/p. 109. *taʿaṭṭalat ghālib arḍihā wa-mukhall ghālib zarʿihā.*

120 Bayt Fāsīn does not appear on the maps consulted. It was said to be near Bayt Ẓulmā, which is to the north of ʿAyn Kārim near Qulūnya (JS 28:184/p.61). A *sijill* entry from 20 Jumādā II 1024 (June 17, 1615) refers to a place called "Dayr Yāsīn, formerly known as Dayr Fāsīn." Dayr Yāsīn was a village just north of ʿAyn Kārim, but the question remains whether in this century one may identify Bayt Fāsīn with Dayr Fāsīn.

121 JS 31:1448/p. 298: *...wa-annahu aṣlaḥ wa-albaq li'l-takallum ʿalā al-qarya al-mazbūra min ʿAlī Bālī al-mazbūr...* Note that while Bayram is now *ustādh* of the village, ʿInab is not a part of the Hasseki Sultan *ʿimaret vakıf* which he administers.

122 JS 31:1448/p. 298.

123 JS 35:815/p. 154.

124 JS 35:885/p. 171 11 Rabīʿ I 965 (January 1, 1558); JS 40:2401/p. 475, 15 Dhū'l-Ḥijja 968 (August 27, 1561).

125 TTD 516/p. 55.

126 See Heyd, *Ottoman Documents*, *passim*, for numerous imperial orders to free the roads from the threat of bandits and unsafe conditions.

127 JS 42/p. 137 (top), beginning of Rabīʿ I 972/mid-October 1564.

128 JS 40:427/p. 85; JS 44:1143/p. 194.

129 JS 27:1200/p. 233.

130 Makovsky's conclusion "that the tax totals the defters display denote the amounts to be paid annually until the next survey," the said amounts being "based on an estimate of average annual production," does not take into account these annual fluctuations. It would seem that the average was used to make appointments, on the assumption that in the grand scheme of things, the *sipahi*s would get by. See "Agricultural Production," 118–19.

5. Between rebellion and oppression

1 *Yasaknâme* from 947/1540. Text in Inalcik, "Adâletnâmeler," 116.
2 JS 1:968/p. 240. The full account of this caustic exchange is given in A. Singer, "*Tapu tahrir defterleri* and *Kadı sicilleri*," 114.
3 JS 44:1280/p. 215.
4 JS 40:590/p. 124: ...*matā tabayyana wa-ẓahara annahu gharasa arḍan min arāḍī al-qarya al-mazbūra bi-ghayri idhni ustādhihi kāna ʿalayhi al-qiyām li-ustādhihi ... bi-alfayn ʿuthmānī bi-ṭarīq al-iltizām al-sharʿī ...*
5 JS 44:1218/p. 206.
6 JS 28:184/p. 61.
7 JS 43:1121/p. 210.
8 JS 30:1841/p. 454.
9 JS 33:2694/p. 506.
10 JS 32/p. 141.
11 The processes of declaration and pricing as part of the overall control of supply and marketing in Jerusalem are discussed in Cohen, *Economic life in Ottoman Jerusalem*, 76–7 (olive oil), 110–13 (barley).
12 JS 28:953/p. 254: ... *wa-shahidā ... anna ghilāl qurā nāḥiyat Quds[-i] Sharif badaʾa ṣalāḥuhā wa-ʾstaḥaqqat al-ḥiṣād wa-ḥuṣida baʿuhā min muddat ʿasharat ayyām ṣābiqatan ʿalā taʾrīkhihi ...*
13 JS 30:1283/p. 356: ... *anna zaytūn al-nāḥiya ... baqiyat jaddādihi maqbūl wa-ʿuṣira wa-ṣāra zaytan ...*
14 See JS 33:2652/p. 499; JS 39:2510/p. 531; and JS 43:1667/p. 306.
15 The August date here, and the July date below for the ripening of olives seem early, in light of contemporary practice, where the olive harvest begins in late September and continues through late December, see Nāṣir, *Zaytūn Filasṭīn wa-mushkilātuhu*, 45. Perhaps the difference reflects changes in climate or cultivation practices which are as yet unelucidated.
16 Including the Shaykh of the villages of Banī Zayd, and *aʿyān* from Ṣirdā, ʿAṭṭāra, Dayr Ghassāna, Mazāriʿ, Batna, Salfīt, and Batāna, the last three being from the *sancak* of Nablus.
17 JS 33:1754/p. 326.
18 JS 33:2133/p. 401.
19 Umm Ṭūba actually supported two different *vakıf*s, whose total share was half the village revenues. Ḥusām al-Dīn seems to have served as the *nāẓir* of both. See TTD 289/p. 112 for the details of the *vakıf*s.
20 JS 43:1834/p. 334.
21 JS 31:1652/p. 334.
22 Mantran and Sauvaget, *Règlements fiscaux*, 52, the *kanunname* of Safad, 1555 (963). This part of the *kanunname* is not found in Barkan's *Kanunlar*. It comes from a manuscript in the Bibliothèque Nationale: ancien fonds turc no. 85, fo. 176 vo. I have translated from Mantran and Sauvaget's translation. See also Mantran and Sauvaget, *Règlements fiscaux*, 34, the *kanunname* of Damascus from 1548 (955) (Barkan, *Kanunlar*, 227) where specific taxes connected with harvesting, presumably Mamluk or earlier practices, are listed as abolished, among them *resm-i hasad* (harvesting tax), *adet-i ricadiye* (tax on the transport of grains to the threshing floor), and *fütuh-ı beyder* (opening of the threshing floors).

23 JS 27:26/p. 6. These lands on the outskirts of the city seem to be the *kit'a-i arz* found listed in the survey registers as belonging to the city, not to particular villages. Although the list may include small plots within the city, it seems to refer only to lands on the periphery, ... *al-arāḍī al-kāina ẓāhir madinat Quds-i Sharif* ... The term *wālī al-barr* reinforces the idea that the lands here are those surrounding the town, *barr* referring to "lands outside," on which see E.W. Lane, *An Arabic–English Lexicon* (London, 1863), s.v. Cohen translates the phrase "*fī'l-barr*" as "outside the city," "in the field," on which see *Jewish Life under Islam*, 180.

24 Threshing might well have been carried out as seen in some nineteenth-century illustrations, in which a donkey or other work animal is driven round in a circle dragging a horizontally-placed board, on which the animal's driver stands or sits. The board is studded on the underside with nails or metal knobs, so that when it passes over the grain ears, it crushes the hulls, thus freeing the seed.

25 JS 27:26/p.6 ...*wa-akhadha min kull baydar min bayādirihim taratan mudd wa-taratan niṣf mudd wa-taratan rub' mudd min al-ghilāl wa-taratan qudrat tibn wa-taratan kharj tibn*...*fa-ajāba annahu akhadha minhum dhalika 'alā sabīl al-shiḥādha* ...

26 MMD 2775/p. 1098.

27 JS 27:26/p. 6, 29 Rajab 960/11 July 1553.

28 JS 30:468/p. 138: ... *wa-naqluhu 'alā al-fallāḥīn 'alā al-'āda* ...

29 A very common sentence reads: ... *mutrakan 'alā al-'āda maḥmulan ilā manzilihi bi'l-Quds al-Sharīf* ... JS 28:1084/p. 281.

30 See Faroqhi, *Towns and Townsmen*, 57 on the general rule and its breaching; and Inalcik, "Adâletnâmeler," 68, and "Suleiman the Lawgiver," 131.

31 JS 31:2989/p. 590.

32 JS 33:2686/p. 505.

33 JS 40:2519/p. 494.

34 JS 33:2536/p. 480.

35 Cohen, *Jewish Life under Islam*, 193.

36 JS 33:1454/p. 275.

37 JS 27:1220/p. 238.

38 JS 28:1694/p. 423.

39 JS 26:451/p. 100.

40 JS 43:2100/p. 378: ... *bi-aydihim qiṭ'at arḍin* ... *wa-innahum 'aṭṭalūhā* ...

41 JS 27:1125/p. 218.

42 JS 40:1457/p. 304.

43 See above, Chapter Four: "Abū Dīs," JS 32/p.124.

44 JS 31:1411/p. 291.

45 JS 27:1295/p. 257.

46 MMD 2775/p. 1257.

47 Imperial concern over peasants abandoning villages is expressed in numerous *fermans*. In any such case, it was important to investigate the circumstances which drove people to move and undertake to correct them. This is discussed, with further examples, in Inalcik, "Adâletnâmeler," 86, 110.

48 JS 40:1200/p. 251. And see R.C. Jennings, "Limitations of the Judicial Powers of the Kadi in 17th C. Ottoman Kayseri," *Studia Islamica* 50(1979):169–71, 176 on the statute of limitations and return of villagers.

49 For a more extensive analysis of peasant migration in sixteenth-century Palestine,

see A. Singer, "Peasant Migration: Law and Practice in Early Ottoman Palestine," *New Perspectives on Turkey* 8(1992):49–65.

50 For a complete picture of Süleyman's building projects in Jerusalem see A. Cohen, "Mif'alo shel Suleyman ha-mefu'ar be-Yerushalayim," *Cathedra* 57(1990):31–51.

51 JS 26:565/p. 124.

52 JS 27:1615/p. 317.

53 The water system, its various channels and the repairs carried out and planned during the Ottoman period are discussed in detail in Salama and Zilberman, "Aspakat ha-mayim li-Yerushalayim." Imperial orders concerning water supply are also found in Heyd, *Ottoman Documents*, 146–50.

54 JS 43:2733/p. 485.

55 JS 33:1840/p. 342.

56 JS 30:1573/p. 428.

57 In Arabic they are called *Birak Süleyman* or *Birak al-Marjīʿ* and in Hebrew *Brichot Shlomo*. (Salama and Zilberman, "Aspakat ha-Mayim," 93.)

58 Cf. A. Raymond, *Grandes villes arabes à l'époque ottomane* (Paris, 1985), 155–67; A. Marcus, *The Middle East on the Eve of Modernity* (New York, 1989), 298–303; H. Inalcik, "Māʾ – Irrigation in the Ottoman Empire," *EI*^{2}, 5:878–84.

59 See Jennings, "Limitations of the Judicial Powers of the Kadi," 167–8.

60 See Barkan, *Kanunlar*, s.v. *su*.

61 JS 33:370/p. 79.

62 JS 40:9/p. 3.

63 JS 30:1035/p. 286.

64 JS 31:700/p. 154: ... *wa-ṭalaba min malik al-umarā ... al-rukūb ʿalā ahālī al-qarya al-mazbūra wa-khalāṣ ḥaqqihi minhum wa'l-khurūj min ḥaqqihim li-yakūnū ʿibratan li-ghayrihim min al-mutamarridīn* ... (11 Rabīʿ II 963/23 February 1556). Alternatively, "*al-khurūj min ḥaqqihim*" may be an Arabic adaptation or translation of the Turkish "*hakkından gelmek*," meaning "to control successfully, to punish."

65 JS 31:722/p. 158. A similar incident from an earlier period is cited by Ḥmūd, in which Jaʿfar *subaşı* rode out against the people of Ṣūbā to help a *subaşı* collect back taxes. But when Jaʿfar arrived at the village, the peasants fled without confronting him. JS 1:4/p.33, in Hmūd, *Al-Askar fī Bilād al-Shām*, 57-58.

66 JS 32/p. 140 (top).

67 JS 40:7/p.2.

68 JS 26:95/p. 22, 27 Ramaḍān 960/6 September 1553.

69 JS 33:2800/p. 525.

70 JS 40:2514/p. 493.

71 JS 28:1254/p. 483, 16 Ramaḍān 961/15 August 1554.

72 See the collection of *ferman*s in Heyd, *Ottoman Documents*, 90 ff.

73 M 6 57/p. 28, and Heyd, *Ottoman Documents*, 143–4.

74 See the examples in Inalcik, "Adâletnâmeler," 77–9 and especially *ferman* #10.

75 M 29, no. 504, dated 14 Dhū'l-Ḥijja 984/4 March 1577, as cited and translated in Heyd, *Ottoman Documents*, 92–3.

76 J. Mandaville cites a similar case where the kadi was ordered to threaten and arrest any villagers who refused to pay their taxes, but no blood should be spilt in the matter. See "The Jerusalem Sharīʿa Court Records," in *Studies in Palestine during the Ottoman Period*, ed. M. Ma'oz (Jerusalem, 1975), 520.

77 M 29, no. 504, Heyd's translation.
78 A collection which includes some of these orders is published in Inalcik, "Adâletnâmeler."
79 Inalcik cites this as one means of peasant protest around the empire, see *The Ottoman Empire*, 99. Faroqhi says of the peasant options: " ... it was usually their only recourse to abandon their lands, join the nomads, or become a follower of a powerful individual." See "Political intiatives 'from the bottom up' in the 16th & 17th century Ottoman Empire," in *Osmanistische Studien zur Wirtschafts- und Sozialgeschichte: in memoriam Vanco Boskov*, ed. H.G. Mayer (Wiesbaden, 1986), 26.
80 JS 35:864/p. 167: *kharabū baldatahumā.*
81 JS 35:854/p. 165 dated 6 Rābi' I 965/December 27, 1557; and see TTD 289/p. 145 (952/1545), TTD 516/p. 35 (967/1560).
82 This market was known as *sūq al-khuḍar wa'l-bāshūra*. After it was renovated by the Ottomans, it was also called the "new market." See Cohen, *Jewish Life under Islam*, 5, and *Economic Life in Ottoman Jerusalem*, 7 and 122.
83 JS 40:427/p. 85: *...min qadīm al-zamān qabla al-fatḥ al-khāqānī wa-ilā yawm ta'rīkhihi adnāhu...*
84 JS 40:325/p. 64.
85 JS 42/p. 137 (top): *...aşcarini islami değuldur küffaridir diyü...* The usage of *küffāri/kafiri* (unbeliever) is the same as that of *rumani* in the Jerusalem *kanunname*, on which see Chapter Three, n. 12.
86 JS 42/p. 27.
87 JS 43:321/p. 58.
88 TTD 1015/p. 241; TTD 289/p. 136; TTD 516/p. 49.
89 A case cited from the *sijill* of Bursa tells of a person who obtained a "false" *ferman* from Istanbul by going there and giving questionable testimony about a local case, dictating the *ferman* to the scribe who prepared it. The *ferman* contradicted the Bursa kadi's decision. See U. Heyd, *Studies in Old Ottoman Criminal Law*, 243.
90 Inalcik discusses the advantages of the percentage calculation to the peasants, as opposed to the fixed rate which favored the treasury, see "Islamization of Ottoman Laws," 112.
91 JS 40:453/p. 91.
92 JS 43:1518/p. 281.
93 JS 42/p. 99 (top).
94 JS 26:345/p. 75: ... *ḥāla 'iṣyānihim*; see also JS 26:278/p. 61.
95 Ludd was a large, productive village of mixed Muslim and Christian population. See also M. Sharon, "Ludd," *EI*^{2}, 5:798–803; and Singer, "The Countryside of Ramle," 61, 64.
96 JS 32/p. 57.
97 MMD 2775/pp. 1047-8, 17 Sha'bān 973/9 March 1566
98 M 5 1017/pp. 382-3, 27 Receb 973/17 February 1566.
99 No tribes were listed in the first two registers. Thereafter, three groups (*cema'at*) from one tribe (*taife*) were listed in the *nahiye* of Jerusalem: *taifet-i 'urbān-i Marādiwa*, including *cema'at Badāh*, *cema'at Rās*, and *cema'at Banī 'Atiyya*. In each survey, they were recorded with a different village, villages which were located from the northern to the southern reaches of the *nahiye*: TTD 289/p. 94, at Bayt

Natīf; TTD 516/p. 32 at Taqū and p. 68 at Jīb; and TTD 515/p. 34 at Kafr Tūt. From the entire Syrian region, the Bedouin appear to be registered in greatest detail in Jerusalem, in some cases with the names of the adult males. For a broad and comparative picture, see W.-D. Hütteroth, "Ottoman Administration of the Desert Frontier in the sixteenth century," *Asian and African Studies* 19(1985):145–55; and Bakhit, *The Ottoman Province of Damascus*, 192ff.

100 Cohen, *Jewish Life under Islam*, 197.

101 For a summary description of the Bedouin in this area during late Mamluk times, see M. Sharon, "The Political Role of the Bedouin," 11–17.

102 See Heyd, *Ottoman Documents, passim*; A. Manna', "Moshlei Yerushalayim mi-Bayt Farrukh ve Yakhaseihem im ha-Bedouim," in *Perakim be-Toldot Yerushalayim: BeReshit ha-Tekufa ha-Othmanit*, ed. A. Cohen (Jerusalem, 1979), 199–202; and M 3 1020/p. 346, 1025/p. 347; M 4 276/p. 30 and 880/p. 86.

103 TTD 516/p. 69 and TTD 515/p. 34. The Turkish says: ... *Riha nam karyenin ve sairlerin terekeleri*... It is thus unclear from which places besides Jericho the Bedouin were expected to collect the grain.

104 Arabs: *'Arab*, *'Urbān* or *A'rāb*, as found in Arabic and Turkish texts, refers to the Bedouin.

105 JS 27:2283/p. 460, 2284/p. 461, and 259/p. 51.

106 JS 47:86/p. 44: ... *hem vakıf ve-hem mal-i miriye nef' olurdu* ...

107 JS 47:86/p. 44: ... *hala eminler zikr olan hisse-i miriyi bazi zi kudret kimesnelere ve-bazi taği arablar şeyhine icareye vermekle mezburler gelüb ahali-i karye enva'-i zulm ve ta'addi etmekle ekseri perakende olub mal-i miriye vakfa zarar müterettib olur*...

108 M 6 55/p. 27.

109 JS 28:1254/p. 483 and 1256/p. 484: ...*wa-qad taḥaqqaqa dhālika min al-jamm al-ghafīr min al-khāss wa'l-'āmm alladhi lā yumkin tawāṭu'uhum 'alā al-kadhib wa'l-ṭalab* ... (Note: There is a mistake in the modern numbering in this volume of the *sijill*. These documents should be located by page number first.)

110 JS 43:2559/p. 454.

111 Hütteroth suggests a continuum "from the 'normally' registered and taxed villager to the uncontrolled nomad," based on the precision with which the tribes were recorded in the survey registers, and the kinds of taxes expected from them; see "Ottoman Administration of the Desert Frontier," 152–3.

112 Manna', "Moshlei Yerushalayim mi-Bayt Farrūkh," 210.

113 Although Dols states that pneumonic and/or bubonic plague recurred on average every 9.5 years in Syria-Palestine during the Mamluk period, he says that the Ottoman period was less certain. Major epidemics are recorded in 1572–6, 1580–2, and 1587–9. Michael W. Dols, "The Second Plague Pandemic and its Recurrences in the Middle East: 1347–1894," *JESHO* 22(1979):169, 176.

114 M 3 481/p. 174 and 929/p. 317. Both are mentioned in Heyd, *Ottoman Documents*, 131–2.

115 JS 40:1250/p. 251, 1559/p. 331, 1700/p. 349. For a local chronicle of locust infestations, see R. C. Jennings, "The Locust Problem in Cyprus," *Byzantion* 57(1987):315–25.

116 JS 31:227/p. 49: ... *wa-taḍarrarū min qillat al-ghilāl wa-min ḍu'f ḥālihim wa-'adam qadrihim [sic: qudratihim] 'alā al-zar' li-qillat mā yajidūnahu 'indahum wa-ṭalabū quwwatan min māl al-waqf*...

117 *Quwwa*: which here could mean either money or seed grain from the *vakıf* stores.
118 JS 44:569/p. 94: ... *fa-'sta'dhana mawlānā al-nāẓir fī dhālika fa-udhina lahu fī i'ṭā'ihim quwwatan lahum wa-libaqiyyat jamā'atihim min māl al-waqf li-ajli maṣlaḥat al-waqf wa-khawfan min ta'ṭīl al-arḍ bi-lā zar'* ... ; and JS 44:781/p. 134.
119 The most detailed account comes from a Hebrew letter published by J. Braslavski in *Leheker Artzenu: Avar ve-seridim* (Tel Aviv, 1954), 227–8. Other information is provided by D. H. Kallner-Amiran, "A Revised Earthquake-Catalogue of Palestine (part 1)," *Israel Exploration Journal* 1(1950-51):229–30.
120 Braslavski, *Leheker Artzenu*, 228. I did not have time to consult the *sijill* on this year. There, one may find appeals from peasants for temporary relief from taxes if the damage in the countryside was serious. No mention of it was made in the survey registers. The third survey was completed before the earthquake; the fourth came almost fifteen years later.
121 The reports of damage to village houses from the earthquake of 1927, thought to be as severe as that of 1546, show widespread destruction. See Kallner-Amiran, "A Revised Earthquake-Catalogue," Part 1, 235; Part 2, *Israel Exploration Journal* 2(1952):50–1.

6. Realities and routines

1 See N. Brown, *Peasant Politics in Modern Egypt* (New Haven, 1990), 1, for a similar observation on Egyptian peasants.
2 Faroqhi has published a study of the phraseology used in the petitions and responses recorded in the *mühimme* registers. She aptly cautions that while the "conversational style" of the petition summary may seem to indicate a direct quotation, it might equally have been only a rhetorical device. See, "Political Activity among Ottoman Taxpayers," 4.
3 H. İslamoğlu-İnan, "Introduction: 'Oriental despotism in world-system perspective'," in *The Ottoman Empire and the World Economy*, ed. H. İslamoğlu-İnan (Cambridge, 1987), 20.
4 See Heyd, *Ottoman Documents*, 4.
5 See Heyd, *Ottoman Documents*, 20, 55.
6 Examples of these may be found in Inalcik, "Adâletnâmeler," 129ff. and Faroqhi, "Political Activity among Ottoman Taxpayers," 17–20.
7 Faroqhi, "Political Activity among Ottoman Taxpayers," 17.
8 A. Manna', "Moshlei Yerushalayim mi-Bayt Farrukh," 210.
9 Brown, *Peasant Politics*, 173–4.
10 G. Veinstein examines the way the standard phrases of the *mühimme* are used to create a particular conceptualization of the sultan. See, "La voix du maître à travers les firmans de Soliman le Magnifique," in *Soliman le Magnifique et son temps*, ed. G. Veinstein (Paris, 1992), 35–6.
11 Faroqhi, "Political Activity among Ottoman Taxpayers," 16.
12 M. Hoexter, "The Role of Qays and Yaman Factions in Local Political Divisions," *Asian and African Studies* 9(1973):301.
13 James C. Scott, "Everyday Forms of Peasant Resistance," *Journal of Peasant Studies* 13(1986):6. Scott's other works elaborate further aspects of his analysis of peasant–government relations: *The Moral Economy of the Peasant* (New Haven, 1976) and "Resistance without Protest and without Organization," *Contemporary Studies in Society and History* 29(1987):417–52.

14 Michael Adas, "From avoidance to confrontation," *Comparative Studies in Society and History*, 23(1981):217.
15 Apostolos E. Vacalopoulos, *The Greek Nation, 1453–1669 (New Brunswick, 1976)*, 12.
16 Lewis estimates the total population in the mid-sixteenth century at roughly 45,000–50,000 households, and suggests a multiplier of five. Gerber estimates a total population of 218,000 in 1800. See B. Lewis, "Studies in the Ottoman Archives – I," *BSOAS* 16(1954):475; and H. Gerber, "The Population of Syria and Palestine in the Nineteenth Century," *Asian and African Studies* 13(1979):77.
17 Faroqhi, "Political Activity among Ottoman Taxpayers," 28.
18 Revolts in Palestine in 1703 and 1834, and that of 1858 in Mount Lebanon were aimed against specific government officials or policies, and entailed far more immediate destruction than these daily acts. See A. Manna', "Mered naqib al-ashraf be-Yerushalayim (1703–1705)," *Cathedra* 35(1989):49–74; M. Hoexter, "Egyptian Involvement in the Politics of Notables in Palestine: Ibrahim Pasha in Jabal Nablus," in *Egypt and Palestine – A Millennium of Association (868–1948)*, ed. A. Cohen and G. Baer (Jerusalem, 1984), 190–213. Y. Porath, "The peasant revolt of 1858–61 in Kisrawan," *Asian and African Studies* 2(1966):77–157.
19 "*Mawlānā al-sulṭān al-malik al-aʿẓam wa'l-khāqān al-mukarram malik riqāb al-umam sulṭān al-rūm wa'l-ʿarab wa'l-ʿajam al-Sulṭān Sulaymān b. Sulṭān Selīm khān* ... " Quoted from the inscription found on the Sultan's Pool fountain which is located below the west city wall of Jerusalem. The fountain was built by Suleyman in 1536. See Max van Berchem, *Matériaux pour un Corpus Inscriptionum Arabicarum*, II, 1 (Cairo, 1922), No. 110. For other elaborate epithets used with Süleyman's name, see, Mantran, *Histoire de l'empire ottoman*, 162–4.
20 JS 1: 968/p. 240; Beg. Ramaḍān 937/18 April 1531
21 See the examples in Inalcik, "Adâletnâmeler," *passim*.
22 See Jennings, "Kadi, Court and Legal Procedure"; Faroqhi, "Rural Society, II," 118; and Faroqhi, *Towns and townsmen, passim*.
23 D. Ze'evi, "An Ottoman Century – The District of Jerusalem in the 1600s" (PhD. diss., Hebrew University of Jerusalem, 1991), Chapter Five, 25 (typescript).
24 Ze'evi, "An Ottoman Century," Chapter 5, 39–41 (typescript).
25 New research on this idea is developed for the nineteenth century by Reşat Kasaba in his paper "A Time and a Place for the Non-state: Social Change in the Ottoman Empire during the 'Long Nineteenth Century,'" (1990), typescript, p. 3.
26 Scott, "Resistance without Protest," 422.
27 Scott, "Everyday Forms of Peasant Resistance," 8.

Appendix 1: The villages

1 Dates of the registers: I 924–5/1518–19
II 937/1531
III 952/1545
IV 967/1560
V 1004/1595–6

Numbers following village names refer to the map. Amounts of taxes, except where otherwise stated, are in *akçe*.

2 In this display I have eliminated categories entirely empty in a given village, in

order to make the charts more readable. In addition, the categories have been given names instead of the original numerical codes.

3 Having entered the data directly into the computer, errors due to copying and recopying figures were also reduced.

4 In them, the left-hand column labelled "village" refers to numbers assigned the villages at an earlier stage in this project. These are only two examples. Such sort-charts were done for each of the thirty-two items identified.

5 "*Hasıl*" in the registers. This does not include the taxes on animals or the *bad-i hava*. Figures are in *akçe*.

6 *Maktu*ʿ (abbreviated here *mak*) and *kısm* are the two means of taxing the total production of crops. *Maktu*ʿ means that a fixed sum is collected from the total yield; *kısm* denotes a fixed proportion.

7 Grain figures are given as "number of *ghirāra*/*akçe*."

8 "*Mal-i seyfi*:" Codes which precede many of these figures are part of the system used to input this information into a computer. A key to the codes follows:

a = *harac-i bustan*	n = goats and bees	16 = *harac-i kurum*
b = *harac-i harnub* (carob)	s = sheep	
d = *harac-i aşcar*	u = marriage tax	17 = *harac-i zeytun*
e = *nil* (indigo)	+ = "other things"	20 = olive oil
m = *mann* (measure)	! = only the code	mak = *maktu*ʿ

The number following the code, or standing alone is *akçe*.

9 *Harac-i aşcar*

10 *Harac-i kurum*

11 Appanage of the provincial governor.

12 Both heads of households and bachelors were liable for the poll tax (*cizye*). The two groups are listed on one line here and in the chart for Bayt Laḥm: households/bachelors.

13 *kısm* = 1/4

14 Recorded as the number of persons taxed at rate of *cizye* in silver *akçe* = total *akçe* due.

15 Imperial domain.

16 *kısm* = 1/4

17 This is 1 *kıntar*; the entry says that *kısm* on olive oil here is 1/2. The entry for #1015 is also in *kıntar*s, but with no note about the *kısm*.

18 A note in registers IV and V says that the grains of Rīḥā are taxed at a *kısm* of 1/3, and indigo (*nil*) at 1/3. TTD 516/p. 66 and TTD 515/p. 34.

Appendix 3: Village leaders

1 "C" indicates that a person was specifically identified as a Christian leader or leader of Christian villagers; occasionally Muslims were identified as such, but rarely and only in mixed villages.

Bibliography

Documents

Başbakanlık Arşivi (Istanbul)
Tapu tahrir defterleri(TTD): 289, 342, 427, 522, 602, 1015
Mühimme defterleri(M): volumes 1–60
Maliyeden müdevver defterleri,
Ahkâm defterleri(MMD): 2775, 7534

Tapu ve Kadastro Umum Müdürlüğü (Ankara)
Tapu tahrir defterleri(TKM): 515/178, 516/112, 517/283

Al-Maḥkama al-Sharʿiyya (Jerusalem)
Qāḍī sijillāt(JS) Turkish: volumes 11, 29, 32, 34, 42, 47, 60, 70
Arabic : volumes 1, 25, 26, 27, 28, 30, 31, 33, 35, 39, 40, 41, 43, 44

Published Works

EI[2] *Encyclopaedia of Islam*. 2nd edition. Leiden, 1954– .

İA İslam Ansiklopedisi. Istanbul, 1940–86

JESHO Journal of the Economic and Social History of the Orient

Adas, Michael. "From Avoidance to Confrontation: Peasant Protest in Precolonial and Colonial Southeast Asia." *Comparative Studies in Society and History* 23 (1981):217–47.

Amiran, D. H. K. "The Pattern of Settlement in Palestine." *Israel Exploration Journal* 3 (1953):65–78, 192–209, 250–60.

Ayalon, David. "Discharges from Service, Banishments and Imprisonments in Mamluk Society." *Israel Oriental Studies* 2 (1972):25–50.

Bacqué-Grammont, J.-L., and P. Dumont, eds. *Économie et société dans l'Empire ottoman (fin du XVIIIe–début du XXe siècles)*. Paris, 1983.

Baer, Gabriel. *Fellah and Townsman in the Middle East: Studies in Social History*. London, 1982.

Bakhit, M. A. *The Ottoman Province of Damascus in the Sixteenth Century*. Beirut, 1982.

Barkan, Ö. L. *XV ve XVI ıncı Asırlarda Osmanlı İmperatorluğunda Zirai Ekonominin Hukuki Ve Mali Esasları. Kanunlar*. Istanbul, 1943.

"*Essai sur les données statistiques des registres de recensements dans l'Empire ottoman aux XVe et XVIe siècles.*" *JESHO* 1 (1958):9–36.

"Research on the Ottoman Fiscal Surveys." In *Studies in the Economic History of the Middle East*, edited by M. A. Cook, 163–71. Oxford, 1970.

"avâriz," *İA*.

"daftar-i khāḳānī," *EI*[2].

Barkey, Karen. *Bandits and Bureaucrats: The Ottoman Route of State Centralization.* Ithaca, forthcoming, 1994.

Barnes, John Robert. *An Introduction to Religious Foundations in the Ottoman Empire*. Leiden, 1987.

Berktay, Halil. "The Feudalism Debate: The Turkish End – Is 'Tax Vs. Rent' Necessarily the Product and Sign of a Modal Difference?" *Journal of Peasant Studies* 14 (1987):291–333.

"The Search for the Peasant in Western and Turkish History/Historiography." *Journal of Peasant Studies* 18 (1991):109–84.

Braslavski, J. *Le-Heker Artzenu: Avar Ve Seridim*. Tel Aviv, 1954.

Braudel, Fernand. *The Mediterranean and the Mediterranean World in the Age of Philip II*. Trans. Siân Reynolds. Vol. 2. New York, 1976.

Brown, Nathan J. *Peasant Politics in Modern Egypt: The Struggle Against the State.* New Haven, 1990.

Burgoyne, Michael H. *Mamluk Jerusalem: An Architectural Study*. London, 1987.

Cahen, C. "La Communauté rurale dans le monde musulman médiéval." In *Recueils de la société Jean Bodin XLII: les communautés rurales, IIIe partie "Asie et Islam"*, 9–27. Paris, 1982.

Cahen, C., and H. Inalcik. "djizya," *EI*[2].

Canaan, Tewfik. *Mohammedan Saints and Sanctuaries in Palestine*. Jerusalem, 1927.

Çetin, Atillâ. *Başbakanlık Arşivi Kılavuzu*. Istanbul, 1979.

Cherif, Mohammed-Hédi. "Témoignage du 'Mufti' Qasim 'Azzum sur les rapports entre Turcs et autochtones dans la Tunisie de la fin du XVIe s." *Les Cahiers de Tunisie* 20(1972):39–50.

Cohen, A. *Palestine in the 18th Century*. Jerusalem, 1973.

Yehude Yerushalayim ba-me'ah ha-16. Jerusalem, 1976.

"Local Trade, International Trade and Government Involvement in Jerusalem During the Early Ottoman Period." *Asian and African Studies* 12 (1978):5–12.

Jewish Life under Islam. Cambridge, MA, 1984.

Economic Life in Ottoman Jerusalem. Cambridge, U.K., 1989.

"Mifalo Shel Suleyman ha-Mefuar be-Yerushalayim." *Cathedra* 57 (1990):31–51.

Cohen, Amnon, and Bernard Lewis. *Population and Revenue in the Towns of Palestine in the Sixteenth Century*. Princeton, 1978.

Cook, M. A. *Population Pressure in Rural Anatolia, 1450–1600*. London, 1972.

Cuno, K. M. "The Origins of Private Ownership of Land in Egypt: A Reappraisal." *International Journal of Middle East Studies* 12 (1980):245–75.

The Pasha's peasants: Land, society and economy in Lower Egypt, 1740–1858. Cambridge, U.K., 1992.

Darling, L. "The Ottoman Finance Department and the Assessment and Collection of the Cizye and Avariz Taxes, 1560–1660." PhD Dissertation. University of Chicago, 1990.

DeJong, F. *Ṭuruq and Ṭuruq-Linked Institutions in Nineteenth-Century Egypt.* Leiden, 1978.

Dols, Michael W. "The Second Plague Pandemic and Its Recurrences in the Middle East: 1347–1894." *JESHO* 22 (1979):162–89.

Doumani, B. "Palestinian Islamic Court Records: A Source for Socioeconomic History." *MESA Bulletin* 19 (1985):155–72.

El-Nahal, Galal. *The Judicial Administration of Ottoman Egypt in the 17th Century*. Minneapolis, 1979.

Elezovic, Glisa. *Turski Spomenici*. Beograd, 1952.

Erder, R. L. "The Measurement of Preindustrial Population Changes: The Ottoman Empire from the 15th to 17th Centuries." *Middle East Studies* 11 (1975):284–301.

Faroqhi, S. "Rural Society in Anatolia and the Balkans During the 16th Century, I." *Turcica* 9 (1977):161–95.

"The Peasants of Saideli in the Late Sixteenth Century." *Archivum Ottomanicum* 8 (1983):215–50.

"Political Intiatives 'from the Bottom Up' in the 16th & 17th Century Ottoman Empire." In *Osmanistische Studien Zur Wirtschafts- und Sozialgeschichte: In Memoriam Vanco Boskov*, edited by H. G. Mayer, 24–33. Wiesbaden, 1986.

"Agriculture and Rural Life in the Ottoman Empire (ca. 1500–1878): A Report on Scholarly Literature Published 1970–1985." *New Perspectives on Turkey* 1 (1987):3–34.

"Political Activity Among Ottoman Taxpayers and the Problem of Sultanic Legitimation (1570–1650)." *JESHO* 35 (1992):1–39.

Finn, Mrs. "The Fellaheen of Palestine." *Palestine Exploration Fund Quarterly Statement* (1879):33–48, 72–87.

Friedman, Yohanan. "Eretz-Yisrael ve-Yerushalayim erev ha-Kibush ha-Othmani." In *Perakim be-Toldot Yerushalayim: BeReshit ha-Tekufa ha-Othmanit*, edited by A. Cohen, 7–38. Jerusalem, 1979.

Gerber, H. "The Population of Syria and Palestine in the Nineteenth Century." *Asian and African Studies* 13 (1979):58–80.

"*Sharia*, *Kanun*, and Custom in the Ottoman Law: The Court Records of 17th-century Bursa." *International Journal of Turkish Studies* 2 (1981):131–47.

Social Origins of the Modern Middle East. Boulder, 1987.

Gilbar, Gad G. "The Growing Economic Involvement of Palestine with the West, 1865–1914." In *Palestine in the Late Ottoman Period*, edited by D. Kushner, 188–210. Jerusalem, 1986.

Goitein, Shlomo Dov. "al-Ḳuds," *EI*[2].

Haldon, John. "The Ottoman State and the Question of State Autonomy: Comparative Perspectives." *Journal of Peasant Studies* 18 (1991):18–108.

Heyd, Uriel. *Ottoman Documents on Palestine 1552–1615*. Oxford, 1960.

Studies in Old Ottoman Criminal Law. Edited by V. L. Ménage. Oxford, 1973.

Al-Hmūd, Nawfān. *Al-Askar fī Bilād al-Shām fī al-qarnayn al-sādis ʿashr wa'l-sābiʿ ʿashr al-milādīīn*. Beirut, 1981.

Hoexter, M. "The Role of Qays and Yaman Factions in Local Political Divisions." *Asian and African Studies* 9 (1973):249–311.

"Egyptian Involvement in the Politics of Notables in Palestine: Ibrahim Pasha in Jabal Nablus." In *Egypt and Palestine – A Millennium of Association (868–1948)*, edited by A. Cohen and G. Baer, 190–213. Jerusalem, 1984.

Humphreys, R. Stephen. *Islamic History: A Framework for Inquiry*. Revised Edition. Princeton, 1991.

Hütteroth, W.-D. "Ottoman Administration of the Desert Frontier in the Sixteenth Century." *Asian and African Studies* 19 (1985):145–55.

Hütteroth, W.-D., and K. Abdulfattah. *Historical Geography of Palestine, Transjordan and Southern Syria*. Erlangen, 1977.

Ibn Taymiyya, Taqī al-Dīn. *Al-Siyāsa al-shar'iyya fī islāḥ al-rā'ī wa'l-ra'īya*. Beirut, 1966.

İlgürel, Mücteba. "Subaşılık Müessesesi." *Journal of Turkish Studies* 7 (1983):251–61.

Inalcik, H. "Osmanlılarda Raiyyet Rüsûmu." *Belleten* 23 (1954):575–610.

"Ottoman Methods of Conquest." *Studia Islamica* 2 (1954):103–29.

"Adâletnâmeler." *Belgeler* 2 (1965):49-145.

"Capital Formation in the Ottoman Empire." *Journal of Economic History* 29 (1969):97–140.

"Suleiman the Lawgiver and Ottoman Law." *Archivum Ottomanicum* 1 (1969):105–38.

"Rice Cultivation and the Çeltükci-Re'âyâ System in the Ottoman Empire." *Turcica* 14 (1982):69–141.

The Ottoman Empire: The Classical Age 1300–1600. Translated by Norman Itzkowitz and Colin Imber. New Rochelle, N.Y., 1989.

"Islamization of Ottoman Laws on Land and Land Tax." In *Festgabe an Josef Matuz. Osmanistik-Turkologie Diplomatik*, edited by Christa Fragner and Klaus Schwarz, 101–18. Berlin, 1992.

"Mā' Pt. 8: Irrigation in the Ottoman Empire," *EI*².

Inalcik, H., and C. Findley. "Mahkama: The Ottoman Empire," *EI*².

İpşirli, Mehmet. "A Preliminary Study of the Public Waqfs of Hama and Homs in the XVIth Century." *Studies on Turkish–Arab Relations* 1 (1986):119–47.

İslamoğlu-İnan, Huri. "Introduction: 'Oriental Despotism in World-system Perspective.'" In *The Ottoman Empire and the World Economy*, edited by Huri İslamoğlu-İnan, 1–24. Cambridge, 1987.

Jennings, R.C. "Kadi, Court and Legal Procedure in 17th-Century Ottoman Kayseri." *Studia Islamica* 48 (1978):133–72.

"Limitations of the Judicial Powers of the Kadi in 17th C. Ottoman Kayseri." *Studia Islamica* 50 (1979):151–84.

"The Population, Society and Economy of the Region of Erciyeş Dağı in the 16th Century." In *Contributions à l'histoire économique et sociale de l'Empire ottoman*, edited by J.-L. Bacqué-Grammont and P. Dumont, 149–250. Louvain, 1983.

"The Locust Problem in Cyprus." *Byzantion* 57 (1987):315–25.

Johansen, Baber. *The Islamic Law on Land Tax and Rent: The Peasants' Loss of Property Rights as Interpreted in the Hanafite Legal Literature of the Mamluk and Ottoman Periods*. London, 1988.

Káldy-Nagy, G. "The First Centuries of the Ottoman Military Organization." *Acta Orientalia Hungaricae* 31 (1977):147–83.

Kallner-Amiran, D. H. "A Revised Earthquake Catalogue of Palestine." *Israel Exploration Journal* I, II (1950–51, 1952):223–46; 48–65.

Kasaba, Reşat. "A Time and a Place for the Non-state: Social Change in the Ottoman Empire During the 'long Nineteenth Century.'" Unpublished Paper. 1989–90.

Köprülü, M. Fuad. "hil'at," *İA*.

"çavuş." *İA*.

Kramers, J. H. "sü-başı," *İA*.
Kunt, I. Metin. *The Sultan's Servants: The Transformation of Ottoman Provincial Government, 1550–1650*. New York, 1983.
Ladurie, Emmanuel Le Roy. *The Peasants of Languedoc*. Urbana, 1974.
Lane, E. W. *An Arabic–English Lexicon*. London, 1863.
Lewis, B. "The Ottoman Archives as a Source for the History of the Arab Lands." *Journal of the Royal Asiatic Society* 3–4 (1951):139–55.
"Notes and Documents from the Turkish Archives." *Oriental Notes and Studies* 3 (Jerusalem, 1953):1–52.
"Studies in the Ottoman Archives – I." *Bulletin of the School of Oriental and African Studies* 16 (1954):469–501.
"Nazareth in the Sixteenth Century." In *Arabic and Islamic Studies in Honor of Hamilton A.R. Gibb*, 416–23. Cambridge, MA, 1965.
"Jaffa in the 16th Century, According to the Ottoman Tahrir Registers." In *Necati Lugal Armagani*, 436–46. Ankara, 1968.
"Ottoman Land Tenure and Taxation in Syria." *Studia Islamica* 50 (1979):109–34.
"Acre in the Sixteenth Century." In *Memorial O.L. Barkan*, 135–9. Paris, 1980.
"ʿarūs resmī," *EI*[2].
"bād-i hawā," *EI*[2].
Little, Donald P. *A Catalogue of the Islamic Documents from Al-Ḥaram Aš-Šarīf in Jerusalem*. Wiesbaden, 1984.
Lowry, Heath. "The Ottoman Liva Kanunnames." *Osmanlı Araştırmaları* 2 (1981):43–74.
Macalister, R. A. Stewart, and E. W. G Masterman. "Occasional Papers on the Modern Inhabitants of Palestine." *Palestine Exploration Fund Quarterly Statement* (1904):150–60; (1905):48–60, 343–56; (1906):33–50.
Makovsky, A. "Sixteenth-Century Agricultural Production in the Liwâ of Jerusalem." *Archivum Ottomanicum* 9 (1984):91–127.
Mandaville, J. "The Ottoman Court Records of Syria and Jordan." *Journal of the American Oriental Society* 86 (1966):311–19.
"The Jerusalem Sharīʿa Court Records." In *Studies in Palestine During the Ottoman Period*, edited by M. Ma'oz, 517–24. Jerusalem, 1975.
Mannaʿ, A. "Moshlei Yerushalayim mi-Bayt Farrukh ve Yakhaseihem im ha-Bedouim." In *Perakim be-Toldot Yerushalayim: BeReshit ha-Tekufa ha-Othmanit*, edited by A. Cohen, 196–232. Jerusalem, 1979.
"The *Sijill* as a Source for the Study of Palestine." In *Palestine in the Late Ottoman Period*, edited by D. Kushner, 351–62. Jerusalem, 1986.
"Mered Naqib al-Ashraf be-Yerushalayim (1703–1705)." *Cathedra* 35 (1989):49–74.
Mantran, R., ed. *Histoire de l'Empire ottoman*. Paris, 1989.
Mantran, R., and Jean Sauvaget. *Règlements fiscaux ottomans: les provinces syriennes*. Beirut, 1951.
Marcus, A. *The Middle East on the Eve of Modernity*. New York, 1989.
Mujīr al-Dīn al-Ḥanbalī. *Al-Uns Al-jalīl bi-ta'rīkh al-Quds wa'l-Khalīl*. 2 vols. Amman, 1973.
Mutafchieva, V. *Agrarian Relations in the Ottoman Empire in the 15th and 16th Centuries*. New York, 1988.
Naima, Mustafa. *Tarih-i Naima*. 3rd edn. 6 vols. Constantinople, 1281–3/1864–6.
Nāṣir, S. F.. *Zaytūn Filasṭīn wa-mushkilātuhu*. Bir Zeit, n.d.

Al-Nuwayrī, Aḥmad ibn ʿAbd al-Wahhāb. *Nihāyat al-arab fī funūn al-adab*. 14 vols. Cairo, 1923–42.

Orhonlu, C., and G. Baer. "ketkhudā," *EI*^{2}.

Pitcher, Donald Edgar. *An Historical Geography of the Ottoman Empire from Earliest Times to the End of the Sixteenth Century*. Leiden, 1972.

Porath, Y. "The Peasant Revolt of 1858–61 in Kisrawân." *Asian and African Studies* 2 (1966):77–157.

Possot, Denis. *Le Voyage de la Terre Sainte (1532)*. Paris, 1889.

Powers, D. S. "Revenues of Public *waqf*s." *Archivum Ottomanicum* 9 (1984):163–202.

Rafeq, Abdul Karim. "Economic Relations Between Damascus and the Dependent Countryside, 1743–1771." In *The Islamic Middle East, 700–1900: Studies in Economic and Social History*, edited by A. L. Udovitch, 653–85. Princeton, 1981.

Raymond, A. "The Ottoman Conquest and the Development of the Great Arab Towns." *International Journal of Turkish Studies* 1 (1979–80):84–101.

Grandes villes arabes à l'époque ottomane. Paris, 1985.

Reilly, James A. "Sharīʿa Court Registers and Land Tenure Around Nineteenth-century Damascus." *MESA Bulletin* 21 (1987):155–69.

Repp, R. C. *The Müfti of Istanbul: A Study in the Development of the Ottoman Learned Hierarchy*. London, 1986.

Salama, O., and Y. Zilberman. "Aspakat ha-Mayim li-Yerushalayim ba-meot ha-16 ve-ha-17." *Cathedra* 41 (1986):91–106.

Sauvaire, H. *Histoire de Jérusalem et Hébron*. Paris, 1876.

Schacht, J. *An Introduction to Islamic Law*. Oxford, 1964.

Scott, James C. *The Moral Economy of the Peasant: Rebellion and Subsistence in Southeast Asia*. New Haven, 1976.

"Everyday Forms of Peasant Resistance." *Journal of Peasant Studies* 13 (1986):5–35.

"Resistance Without Protest and Without Organization: Peasant Opposition to the Islamic *Zakat* and the Christian Tithe." *Contemporary Studies in Society and History* 29 (1987):417–52.

Shanin, Teodor. "Short Historical Outline of Peasant Studies." In *Peasants and Peasant Societies: Selected Readings*. 2nd edn., edited by Teodor Shanin, 467–75. New York, 1987.

Sharon, M. "The Political Role of the Bedouins in Palestine in the Sixteenth and Seventeenth Centuries." In *Studies on Palestine During the Ottoman Period*, edited by Moshe Maoz, 11–30. Jerusalem, 1975.

"Ludd," *EI*^{2}.

Shaw, S. "The Land Law of Ottoman Egypt (960–1553)." *Der Islam* 38 (1962):106–37.

The Financial and Administrative Organization and Development of Ottoman Egypt 1517–1798. Princeton, 1962.

Singer, A. "The Countryside of Ramle in the Sixteenth Century: A Study of Villages with Computer Assistance." *JESHO* 33 (1990):51–79.

"*Tapu Tahrir Defterleri* and *Kadı Sicilleri*: A Happy Marriage of Sources." *Tārīḫ* 1 (1990):95–125.

"Peasant Migration: Law and Practice in Early Ottoman Palestine." *New Perspectives on Turkey* 8 (1992):49–65.

Stephan, S. H. "An Endowment Deed of Khâsseki Sultân, Dated 24th May 1552." *Quarterly of the Department of Antiquities in Palestine* 10 (1944):170–94.

Stillman, N. "khil'a," *EI*[2].

Svanidzé, M. "L'Économie rurale dans le Vilâyet d'Akhaltzikhé (Çıldır) d'après le 'registre détailé' de 1595." In *Contributions à l'histoire économique et sociale de l'Empire ottoman*, edited by J.-L. Bacqué-Grammont and P. Dumont, 251–66. Louvain, 1983.

Thomas, Lewis V. *A Study of Naima*. Edited by Norman Itzkowitz. New York, 1972.

Tibawi, A. L. *The Islamic Pious Foundations in Jerusalem*. London, 1978.

Toledano, E. "The *Sanjaq* of Jerusalem in the Sixteenth Century." *Archivum Ottomanicum* 9 (1984):279–319.

Vacalopoulos, Apostolos E. *The Greek Nation, 1453–1669: The Cultural and Economic Background of Modern Greek Society*. Translated by Ian and Phania Moles. New Brunswick, 1976.

Valensi, Lucette. *Fellahs Tunisiens*. Paris, 1977.

Venzke, M. L. "Aleppo's Mâlîkâne-Dîvânî System." *Journal of the American Oriental Society* 106 (1986):451–69.

"Special Use of the Tithe as a Revenue-raising Measure in the 16th-century Sanjaq of Aleppo." *JESHO* 29 (1986):249–334.

Wickham, Chris. "The Other Transition: From the Ancient World to Feudalism." *Past and Present* 103 (1984):3–36.

"The Uniqueness of the East." *Journal of Peasant Studies* 12 (1985):166–96.

Winter, Michael. "Military Connections Between Egypt and Syria (including Palestine) in the Early Ottoman Period." In *Egypt and Palestine: A Millennium of Association (868–1948)*, edited by A. Cohen and G. Baer, 139–49. Jerusalem, 1984.

Ze'evi, Dror. "An Ottoman Century – The District of Jerusalem in the 1600s." PhD. Dissertation. Hebrew University of Jerusalem. 1991.

Index